CUSHTY

A ROMANY LIFE

JOE SMITH

& MARTIN KNIGHT

A ROMANY LIFE

LONDON BOOKS

LONDON BOOKS
39 Lavender Gardens
London SW11 1SE
www.london-books.co.uk

Originally published in 2009 as
Gypsy Joe: Bare-Knuckle Fighter, Professional Golfer
This revised and expanded edition 2021

A catalogue record for this book
is available from the British Library

ISBN 978-0-9957217-5-3

Printed and bound in Great Britain by
CPI Group (UK) Ltd, Croydon, CR0 4YY

Typeset by Octavo Smith Publishing Services
www.octavosmith.com

I would like to dedicate this book to my grandparents
Joe, Rymer, Ria and Mary, my Uncle Neville
and to my wonderful parents
Aaron and Mary, aka Sissy.

Thank you to the following people who have inspired, encouraged
and in some cases tolerated me: Mices Joe, Jimmy and Wally Stockin,
Matty's Matty, Charlie, Billy, Joe & Emily's Joe & Bill, John Fagan,
Tony O'Brien, John Snook Jnr., my brothers John and Aaron,
Graham Stevens, John Moor, cousin Albert Stockin,
cousins Johnny French, my uncles Freddy, Johnny, Cliff,
Charlie, Joe, Ruffy. Not forgetting all my pals at West Drayton
British Legion and all the boys down at the yard.
GOD BLESS

CONTENTS

ILLUSTRATIONS

Between pages 112 and 113

Unless stated otherwise all pictures © Joe Smith

Esteban Toledo and me with our sons.

'Birdman Series No. 8' and 'Ned the Neck'. Charles Bronson sent his own special encouragement from prison. *Courtesy of Charles Bronson.*

Young Rymer after a very competitive football match.

All about me.

Mum and Dad. God rest.

Muhammad Ali. He probably *was* the greatest.

BORN FREE

In the June of 1965 Aaron Smith and Mary Eastwood jumped the broomstick. This is, or was, the gypsy way of making a commitment to each other for life. Courting couples, or even two young people who had only just met each other but found a spark between them, elected to disappear off somewhere and live together for some days or weeks to see how they get along before deciding to become partners for life. Years ago, before sex before marriage became compulsory, outsiders would have frowned upon such a practice. Now it seems like a beacon of common sense. Their flight had both sets of parents' blessing with all of them being Romany and friends. Aaron senior and his wife Maria (known best as Ria) had travelled from Surrey and Essex and Joe Eastwood and his wife Mary had arrived with their family from their yard in Hanworth, Middlesex to the annual hop-picking working holiday in Kent. Here, like generations before them among the vines and in the shadows of the oast houses, young Aaron and Mary cemented their relationship.

That hopping holiday where Aaron and Mary fell head-over-heels in love would have been one of the last had by my family or any family as by the 1960s the annual ritual of the working-classes, and gypsies, arriving in their hordes in to the Kent countryside to harvest the hops was almost dead as the British had developed an increasing taste for imported beer (lager) and farming practices became almost completely mechanised. Even though hopping was a thing of the distant past, when I grew up the adults still talked about it, and the magical romance was part of our history. I regretted not being a witness to it all, choosing to overlook the fact (as they did) that it represented back-breaking toil and we and the cockney masses were merely a handy source of cheap labour for the farmers and landowners to exploit. I can remember our elders standing around a blazing, spitting fire singing various songs handed down from those days. One in particular went something like this:

Now, early Monday morning,
The measurer he'll come round,
Pick your hops all ready,
And you'll pick them off the ground.

Now, early Tuesday morning,
The bookie he'll come round,
With a bag of money,
He'll flop it on the ground.

Says, 'Do you want some money?'
'Yes, sir, if you please,
To buy a hock of bacon,
And a roll of mouldy cheese.'

They all says hopping's lousy,
I believe it's true,
Since I've been down hopping,
I've got a chatt or two.

Early Saturday morning,
It is our washing day,
We boils 'em in our hopping-pot,
And we hangs 'em on the ground.

Hopping's all over,
All the money's spent,
I wish to God I'd never done,
No hopping down in Kent.

I say one, I say two,
No more hopping shall I do.

'Pick 'em up, pick 'em up off the ground!'
When he starts to measuring,
He never know when to stop,

'Why don't you jump in the bin,
And take the bloomin' lot.'

In May of 1966, just in time for England's glorious victory in the football World Cup final, Aaron and Mary's first child was born. Aaron the younger popped out in Barking as the young couple travelled around the Home Counties in their beloved caravan. Mary, their second child, followed in 1967 and was born in Isleworth, Middlesex. Aaron was getting a living as a scrap dealer and Mary was helping the young family to keep their heads above water by selling lucky white heather and wishing people good fortune. It was a happy time and a good start to their union.

The following year the harsh reality of life (or death) closed in on them when Mary's father Joe was diagnosed with cancer and, despite putting up a tremendous fight, he subsequently died. I don't like using the term 'fight' because in most cases it is not a fight when cancer is the opponent. It is very often a fight you *cannot* win. A mismatch, and to say he or she 'lost their fight' implies some sort of failure when in reality they have been shot in the back. Although he had spent time in hospital, Joe's final days were passed in their caravan nestled under the Beckton flyover as was his wish. Born in a caravan and died in one with the lorries and cars trundling overhead. He and his daughter Mary enjoyed a special bond as she was the only girl among his seven children and he had affectionately called her Sissy. She was completely devastated as was his widow and sons who had lost that great presence in their lives at what is now considered the young age of fifty-three years, although back then it was not unusual for gypsy men not to see out their three score years and ten. Aaron too was cut low by the death as he had a great admiration and love for his father-in-law. Only the support of many friends from their Christian faith and then the imminent arrival of a new child for the young couple lifted their spirit. Should the baby be a boy they vowed to call him Joe after the man that had left them so sadly and prematurely. Nature knows best, though, and Maria was born on the 10th May 1970. Three children named after three grandparents. They had to finish the jigsaw and practically forbade the fourth child to be a girl. Finally, on 7th July 1971, a big bouncing baby was born weighing in at 10lb 4oz in Isleworth, Middlesex. They called him Joe. That was me. Hello.

Being a curious person by nature I have since tried to find out what I can about the outside world at the time of my birth. In sadder more recent times that date of 7/7 has taken on a tragic significance being the date of the London bombings. It tied up a knot in my stomach when I flopped open an encyclopaedia in my local library and discovered also that it was in that month in the year of my birth when the final floor of the World Trade Centre in New York, later to be destroyed by terrorists, was finally completed. I learnt, as soon as I was old enough, that my cousin Jimmy Stockin, a legendary bare-knuckle fighter, was also born on 7th July. Louis Armstrong, the trumpeter, died hours before my birth. Later in the year Cher would make the song charts with 'Gypsies, Tramps And Thieves', *Fiddler On The Roof* with Topol gurgling 'If I Were A Rich Man' was the top film, Mill Reef ridden by Geoff Lewis won the Derby, Arsenal spearheaded by Charlie George won the Double, Lee Trevino took the British and US golf opens and Joe Frazier and Joe Bugner were the respective world and British heavyweight boxing champions. I see significance everywhere. As I write this I am welling up with tears as another coincidence occurs to me. My Granny Mary has just died and she has left us on Oaks Day. The Oaks, which sorts out the leading fillies, is the second biggest horse-race after the Derby Stakes at the Epsom Derby meeting which has been the most significant meeting place for gypsies for generations. Granny Mary was a quality filly herself, loved by all who knew her, and it is right she leaves us on the day of the Oaks.

Back in 1971 the British economy was running into choppy waters and our first soldier had been killed in Northern Ireland. 'Chirpy Chirpy Cheep Cheep' was atop of the hit parade. Yes, there was bad news everywhere but we, the Smiths, were insulated from all this. We were Romanies and recessions didn't impact on us. We were always up against it and we didn't have a record player. Coming to think of it we didn't have mains electricity, either. Being self-sufficient and self-reliant and living on the land and living off it does have its advantages. Words like redundancy, pension, wage cut, power cut, unemployment, inflation, house-price and investments were rarely uttered in a gypsy caravan. Life was austere but we knew no different and if you don't have a lot to lose there's not much to be taken away.

Many of my earliest memories are of staying with my Aunt Lou and Uncle Neville in their caravan on the Hampton, Surrey gypsy site. This was the place to be. Aunt Lou and Uncle Neville had had only one baby, Anthony, who had tragically lived only seven hours and afterwards Lou could have no more children. I think they over-compensated with us. We were spoilt rotten and I was the luckiest toddler alive because I effectively had four parents. Uncle Neville owned a prosperous scrap-metal business and they lived in a top-of-the-range sparkling and stylish Jubilee caravan which even at that young age I could appreciate. I soon learnt how to ring their bells.

'Aunt Lou, can I have that?' I'd look up doe-eyed as I held her hand asking and pointing to a toy in a shop window.

'Neville,' she'd say. 'Young Joe, he wants that.' He'd look down at me and smile and ruffle my blond curly hair with his big, strong hands.

'If my Joe Bugner wants it, he can have it. Go on Lou. Go in and get it for the boy.'

He started calling me Joe Bugner because he said I looked like him, which is not too flattering to any toddler to be likened to a flat-nosed and battle-scarred boxer, and Bugner was then, in 1971, our heavyweight boxing prospect. He'd beaten Henry Cooper in a controversial points-decision fight and had even fought Muhammad Ali, arguably the greatest boxer of all time. Bugner was a good, brave fighter and sadly is pretty much overlooked today. Family people still call me Bugner and when they use it now younger people who don't know me and have never heard of Joe Bugner, think, perhaps, I'm of eastern European extraction and just arrived in the country to pick fruit.

At the age of just thirty-five in 1975 Uncle Neville was scythed down with a massive heart attack and died. Those dreamy days of hot milk and cornflakes were gone in a blink. I can remember asking poor, mourning Aunt Lou when is Uncle Neville coming back? When are they going to mend him? You said my milky white hair would go black like Uncle Neville's. Why hasn't that happened?

'Eat all your cabbage,' Lou would say, 'and it will, slowly.'

It never turned black and for many years I believed I stayed blond because Uncle Neville had died. They told me he'd gone to live with the angels and we could look after his garden. They said we'd see him again when we were older and I believed it. I still do.

Aunt Lou moved site to be with Grandfather Rymer and Granny Ria. Aunts Phyllis and Mary Jane also lived on their yard. I stayed there too, but also went travelling with my mum and dad and brothers and sisters more and more now I was older. Home was Epsom in Surrey and Hanworth in Middlesex and in between times we'd spend the summer down at Portsmouth where Mum would get on the hovercraft and sell heather to the holidaymakers, and because there was no way off the craft (except diving in the Solent) and away from her they'd buy some. They call it a captive market, I believe. We kids would keep out of the way gnawing on sticks of rock that said Sandown in the middle and I remember thinking they're even mad about horse-racing down here.

As we got a bit older Dad would allow us to tag along with him when he went out selling scrap metal and once he said if he did well he'd get us a second-hand bike and he was as good as his word. In the evening Aaron and I would ride up and down the sandbanks on the bike and play with the local children. I can still remember the thrill of seeing, mounting and then riding that bike for the first time. Second-hand, third-hand, fourth-hand – it never bothered me. Who knew except the person who sold it to you that an item was second-hand? Who's to say when you're gliding down the street that you did not buy that bike *new* two years ago? It's all in the mind and it was an early lesson for me in the psychology of prices. How can a £20,000 car be worth £17,000 the second you drive it off the forecourt? Is the first price too high or the second too low?

Dad would go to the pub while we brothers shared the bike and Mum and the girls would clean up the caravan and polish the chrome until it glowed in the moonlight. Then we'd go together and fetch Dad who'd been playing pool in the nearest pub. We'd watch him in the doorway as he brushed the tip of his cue with a cube of blue chalk, lean over the table, squint one eye and pot the black. Or not. Win or lose he'd always shake his opponent's hand at the end of the game. He never got in any trouble. He liked people and they liked him. Times must have been fair because we could even afford a Chinese takeaway that we'd eat around the table in the caravan. This was being a gypsy at its best.

Chinese food was a luxury, but it was our Sunday meat pudding that we all looked forward too. If any of us was offered Chinese or Indian or fish and chips in place of our meat pudding we'd have declined. We anticipated it so much that we measured time by it. If I said 'Dad, when do we move off back to Epsom?' he'd reply 'Not long boy. Just two more meat pudding days and we'll be there.'

We had a wonderful, unstructured, outdoor childhood. There was no routine to speak of and we were often left to our own devices although we always knew where our boundaries lay and the adults equally knew we would not cross them so they did not worry. In reality we wanted to be with the grown-ups more than we did each other because they tended to have more fun than we did. For example, I was taken hare-coursing from an early age and you can imagine how exciting this was for a wide-eyed kid. Gypsies have been hare-coursing for centuries and originally, I guess, it was an important food source, but in latter years it became a sport although I can remember the hare being taken home for the pot on the occasions we did catch one. The adults would wager one another on whose dog would catch the animal and spectators too would join in the betting and there were cups and trophies in properly organised tournaments. In these competitions the landowners would be aware of what was happening and the dogs were mainly owned by the gentry. They maintained that the aim was to turn the hare rather than kill it and they awarded points for stamina, skill and other attributes. Also hares were actually brought and let out for the occasion whereas when we coursed we just went to the land where we knew they lived and flushed them out. Grandfather Rymer had a lovely lurcher called The Ghost who won countless trophies and in his time was considered one of the best dogs in the country. Dad also bought me a dog but we didn't get around to taking it hare-coursing very often, especially as you had to go further and further afield to find the hares as the years went by.

This sport was banned in 2005 when all hunting with dogs became prohibited by law. It threw up an unlikely alignment. For when pro-hunting and Save The Countryside groups marched on London in their masses to protest about these fundamental changes to their centuries-old way of life, poachers and gamekeepers and squires and gypsies stood together united in their anger. It was not always so. In my lifetime there was an incident when a distant relative of mine, only a boy, was found on private land with his lurcher by a gamekeeper who without compunction shot the dog dead. Distraught, the kid ran as fast as he could back to where his family were pulled up and poured out the terrible story to his dad. Understandably the father was incensed, rolled his sleeves up, and set off to challenge the gamekeeper. When he did a huge row ensued and the father, like his dog, was shot dead in front of his traumatised son. In court the gamekeeper was acquitted of murder when he claimed self-defence. Self-defence? There was only one of the two men holding a gun.

It was down in Portsmouth when a man came on to our site who would change my life. I guess he changed lots of people's lives. I imagine it must have been hard for him when he first walked on the camp because the welcome given to strangers can be cold at best and downright hostile at worst. This is because the majority of non-gypsies who came on to the site did not come in peace or bearing gifts. They were normally policemen bearing charge sheets; council officials bearing clipboards; bailiffs bearing eviction orders; residents bearing grudges about the prices of their houses being adversely affected by our presence; pet lovers bearing suspicions about missing cats; officials from the Hedgehog Protection League and so on. This man, Jim Needle, simply came to teach the children to read. He explained he was not from the Government or the Council, or anyone else for that matter, he did not want paying, he did not want anything, but he would teach the children to read. My parents took him at face value and made him welcome in our caravan and he sat me down and patiently taught me to read over a period of months. He showed me how to break down words into sounds and then put them back together again. I was excited about it and each time I could pick up a word from the television or a road sign and I got it right it gave me great satisfaction and confidence.

Learning to read and write opened up a whole new world to me and once I could it was hard to believe that I might have gone through my entire life without ever reading or writing, as many gypsies did then and still do today. Even when we moved sixty or seventy miles inland to Epsom in Surrey, Jim would make the journey to see us and continue my tuition. What a good man. Of course, I just accepted he came and visited at that young age, and had no idea of the efforts he made on mine and others' behalf, but now I realise what an extraordinary, generous man he was. Throughout my life I have met such people in various spheres and they are the unsung bedrock of our societies: people who help others for no monetary gain or reward, people who give far more than they take. There are fewer of them with each passing year. Jim Needle gave me a head start in life and I am eternally grateful. Mr Needle, if you're out there, thank you, sir.

Another extraordinary chap who befriended the gypsies and fought our corner was Grattan Puxon. I saw him a few times but never knew him like I did Jim Needle. To this day gypsies are grateful for his efforts on our behalf. I don't know where he came from, I don't know why he championed us, but he did and I'm told he still does. As attitudes towards gypsies hardened in the 1960s and the countryside became more developed and our travelling and stopping age-old lifestyle was curtailed as the available space for all the residents of this wonderful country shrank, clashes between gypsies and the authorities intensified. Grattan Puxon was educated, articulate, and most importantly charismatic. He could utilise the legal system in a way we could not. He could present our side of a dispute eloquently in a way we often could or would not. A fine man.

There were others that spoke out at what they saw as the unreasonable treatment of gypsies who I have learnt about since but never met to my knowledge. There was a lady called Diana Allen who after the war persuaded gypsies that they needed to take driving tests when cars were rapidly pushing their traditional form of transport – horses and carts – off the road. Although we knew there was a legal obligation to take the test we shied away from it, not from disregard for the law but in the knowledge that questions on the Highway Code could not be answered as so few of us could read or write. She coached gypsies before the test and was instrumental in making sure we were not completely criminalised as we joined the driving classes. She often worked with an MP called Eric Lubbock who fought tirelessly for councils to provide permanent gypsy sites.

In the winter we'd pull up at Epsom, where Granny Mary lived, and Dad would find a field near where Granddad Rymer's brother, Muggy Jim, would be staying with his family. Epsom was always a home for gypsies and is probably *the* place in England that people associate with gypsies more than any other. There is a long tradition of gypsies gathering at Epsom for the Derby classic horse-race that has been run there since the 17th century. Over the generations many have stayed and intermingled and interbred with the local population. The Epsom people were a tolerant and laid-back lot. Way ahead of their time. There has been permanent gypsy sites there for generations, notably at Cox Lane and more recently Kiln Lane, and the town was encircled almost by a cluster of imposing, red-brick Victorian mental hospitals. Patients, some of whom had been incarcerated for years for the crime of becoming pregnant out of wedlock, for example, were part of the town's fabric as were the army of small, wiry men who worked thanklessly in the town's thriving horse-racing industry. It may have been affluent stockbroker belt, but it was the 'gypos', the 'nutters', the 'stable rats' and others that contributed as much to Epsom's unique character.

It was through Muggy Jim at Epsom I had my first experience of boxing. I was five years old. Muggy's two sons were Jimmy and Wally, and Muggy had trained them as boxers and they were both very good. They were strapping teenagers already with big reputations and I just watched in awe when Dad would take me over to Slough Boxing Club to see them spar. Boxing and bare-knuckle fighting has been another tradition among gypsies since the beginning of time. The fights could be violent but it was rarely violence for the sake of violence. It was one of the things our community did and always had done. Boxing was one sport where Romanies could excel and break through. It was no wonder we embraced it so enthusiastically.

Bare-knuckle fighting as a sport is now seen as an underground and brutal pastime of mainly the criminal classes, but not so many years ago it was legal, widespread and accounts of fights made the pages of *The Times*, and the pugilists themselves became celebrities on a par with the top sportsmen of the modern age. It was also the predecessor of the sport of that we now know as boxing and was then commonly referred to as prize-fighting. It was called this because a purse was put up for the eventual victor. Purse-fighting does not have the same ring to it and could have led to confusion. Fights became so popular that they attracted huge crowds, who would often become rowdy, and large amounts of money were being wagered on the outcomes. For this reason the Government of the day in the middle of the 18th century banned prize-fighting. This only had the perverse effect of it becoming more organised in order to outflank the law and more attractive to its followers. The sport was patronised and funded by aristocrats and even royalty, and primitive gymnasiums sprung up across the country, often in public houses run by former fighters. Champions emerged whose names would go down in history: Tom Johnson, Jack Broughton, Tom Cribb (whose name is commemorated in Bristol's Cribb Causeway shopping centre), Tom Sayers, Daniel Mendoza (an ancestor of Peter Sellers), Jem Mace, Tom Molineaux (the first black boxing champion), Gypsy Boswell, Tom Sayers and many others.

The aforementioned Jem Mace was known as The Swaffham Gyspy, although during his life he denied having Romany blood in him. Yet in his own autobiography published in 1908 he acknowledges that his own uncle was 'half-a-gypsy'. Experts and biographers believe Jem clouded his gypsy heritage during his later lifetime through fear it may have impeded his career. Mace is a gypsy name and by all accounts Jem was a swarthy, dark-skinned individual. So in my mind, at least, I feel sure he was. Whatever, he was a key figure in prize-fighting and very much involved in the transition to the gloved boxing that we enjoy today. In his life story Jem talks about a bout he had with Farden Smith, known as King of the Gypsies, in Norwich. Now Smith is a common name in England and the Smiths are the biggest gypsy clan. Nevertheless I do not think it too fanciful to believe that old Farden Smith was a relative of mine. Somewhere along the line we may well have shared the same blood. When Jem retired from the prize ring he travelled around the world giving exhibition bouts and spotting and developing new talent. In New Zealand he came across a young Cornishman whose family had been thrown out of work by the closure of the tin mines and emigrated. His name was Bob Fitzsimmons and with Jem's early encouragement and promotion he went on to become the third ever World Heavyweight Champion of gloved boxing and Britain's first great *boxer*. In a surreal twist to the evolution of this fascinating sport the first fight between Fitzsimmons and his arch-rival Tom Sharkey was refereed by Wild West legend, Wyatt Earp. Fitzsimmons fought Jack Jeffries, Jeffries fought Jack Johnson, Johnson fought Jess Willard, Willard fought Jack Dempsey, Dempsey fought Jack Sharkey, Sharkey fought Primo Carnera, Carnera fought Joe Louis, Louis fought Rocky Marciano, Marciano fought Archie Moore, Moore fought Muhammad Ali, Ali fought Larry Holmes, Holmes fought Evander Holyfield, and he recently made a comeback at forty-six years of age that brings us nicely to the present day.

Although there has been a century of gloved boxing now and prize-fighting has been consigned to the box marked Uncivilised Things We Used To Do But Pretend We Didn't, like cock-fighting, burning old ladies with facial hair as witches and watching *Love Thy Neighbour* it has been sustained in the gypsy community and elsewhere, away from the eyes of the law and uninterested citizens. A whole subculture flourishes around it and the sport can still boast large crowds, huge amounts of money staked and its exclusive heroes, villains and champions. We gypsies practise it as a matter of course to settle family arguments and general disputes, and as it is so ingrained it is no surprise that there are so many of us that become regular and well known bare-knuckle fighters. The names of some of the fighters we'd hear about as children, both gypsies and Gorgios, included Jimmy Frankham, father of Johnny and Sam who became established boxers, Les Stevens, Donny 'The Bull' Adams, Roy Shaw, Boxer Tom, John-John Stanley, Kenny Symes, Lenny McLean, my own grandfather Rymer Smith and of course more recently my cousins Jimmy and Wally Stockin. Wally had fought Johnny Docherty on Epsom Downs in a classic bare-knuckle fight and Jimmy's fight with Johnny Love in the 1980s has gone down in history as one of the bloodiest ever with Jimmy discovering afterwards that he had fought for an hour or more with a fractured skull. That's one of the key differences between bare-knuckle and boxing (other than that one has gloves and one doesn't) is that there are no rounds, no pre-set time. A fight continues until one man gives best (signals he has had enough and concedes defeat) or is unable to continue through being knocked unconscious. Some bouts can and have lasted hours.

Dad, while proud of Muggy and his sons and their achievements, never particularly encouraged any of us to box. Aaron had some fights at Slough Gym and was accomplished but Dad was never a fighting man. He showed us that you didn't need to be physically powerful or prepared to resort to violence to command respect. He taught us that to be polite and courteous to people normally produced better results than to be aggressive or threatening. He could not see the point of fighting for fighting's sake and disliked confrontation. He was essentially a gentle man and a gentleman. Unfortunately, as is the way with the world, not everybody responded in kind. The only act of violence I ever knew about was when Dad struck a pub manager for disrespecting our beloved Husky/Alsatian dog, Blacky. I think it says a lot about the man that only the mistreatment of an animal ever drove him to violence. For this act he received seven days in Wormwood Scrubs prison. Blacky went missing soon after and Dad searched for him in vain from police station to police station and regularly calling at Battersea Dogs Home to see if he had been handed in. Blacky was an old dog and Dad believed that he was so miserable at having bought such upset to the family he had taken himself off to some quiet place to die and cause us no further heartache.

LEARNING TO SWING

My first experience of golf came when I was six years old. 'Do you fancy nine holes, Fish?' Grandfather Rymer asked my dad, calling him by a nickname that only Grandfather used and had no obvious explanation for.

'What's nine holes?' I asked.

'Golf, mate,' came the reply. Dad clearly fancied a game, but taking me wasn't part of the plan.

'If you're ready Fish, we'll take Joe round to Sissy and we'll go.'

I was having none of it. Golf, whatever it was, sounded interesting. Or rather nine holes did. Perhaps they'd let me climb down them too. 'Please let me go, Dad,' I pleaded.

'You're too young to walk round a golf course.'

I tried another tack. 'Please, Grandfather, please. I'll walk and be quiet. I promise.' It worked.

'He'll be all right, Fish. You can pull my trolley, old son.'

And with that we were off, and my love affair with golf began. With no school, I was quickly caddying at every opportunity around Twickenham, Fulwell, Esher and in the money games at Epsom Downs, mostly between Uncle Jasper Smith, who married Rymer's cousin Binky, aka Priscilla, and Rymer. I didn't care who I went with and where, I was just bewitched by the rolling greens, the little flags and the thwack of the ball. I may have been only six or seven but I ensured I made myself useful to the men and did not get in the way as strictly it was the done thing not to have kids around and so I became a good caddy.

I clearly remember my first shots on a golf course as if it were yesterday. Grandfather Rymer, Uncle Jasper and Grandfather's brother, Joe, up on Epsom Downs. Behind me stood the whitewashed old grandstand, now replaced, and out to my left was a wonderful view of the landscape peeling backwards to London town. 'If you look carefully you can see the Post

Office Tower,' Dad was pointing in the general direction of the skyline.

'Oh yes,' I'd say, not having the faintest idea what the Post Office Tower was or what it looked like. I would then hang back behind the men, quickly get balls out of the bag, take swings and wallop one as far as I could.

'Where's this ball come from?' asked Uncle Joe.

'That's my little caddie mate,' replied Grandfather, laughing.

'But he's hitting it a hundred yards.'

'He always does, consistently.'

'He's a right little Tony Jacklin,' added Dad, patting my head. (I would later learn that Tony Jacklin was England's top golfer at the time and later still that we too shared the fabled 7th July birthday.) It wasn't long before I was allowed to play the par-threes when out of sight of the clubhouse.

One night at the yard after a good few beers with all the family in the front room of the caravan, Grandfather scooped me up for a hug and a kiss in his tree-trunk arms, rubbing my face as usual with his prickly stubble.

'Do you know what tomorrow is?' he asked.

'No.'

'Tomorrow is my Winchester trip, and I am going to buy my wonder boy some golf clubs.'

I yelped with excitement. 'But only if you tell me "Who loves ya, baby?"' I think he was a fan of Telly Savalas and *Kojak* on the telly.

'I dunno, Grandfather.'

'Yeah, Grandfather do!' and with that he let out his huge belly laugh that resounded off the metal walls that will stay with me forever. This big man, so happy, although he looked like he'd been through ten world wars, with a cauliflower ear beaten into one piece of flesh and a nose spread across his face. And when I looked in that face I could see white lines everywhere. Sitting on his lap I would trace them with my little fingers.

'What's that white line near your eye?'

'Just another scar my old mate.'

I was fascinated. I didn't know why he had so many of these different markings but found out that each one could yield a tale when I was older.

Riding around the country in Dad and Rymer's old truck was heaven for a young kid. They would collect the shavings and waste from factories, plants and sheet-metal works and then take it off to dealers to get the best price they could and the difference between what they paid and what they sold it for was their wage. The factories that were making bespoke metal products could not be arsed to tout around their off-cuts so we were welcome and to watch Rymer, and later my dad, build up relationships with the gaffers and the owners taught me a lot about how to deal with people. We were not the only gypsies and totters approaching them for 'Any old iron?' so to make a living you had to make them comfortable with you. Rymer was a master at it and he dealt with the same people, sellers and buyers, for years and they liked him and he liked them. There was absolutely no sense in ever trying to have someone over because you would not get their business again. In those days there was plenty of industry around and you did not have to travel too far to make a living unlike later when Britain stopped making things and started to import from abroad instead. Then the distances you had to cover to buy up the same amount of scrap ate into your margins considerably.

Rymer's customer in Winchester would produce enough scrap metal every two weeks for him to live very comfortably, so this was a regular trip for us. Next day, pockets laden with cash, we went straight to the pro-shop at Epsom Downs looking for Mr Rutter, the proprietor. He was out but the assistant said we could wait for him. Grandfather asked if we could borrow a putter while we waited and he agreed. I aimed for hole seven on the practice green and down it pops from a full fifteen yards away. We returned the man's putter and the assistant remarked: 'He may have taught my putter something there.' My little chest puffed out with pride. Giving up on Mr Rutter we whizzed over to Rodney Hutton's pro-shop in Thames Ditton and were welcomed by an old man helping out in the shop. Mr Hutton was out but should be back soon. Perhaps, he was with Mr Rutter?

'We're looking for some old clubs for the boy,' said Granddad. The old man showed us some second-hand putters and there was a putter exactly the same that I'd just used to drain the forty-five-footer on the practice green at Epsom.

'Look, Grandfather,' I squeaked excitedly, 'it's the same one.'

'Then that's our putter,' smiled Rymer.

He found a few more clubs and agreed a price of £12 and I was the proud owner of my first set of clubs. Looking back golf was not as popular a sport as it is nowadays, especially with children. I can't imagine there were many eight-year-olds getting as excited about a set of clubs as most other boys were over acquiring their first pair of football boots. It was unusual. Things are different now. Many youngsters are introduced to golf at an early age, normally carrying the hopes and dreams of their fathers that they might become the next Tiger Woods, and these kids will have a brand-new set of Callaways or Nikes. But, for me, those clubs bought from the proceeds of a scrap-metal dealer meant everything and gave me fantastic pleasure. I practised like mad in the park at Hanworth; a solitary figure while other children climbed trees, fought and played ball games. Soon I could play a few holes with my father and grandfather on balmy summer nights and know they weren't lowering their game to accommodate the kid.

In the meantime, in county Surrey, there was a permanent Romany site built in Epsom where my mum's side of the family lived. It was called Kiln Lane, presumably because a brick kiln of some sort was originally on the site. However, Epsom people recall that immediately before the gypsies were allocated the area, a large steaming rubbish tip existed there and this may or may not say something about council thinking at the time. The Waterloo to Epsom railway line was not just at the bottom of the garden; it was that close that if you opened the window and someone was flicking a fag-end out of the train window it may well have landed in your lap. The area was peppered with industrial yards, car showrooms and electricity sub-stations. Nevertheless, this became Granny Mary's home and there wasn't a day went past when she didn't have a sweet for all the grandchildren and, later, great-grandchildren. She would sell lucky heather when things got a bit hard, and being widowed herself with young children, times were generally that. I was more than happy to play and tumble around the site and its surrounds with my cousins but it was here I was inducted, unwillingly and unwittingly, to a sport or pastime that could not have been further away from the bucolic, graceful and placid enjoyment of golf. Like golf it would come to dominate my life for many, many years.

One cousin, Charlie, who was four months older than me and a bit bigger, had discovered the thrill of fighting and loved it and to be fair to him there was no reason for him to think any of us were any different. I can remember the first time he clumped me in the face. It was the most rude awakening. Here I was – Little Joe – loved and pampered by all. I nestled in the bosom and under the protection of my extended family. I was not prepared for physical pain; my father never hit me and never had anybody else. If I overstepped the mark a raised voice from Dad was enough to send my bottom lip quivering. That first punch from cousin Charlie sent me scuttling into the arms of Granny Mary, sobbing and shaking like a baby.

The next day as is the way with kids I was back outside joining in the horse riding, bike riding and other games with all the children. Charlie seemed keen to take up where he left off and at one point after playing happily, and again when I least expected it, he delivered another well aimed punch to my head. This time I rode the blow and continued to play but keeping my distance from my tormentor. There was no malice on Charlie's part. He seemed to be getting a kick out of giving me a dig when nobody was looking and after he had regained my confidence. It happened time and time again and I was at a loss what to do about it. I couldn't run in again and tell an adult, because even at that young age we knew that being a 'grass' was the lowest of the low. Besides I adored Charlie's dad, my Uncle Ruffy, and wouldn't want him to hear about this. Looking back it was my first challenge in social relations and I had to deal with it myself.

I remember the day well. Another cousin from Dad's side, Dido's Henry, had devised an exciting game of horse-racing. We made up jumps and we children were the jockeys and horses. We even gave the slower and smaller children head-starts to create a proper handicap race. It was truly exciting stuff, a proper game of *Escalado* but with real human beings. I looked out the caravan window and watched the kids breaking up into horses and jockeys, I wanted to run out and join them but Charlie was in the middle and I knew what would happen. 'Can I go out and play?' I asked Dad.

'Course you can, boy. But, remember, you have to stick up for yourself.'

It was a strange moment. I had said absolutely nothing to Dad yet he knew exactly what was going through my mind as clearly as if it was written in big letters on my T-shirt. Of course, I knew about fighting, it was all around me. As I said my cousins Jimmy and Wally Stockin were climbing the boxing hierarchy, professional boxing champion Johnny Frankham was a family friend and at the peak of his career, so you can imagine the pride he inspired in his wider family and Romany communities generally, and fights among the boys and men were a common occurrence on the sites and anywhere where we gathered and drank. My older brother Aaron boxed well and sometimes he'd spar with me but he pulled his punches as he danced around me as I in turn tried to land one on his elusive body. It was a game, though. Same as jockeys and horses.

I walked outside intending to break into a canter and overtake the others on the rail but then decided to turn Charlie's tactic of surprise on himself and banged him as he approached me. I was eight years old and I had struck a fellow human being for the first time and unlocked something I wish I hadn't. Striking my first blow was a memorable experience for me. It unleashed a feeling of achievement inside. Like mastering tying your own shoelaces or riding a two-wheel bike. Once I had used my fists I was conscious of them and the power they could yield.

In an ideal world, or even a normal world, that would have been the end of it – both kids would have learnt a life lesson and they'd have embraced and stayed the best of friends. Our world was not like that. Like it or not if gypsy kids showed an aptitude to fight they were often encouraged to do so. This was just the beginning of a three-year rivalry that saw Charlie and myself become seasoned fighters with and without gloves before we were old enough to take our eleven-plus. Of course, we would never take our eleven-plus because we never went to school, not for any sustained period, but I'm trying to paint a picture here.

That day we fought like a pair of animals and as regularly as clockwork thereafter. The adults sometimes split us up when they saw us but we'd just resume whenever the opportunity arose. Our respective brothers Aaron and Champ took us to Foley Boxing Club and put gloves on us to try and channel the aggression and teach us about boxing but this didn't stop us lapsing back into bloody fights back on the site. If you could add up all the minutes Charlie and I spent bashing each other's brains in it would have run into weeks.

By now I was no longer frightened but I fought with fear. Fear of losing. I tried to use my brain – thinking about tactics rather than brute force. I worked out very early that speed was often the greatest weapon in a boxer's armoury. Also, mental attitude. Mental strength. I decided if Charlie hit me twice I'd hit back three times. The flaw in this strategy was that Charlie must have developed a similar one: I hit him three times and he came back with four. Our fights became bloodier as we got bigger and better and they provided good entertainment for everyone on the Epsom site. At the Foley Boxing Club, where Frank Bruno began his career, the trainers said our bouts were among the best they had seen. One of the trainers was Paul Bradley, a blond-haired Scouser, who possessed a beautiful left hook – one I tried to mimic

– and he gave us much praise and encouragement. Tragically, he was to fall to his death while out roofing at the young age of thirty-eight. He was a real nice man, and I'm still sad he is not around today.

Premature death was all around us children and I have read that even today the average gypsy male only attains forty-eight years of age though I don't know where those figures have come from as I'm not convinced that it says anything about being Romany on a death certificate. If it's true I better get a move on as I've only ten years left. What is true is that a gypsy man is far more likely to die in a violent confrontation than a Gorgio man and as an eight-year-old I found out about that first hand. In 1979 Rymer's brother, Dad's uncle, my great-uncle and cousins Jimmy and Wally's father, Muggy Jim, was murdered in an incident over a pool match at Southall Market. He was killed by a hammer-blow to the head. I was very young when this happened and the details and the raw grief was kept from me and the other children as much as possible, but we knew that Muggy Jim, a lovely man and a great character, was gone for ever and that his wife and children were distraught and would never properly recover, and that a black cloud descended over the whole extended family and community.

In 1981 Charlie and I had our last and most violent fight. I was now eight stone and Charlie a little more. We both had our fair-play men. Fair-play men were required in bare-knuckle matches to ensure fair play, and were vital in adult fights to ensure nobody got killed, especially if there was animosity involved. This was different here – we were family and there was no real animosity. Competitiveness, yes. Animosity, no. Therefore Uncle Dido, Grandfather Rymer's brother and a top fighter in his day, was my second rather than fair-play man and Champ, Charlie's brother, who was about to fight professionally, was his.

'Give it to him, Charlie!' urges Champ.

Uncle Dido is leaning out of his caravan window eyeing the proceedings. 'Go on, Joe,' he encourages. Others from the site have gathered around, as they always do when Charlie and I fight. Today we are both keyed up more than usual. Don't know why. The fight starts. We don't take each other by surprise any more. We play fair. He comes in with a left straight around the ear and follows with a double-left jab in the face as I move back. We get in a clinch and... boom! I catch him with a big right uppercut. Charlie shakes his head and steps forward purposefully. A snappy right from him hits me in the mouth and this pattern repeats itself for about twenty minutes until I miss him on the way in with a left and crash right. I get him full force in the nose and first blood is to me. Dido shouts: 'You got him, Joe.' Like fuck, I have. He clocks me with a massive right hand and left hook to both sides of my jaw and I feel like I've walked out into the road and been struck by two cars coming in opposite directions. He's bleeding heavily though, but this doesn't bother Charlie. Never has. Thirty minutes have gone and maybe I'm winning on points. But points are as useful as bicycles are for fish in bare-knuckle fighting. A crunching right hand seems to penetrate my eyeball – a big flash of blue light like you see when the paparazzi doorstep Madonna, or someone, electrifies my skull and my eyeball feels like it has been stabbed. I am blinded.

'Go on, Charlie boy, finish him off!' I hear. I stagger backwards struggling for balance.

'Come on, Joe, you OK?' says Dido, concern in his voice.

He does not want me to fold but he's worried for me. 'I'm all right, Uncle. It's no problem.' But it is. I manage to keep Charlie at bay with some piston-like pops at his face and I begin to settle as darkness clouds my left eye. My face is closing up and Charlie continues to bleed from the nose. The fight is entering its next phase as dusk envelops the site. 'Joe, come on in now, it's dark.' The sweet voice of my mum popping the violence like a balloon.

'I'll have to go in now,' I say. 'We'll finish it tomorrow.'

'You win Charlie, you done him,' interrupts Champ.

'No, we'll fight on tomorrow,' I protest.

'You're beat Joe,' says Champ firmly.

'Nobody's beat,' shouts Dido, who is still watching from the window. 'Don't do that to the boys. It's a fucking good fight and a draw is the only right result.'

Charlie nods, Champ nods, I nod.

The morning after that fight with Charlie we moved on as travellers do. The two events were not connected. It meant that Charlie's and my fast-growing bodies would have some respite from regular battering, at least. Our destination was Cranford and although it bore little resemblance to the fictional country town populated by Judi Dench on the television, it was an idyllic gypsy site. There were, inevitably, cousins from both sides of my family to knock around with but there were also huge playing fields with long-jump pits and goal nets everywhere. I was no Carl Lewis or Kevin Keegan but I'd join in sometimes. More interestingly there were sweeping swathes of short grass where I could practise my golf in peace.

Getting involved in scraps was the last thing on my mind. I was excited to be among a new set of people and I started to attend a youth club in the grounds of Cranford Community School. Here we had pool tables, darts, table tennis and sweets and lemonade pop. I took a liking for the green baize. There were similarities between the games of pool and golf. Potting and putting. Hitting the white ball. Lining up shots. The club was run by a young man called Hayley and he had a younger brother called Hayden. Hayley was a pleasant man but Hayden was a cocksure type who tended to push us around a bit. One day we had a bit of a row. Can't remember over what and we were about to rip into each other when Hayley intervened. 'If you boys want to fight, let's do it properly.'

He arranged a ring there and then on the disco floor with chairs and ushered us in like a circus ringmaster. He made us touch fists before pushing us apart and then raised his hand and brought it down signalling us to start to box. I think he may have been watching too much *World Of Sport* on a Saturday afternoon. Everyone had gathered around though they were less enthusiastic than the audiences at the Epsom site. I probably didn't realise it until then but I was by now a very good boxer for my age and Hayden was no match for me at all. Hayley realised this quite quickly and conscious that he had just thrown his brother to the lions, so to speak, stopped the fight quite rapidly. We were presented with a 50p piece and bottle of pop each and I thought – this is good. Cranford, Middlesex was turning out to be fun. Back in the caravan I told my brother Aaron that I had been paid for a fight.

'Really?' he said. 'Well, Joe, you're a pro now. If you got paid that was your first professional fight.' I felt good about that. I looked forward to the next one. It seemed so easy.

I soon made pals with two brothers, Paul and Jason Loveridge. They were always up for a lark and attended the local school. I never went to school but during the lunch hour I would creep through a hole in the fence and mingle with my new friends in their playground. I suppose, technically, this is the opposite to playing truant. One day they pointed out another boy in the playground.

'Do you reckon you could fight that boy, Joe?'

He looked older than me. 'Yes, I reckon I could.'

'I think he's quite hard...' said Jason. I was being goaded, even set up, but I was keen to please my new friends.

'Do you want to fight me, mate?' I called over.

'Fuck off, you little pikey.'

'Come on then you Gorgio bread.'

He was standing on a wall about a foot above me – a fact I should have borne in mind as I swaggered towards him. He unleashed a round house kick to my jaw and somehow I didn't go down. I pressed forward but only walked into a hail of fists.

A lady teacher blowing on a whistle ran towards us very flustered. 'Stop this! Stop this at once! What on earth is the matter with you boys?' She looked at my opponent and then at me. She was confused as she did not recognise me and I had nothing resembling a school uniform on.

'Go away,' she eventually demanded, pointing in to the distance like I was some sort of stray dog.

I was finding the reaction confusing. Back in Surrey they clapped and slapped my back when I fought but here in Middlesex they either gave you a fifty-pence piece or stopped you and treated you with contempt.

Now, with the family growing – John having been born in 1979 and Mum expecting again – Dad had little choice but to move into a house. There was always pressure on Romanies to give up their lifestyle and ditch the caravans and take houses and more and more did. It made sense. There were fewer and fewer sites where we could pull over and stay without arousing tension and it wore you down. We found a perfect house close to Grandfather's yard and also to Feltham swimming baths. It was on one of my first visits to the baths where I recognised the boy from the playground. He had grown even bigger and was on the top diving board and I was a few dripping bodies behind. I dived off before my turn not liking heights at the best of the times and a resumption of hostilities on a plank of wood balanced at a great height filled me with dread.

With my feet firmly on the ground I made sure he saw me as he lifted himself out of the pool. 'Hello, mate,' he said. 'I recognise you from Cranford School. I'm Chris. Shall we shake hands?'

'Yes mate, sure.' And we stood there in our trunks pumping hands.

'How old are you, Joe?'

'I'm eleven now, Chris.'

'Eleven. Fucking hell! Your two years younger than me. I normally fight fourteen and fifteen-year-olds.'

Two years isn't much when you're an adult but at that age it's practically a generation gap. Chris challenged me to a swimming race and I obliged. Can't remember who won.

Even at that young age I was aware that gypsies were experiencing the biggest cultural changes in their history and that my parents and grandparents' generations were finding it hard to abandon a way of life that had been practically unchanged for five hundred years. We gypsies are first recorded in this country in the 1500s arriving via a long trek across the Middle East and Europe having originated, it is believed, in India. I can go along with this as I know when I go down my local curry house they call the water *parni* as we do and there are other language similarities. At first we were welcomed as an exotic and colourful novelty, but then we were seen as a threat and a law was passed in 1530 banning us and ordering us 'home'. In 1554 when it was realised that the law was not really working it was strengthened a tad when the death penalty was introduced for being a gypsy and also for consorting with one. No wonder we kept on the move. Only in 1791 when William Pitt the Younger was Prime Minister were those laws repealed. Now if there is a touch of the persecution complex bubbling under in the gypsy DNA this might go some way to explaining it.

Thereafter we settled into a happy nomadic existence travelling around in brightly-painted wagons drawn by horses and getting a few coins selling heather and pegs, dealing in horses, picking fruit, sharpening knives and forks and living off the land. We didn't take anybody's jobs nor we did we move in next door to anyone, therefore the Romanies and the rest of the population rubbed along together reasonably well for a few hundred years.

In the last century governments became increasingly vexed by a group of people in their midst who did not register their births and deaths, were absent from the census, rarely showed up in schools or hospitals, and perhaps most significantly were difficult to tax. By the middle of the 20th century, even though many of us could not read, we could see the writing on the wall as traditional rural lifestyles had all but disappeared and started to buy land to park our caravans on and live a more settled existence. This is when the real problems began and buried prejudices came to the fore as few people wanted us settling close to them. Laws were passed to prevent us doing this which soon extended to merely stopping anywhere for a period of time. Even though local councils were ordered to provide sites for us they often didn't, or what they did provide was inadequate, and it is this failure in planning that led to the deteriorating relationship between gypsies and Gorgios that, although improving year on year, persists to this day.

Before all this though was the Second World War. In Europe Adolf Hitler's Germany nursed a particular hatred of Romanies and as his army swept through the continent an estimated half a million were put to their deaths in the concentration camps. Had he of made it across the English Channel then I would most probably not be here, but then again neither, perhaps, would you.

GOODBYE, RYMER

My brother Aaron was improving steadily as a boxer. Physically he had grown into a lean young man from the chubby boy he had been and together we had moved from Foley Boxing Club to one back at Epsom and Ewell. Pitt House stood on the edge of Ewell Village and old Joe Taylor was our trainer. He looked like he was in his eighties but he still had the poise of a fighter and I would have not liked to have taken a right-hander from his wrinkled old fists. Aaron was the top fighter there and rated at third in the country for his age and weight. I was too heavy to get registered fights, so I continued to have gym bouts often giving away as much as four years in age. At eleven I was a veteran of more than twenty of these gym fights and many knuckle contests. But suddenly Aaron decided to quit boxing; even though he was at the top of his game, forever improving and never having been decked. This disheartened Dad who, although he had not been over keen on the boxing game, recognised his son's sophisticated talent in the ring. He and I did not have the same connection as a team when it came to boxing. We were a three-man operation and when Aaron bowed out Dad and I were not so motivated to go to the club. Anyway, Grandfather was gently pushing me a little harder towards the altogether more gentle sport of golf.

Rymer Smith, my grandfather, was a remarkable man. Legend is an overused word in most contexts but Rymer *was* a legend among Romany folk. Mainly as a fighter: he had worked the fairground booths and cut his teeth (and his eyes, mouth and ears) as a bare-knuckle warrior before turning professional as a boxer. The boxing booths on the travelling fairs that were once commonplace were the starting point for many young fighters that went on to greater things: Randy Turpin, Tommy Farr and Jimmy Wilde were just some of the illustrious names that started out taking on up to twenty-five people a day in the three-round bouts that were staged for a bloodthirsty crowd of fairgoers, day-in and day-out. You can imagine it:

Rymer sitting on his corner stool, his arms stretched out and resting on the ropes while the showman shouting through a loudhailer whips the crowd up into a frenzy simultaneously attempting to goad some young chap in the audience to step in with his man – the incentive being a couple of pounds if he could survive three rounds and a few minutes of glory. Inevitably there was always someone fuelled by drink or youthful bravado, probably both, who would throw up his hand and, to much cheering from his mates, climb into the ring. Rymer would measure him up mentally and try to balance the need to entertain the crowd and the desire to dispatch him as quickly as possible. It was a long night ahead. The closing seconds of the first round or the opening ones of the second was his preferred time to unleash the knockout punch.

The boxing booths are interwoven with gypsy and fighting culture as are the travelling fairgrounds themselves. There is a famous painting by William Hogarth showing debauched Londoners at play called *Southwark Fair* and a boxing booth is visible. This is 1733. They survived until recently although in the last few decades only a showman called Ron Taylor, who died in 2006 well into his nineties, kept it going. He said: 'The boxing booth is good training for a boxer because he never knows what kind of opponent he will get and it keeps him alert.' I should say so.

Rymer went on to fight professionally under the name Jack Daley though I'm not sure why he felt he had to change his name. Maybe as Rymer Smith he needed to avoid the attentions of someone or other. He met and knew many of the boxing greats of his era. Some of his fights were at the Winter Gardens in Bournemouth and inevitably he met up with the local boxer who was to become a champion – Freddie Mills. Freddie too had worked the fairground booths before turning professional and they were scheduled to fight each other professionally in 1939 and for many years a poster existed in the family promoting the event. However, war broke out and the fight never happened. Years later when Rymer was parked up on a site near Shepperton, Freddie cruised past in his Roller on his way to the film studios and he spotted Rymer and stopped his car and greeted his old pal for a chat. He pressed a white fiver into the hand of Wally, Rymer's son, declaring he'd be a world champion boxer. By this time Freddie was a TV star and was a panellist on the *What's My Line?* quiz show along with Gilbert Harding and Lady Isobel Barnet. Strangely and very sadly two of these celebrities committed suicide although Rymer always maintained that Freddie did not take his own life, claiming he'd been murdered. He'd been found dead in his car with gunshot wounds to his head outside his nightclub in Soho. The verdict said the wounds were self-inflicted but Rymer was having none of it. Even a decade or two after Freddie's death Rymer would talk about his death and lower his voice so my young ears could not hear the names he mentioned in connection with it.

Many said that if the war had not interrupted Grandfather's boxing career he'd have become a Middleweight Champion. His first professional fight had been against Scouser Ernie Roderick in 1934 which he lost on points. This was no bad showing as Rymer was only sixteen years of age at the time and Ernie was in his early twenties and a fine boxer who went on to become British Welterweight Champion and a challenger for the world title. That fight was at the old Liverpool Stadium and would have been well attended. I would dearly love to find the poster for that one. Finding his records all these years later on the internet I have discovered that many of his fights were staged at The Ring, Blackfriars, in London. This venue was immensely popular in the early part of the century, providing quality boxing at cheap prices and Rymer fought there after. The names of other fighters give you a feel for the place: Lefty 'Satan' Flynn who was a Jamaican, Battling JoJo, Ginger Sadd, Stoker Fred Clark, Trooper Jim Gully and so on. The Ring was demolished by the Luftwaffe in 1940 and today a pub of the same name stands across the road where many pictures of those old fighters adorn the walls. According to the records Rymer's (or Jack's) last professional fight was in 1940 against Sid Hart in the Town Hall at High Wycombe, which he lost.

However, Rymer had also taken up golf, which was an upper-middle-class sport in Britain and therefore one that gypsies had no access to. The game had been invented in Scotland, spread to England and was then exported to the rest of the world along with the British Empire. Back in the 15th century when it all started the Scots took to it so enthusiastically that King James II banned it because he believed it was distracting the people from practising their archery, a skill he wanted them to hone as he felt an English invasion was imminent. In Victorian times when the railways facilitated access to courses the game grew in popularity. The first British Open was played at Prestwick in 1860 and the first golfing superstars were born. 'Old' Tom Morris won the event in 1862, 1864 and 1867, but his son 'Young' Tom Morris went better winning it four years on the spin from 1869. They remain the oldest and the youngest winners ever of the tournament at forty-six and seventeen respectively. Shortly after the Americans began to sponsor tournaments and the USA became the leading force in the sport, although the British tournaments remained the prestigious ones to win. In 1900 it became a recognised Olympic sport. American players such as Bobby Jones, Henry Cotton, Ben Hogan and Walter Hagen became superstars and the latter showed all the necessary flamboyance by using his Rolls-Royce as his changing room and, when winning the British Open, giving all his prize-money to his caddy. The 1960s and 1970s were dominated by Americans Arnold Palmer and Jack Nicklaus and the South African, Gary Player. Only when Seve Ballesteros won the British Open in 1979 and the US Masters in 1980 did Europeans start to get a look in. Since then Colin Montgomerie, Ian Woosnam, Sandy Lyle and Nick Faldo have made Britain a force again on the world golfing stage.

As the game developed in this country it became the preserve of the reasonably well-heeled. This was natural as there was expense involved in getting the equipment together, joining clubs and travelling and playing other courses. Whereas the working classes concerned themselves mainly with playing football and the aristocrats kept themselves amused with their croquet, the emerging middle-classes claimed golf as their own participant sport. Clubs sprung up all over commuter land and were embraced enthusiastically. Unfortunately this led in many cases to golf snobbery where clubs were run more along the lines of a freemason's lodge than a sports club. What you wore, who you played with, who was captain, committees and rules and regulations became more important than the playing of eighteen holes. Memberships were rationed and the strands of society they thought might lower the tone were vigorously excluded. First and foremost of these strands were often women. For many years (and to some extent still today) it was hard to practise golf without jumping through countless hoops and meeting various criteria which had nothing to do with enthusiasm or ability.

A little matter like the English class system would not deter Rymer though. One day he merely pulled up on some land that happened to be adjacent to a golf course and he and his cousin Nelson peered over the fence and watched the golfers in their silly floppy caps and plus-fours play the course. When they'd all finished and headed for the nineteenth hole and their scotch on the rocks and communal guffawing, Rymer and Nelson sneaked on the greens and practised themselves using sticks broken off nearby trees. Catching the bug they acquired some crude clubs and returned to snatch quick games and practise around deserted holes time and time again. They became competent – Rymer especially. On one occasion one of the members spotted Nelson get a hole in one and was so impressed that the two men were allowed to play as much as they wanted as long as nobody else was around. Rymer practised continually and became more accomplished. He was very good. As far as I know he never attempted to join a club because he would have known that it would have been a lost cause and therefore his game was unable to develop any further.

Gambling was another of Rymer's passions and as long ago as 1938 he put a grand on a horse. Seventy years later a wager of a £1,000 on a single horse is a bit racy but in 1938, in austere times when a £1,000 was like £40,000 in today's money, it was absolutely ridiculous. The horse lost. In 1956 he befriended a German prisoner of war who had chosen to remain in this country when the conflict had ended (which speaks volumes for how we treated our enemy prisoners – I don't imagine many of ours stayed in Germany), and this man told him that Bert Trautmann, the German Manchester City goalkeeper would be instrumental in helping his side win the FA Cup. Rymer started backing City in each round of the competition, reinvesting his winnings each time. By the time City reached the final Rymer stood to win £22,000 if they won. Rymer's less headstrong family and friends urged him to back finalists Birmingham as well and this way he could not lose but Rymer ploughed ahead, went to the game at Wembley, and saw City win 3-1. Don Revie, later to become England manager, bossed the field that day and Rymer revered him ever after, but the man who was unlucky that historic Saturday afternoon was Bert Trautmann. He broke his fucking neck. Twenty-two thousand oncers in 1956 would be worth close to a million pounds today and what Rymer did with all the cash is anyone's guess. He was always generous to a fault and no doubt the bookmakers that protested so when he cleaned them out got it all back over time.

When he was riding high as a professional boxer or soon after he packed up he was 'adopted' for a spell by Jack 'Spot' Comer. Spot was a notorious

Jewish gangster famed for standing up to Oswald Moseley's anti-Semitic Blackshirts in the Battle of Cable Street in 1936, and feared in the underworld for his protection rackets and racecourse razor antics. According to Rymer, Spot liked having boxers and hard men around him and as Grandfather was a gypsy too he was doubly interesting to Spot. He was not used as a bodyguard or enforcer, more of a trophy from what I could gather. Grandfather said he was truly astonished by the amounts of money he saw Spot take, carry and spend. This was the 1930s when we were supposed to be in the worst economic slump of modern times and Spot would take thousands of pounds each week from his 'clients'. Jack's control of the London underworld continued into the 1950s when he was finally attacked by Billy Hill's men Albert Dimes and a young Frankie Fraser. Unusually for a man in his line of work, though, he lived in to ripe old age dying as late as 1996 when he was in his eighties.

By the time I knew my grandfather he had calmed down and his fighting, gambling and carousing days were over. He exuded wisdom and gentleness. He took a great interest in all his grandchildren and would watch Aaron and myself at the gym and in bouts, but he was disapproving of fights outside of that environment.

'The best man is the one that walks away,' he said, although I did not yet understand his logic. I bathed in the glow of his gentlemanly presence and listened transfixed and wide-eyed as he told stories of his youth, his boxing, his golf and his many escapades. The family history was passed down by him and great, great, great-uncles and aunties sharing names but all with distinct characters and stories came to life in my fertile imagination. For a man steeped in the rough and tumble of life and bearing countless scars, bumps and bruises as proof, he was surprisingly serene and graceful and I never heard him swear. He took me everywhere with him and I was his mate. Down his local he taught me to play cribbage and at twelve years of age I won a tournament. It was a source of amusement and puzzlement to the locals as cribbage is one of those pub games (played with cards, a board and matchsticks) that require a bus pass and smoker's cough to partake.

'My grandson pars eleven holes at Fulwell today,' he'd announce as we walked into the bar, his chest puffed up. He was very proud of me and I was proud to make him proud. One day he said to me that if I beat him on a nine-hole round he would hand me his clubs and retire. We played the game at Twickenham and he played his best, in fact he played better than normal, so I thought this retiring thing was a joke. On the last hole, a 520-yard par-five, he was one down on me and I cracked one straight down the middle then knocked my second shot within a hundred yards and then put my nine-iron to within about ten feet of the hole and he missed the green in three. I was the winner with a round of forty-two shots and Grandfather did it in forty-four. He smiled and put his arm around me. 'These clubs now belong to you, young man.'

One Monday night in November 1983 Grandfather arranged for me to play a couple of men from his local pub. He had obviously backed me to beat them and on hearing I was only twelve they probably could not resist the punt. It was all very friendly. As we drove home from the pub he seemed lost in thought. 'You will become a professional golfer, Joe. Of that I'm sure. But I won't live to see it.'

He had some heart trouble a few years earlier but was in rude health as far as we were concerned. He was not a man given to melancholic musings and him saying this was quite weird and discomfiting.

'Don't be silly, Grandfather. Course you will.'

'No old mate, I won't. You had two grandfathers, and now one is gone and I won't be here for much longer. You will have to accept this. And I want you to golf, Joe, not fight. Golf's for you. Will you remember that? Will you promise me that?'

I was scared he was saying this and looked to Dad in front of the car to say something, to tell Granddad not to be so stupid, but he didn't. He looked scared and upset too.

The following morning it was cold, with the frost on the grass and the breath from my mouth almost freezing mid-air in front of me. The old heater in the car was stubbornly refusing to emit hot air as the two of us drove towards the rendezvous with our two golfers. 'I don't think I'll bother today,' he said.

'Please Grandfather. I want to play golf. I want to play those men.'

'I will drop you there, mate. Don't worry. It's just a bit cold for me today.'

I didn't want to play them without Grandfather there. Not because I was shy or worried or anything; I wanted to please Grandfather and I wanted him to be there when I beat them and won him some money. I noticed Dad's thick chunky blue cardigan lying on the back seat. 'Wear Dad's cardigan, Grandfather. Wear that. It'll keep you warm.'

'OK, boy. I'll put that on and walk the first three holes.'

The men were there as arranged and we teed off. Grandfather spoke to the men. 'Look I'm going to go after the next two holes. Make sure you look after my grandson and drop him back, please.' The men nodded.

'Is that OK, Joe?'

'Course it is, Granddad. Are you OK, though?'

'Yes, I'm OK.'

I made five on the second hole and hit my tee shot down the left of the third my ball finishing short behind some trees. I then hit a beauty over these trees with some drawn spin to within about eight feet of the flag. 'Grandfather will be pleased with that one,' I thought.

I looked for him and then noticed someone lying in front of the trees across the fairway. The way the body was positioned told me they were unwell. It didn't look right but I was not immediately alarmed because although my first thought was for Grandfather this man had different clothes on and then in a flash I remembered he was wearing Dad's cardigan. I panicked and shouted to my playing partners who ran over to him. I didn't go. I couldn't. I was frozen to the spot and then I ran to the clubhouse and phoned 999 and asked for an ambulance. It seemed to arrive in a blink of an eye and bolstered by the presence of the ambulance men I followed them over to my grandfather. As I crouched down beside him I welled up as I saw that old battered fist gripping my three iron; my club that he was using to aid his walking. He hadn't let go. He had a pulse. I heard someone say that. There was a cut above his eye just like another boxer had opened him up but this was from the fall and the blow having been delivered by the Good Man above. The only man who could fell him.

When I phoned the ambulance I had also alerted my family and they started arriving as the ambulance men gently lifted Grandfather on a stretcher into the vehicle. My dad, Aaron and I followed the ambulance, and Dad assured me he would recover, but Aunt Phyllis, who had travelled with Rymer in the ambulance, broke the news when we arrived at the hospital that Rymer was dead. It was the 14th November 1983. I will never ever forget it. The family wailed and cried, holding one another, not able or not wanting to absorb that Rymer had gone. By the time we got back to the yard, our happy little world crushed, word had spread already and family and friends had started to arrive by the score. They came to offer comfort and condolence or, as we have the biggest family in the country, share their heartbreak.

I have heard it said that we gypsies make a meal of death, the days after passing and the funeral, and perhaps we do. But we would have it no other way. I cannot see the sense in swift burials, bottled-up feelings, stilted conversation and discreet pots of tea and ham sandwiches back at the house. This is the end of a life! The single biggest thing that happens to anyone after birth. It needs to be marked and that life should be celebrated and mourned. Family and friends should be allowed time and opportunity to be with the body and share their feelings. Stories need to be told and retold. Grief has to be exposed and aired. The funeral has to be an event. It is the man or lady's last hurrah and we owe it to them to push the boat out. And we do. If this disrupts a town's routine for a few minutes as a procession snakes through the high streets and on to a graveyard, then I'm sorry, but in my eyes the marking of a passing of a loved one should disrupt the routine for a few seconds or minutes.

Another element of how some gypsies mark a death that seems to fascinate and horrify in equal measures is the custom of burning a person's caravan following the death. Of course in the early days it would be the person's vardo or wagon and the reason was that many felt that they did not want to be living in and using the belongings of a dead man or woman. It was like there was a desire for finality. We never went in for it in my family and I would estimate that only about one in ten gypsies do today. It's not practical for one. Now that most gypsies are in houses or mobile homes I'm not sure the council would be rushing to re-house us if every few years we burnt the house down. A custom we do adhere too is never looking backwards when walking in a funeral march or in a cortege. There is a suspicion we gypsies have is that if you look behind you then you will be seeing another funeral soon. It's probably codswallop but why take the risk?

On the day of Rymer's funeral we all drew comfort and support from one another. There were literally hundreds of people attending. Grandfather had been lying in the yard for four days as people from all over the country came to respect his body and share some last time with him. Being travellers, people came from far away and we were not going to deprive anyone that loved the man from seeing him. It was time to take him from the yard to be buried. My dad put his hand on my shoulder and said: 'Come with me, Joe. Come and say goodbye to your grandfather for the last time and make him that promise.' We went inside the tent and I held one hand and Dad held the other, both of us choking back tears.

'Grandfather, I will become a professional golfer, I promise you.'

There we were, three generations linked by hands, two of us crying. We were a team. Inseparable like three old mates and now one was leaving. We walked outside in a trance and joined the cortege as Grandfather was put into a hearse and drove slowly away. I learnt from a press article afterwards that one old man standing at the side of the road removed his cap at this point and sighed: 'My God, that man could fight.'

PLAYING A ROUND

With my promise to Grandfather in mind, Dad shortly after fixed me up with a golf membership at Twickenham. It was a great tonic for me and helped me deal with the death of Rymer. My first handicap was eighteen and I quickly got that down to thirteen and then twelve. The structured environment and good facilities were working wonders on my game and when I played in my first Open event in 1985, The Richmond Open, I won it. My handicap was now down to seven but I seemed to stick at that. With all due respect to Twickenham Golf Course the condition wasn't suitable for a short game with its small bumpy slow greens. I practised for hours on my chipping outside our house and on the green next to it. I would make my holes up, playing blind over walls and through tiny gaps in trees. However, I could not push that handicap below seven at Twickenham and one of my friends, Paul Champion, suggested I should come with him and join Home Park in Kingston, Surrey. The club was situated in the grounds of Hampton Court and to make it more interesting there was always the possibility that your shot might ricochet off a roving deer's antlers.

I was excited on my first visit and Mum gave me a lift there. We pulled into a nearby garage to fill up with petrol and while Mum held the pump I joined the queue inside to pay. I could see through the window that a man in a van behind Mum's car was leaning out of his window and shouting. I stepped outside and could hear 'Fucking well hurry up!' and more. He negotiated around my mum to leave the garage and we made eye contact. I raised my fist to him as he sped off and he did a handbrake skid and stopped and jumped out of his van and charged at me. I had never seen anyone so angry. He was about forty years of age with a shaved head and generous tattoos. Large muscles twitched in his upper arms and angry veins bulged in his forehead and neck.

'I will fucking kill you,' he growled.

I was fourteen or fifteen years old now and had not had a fight for a couple of years. Golf was my passion and I had not been mixing with people who wanted to bash your brains out at the first opportunity. I was terrified at his anger and at his power and he came at me lashing out and connected with my chin and although it rocked me I remained standing. I adopted the traditional prize-fighting pose: fists high, one foot forward which confused him and came back with a combination of lefts and rights, one of which made his mouth bleed. Mum charged between us. 'Leave him alone, he's only fourteen!' she screamed.

'No, he's older than that, Mum,' I joked, getting into my stride. 'Come on you bald-headed cunt, let's finish it off.' I was pushing him around the forecourt with my punches and he could not get near me. Mum came on his blind side and attacked him with her shoe and handbag and the man gathered himself and ran off in the direction of the golf course leaving his van with the door hanging open and the engine running.

Home Park, when we finally got there, was near perfect; speedy, smooth greens with the very best of practice grounds. I was so much at home immediately and my handicap quickly tumbled to four. I loved the place and practised non-stop even if I wasn't playing the course. The head pro at Home Park was a man called Len Roberts and he soon got to know me. 'Come on Joe,' he would say, 'it's not that important. Haven't you got a home to go to?'

'I want to be good Mr Roberts. I want to be the best.'

Len would smile and just say the gates would be closing soon. Grant Harrison was an attached pro at the club and he took me under his wing. He was a former champion tour player and I looked up to him as my coach and even his wife Morrie took a lively interest in my development. I knew they discussed me because Morrie would say things like 'I hear you've learnt your punch and spin shot,' and I would feel great knowing I was worthy of their discussion.

One blustery and unpleasant afternoon I was playing a stinker when one of my partners, Jack Strange, said: 'Club Championship next week then Joe. I suppose Bill Cooley will win again.'

'No, not this year,' I replied.

'Can't see who'll beat him,' Jack mused.

'I will.'

'You'll have to play better than you are today,' laughed Jack. But I meant it. I was not being deliberately arrogant, I felt I could win. Mr Bill Cooley had won the Club Championship eight times out of nine and nobody was betting against him.

The format was that the top sixteen qualified from thirty-six holes and seeded accordingly. I shot seventy and seventy-four and Bill shot seventy-one and seventy-two. We were therefore seeded first and second but before we could meet we had to play the other seeds. We both came through this and the final match was set over thirty-six holes.

It was my first big game and on the day of the final my dad tried to get some of the gamblers to bet against me, but I was soon four holes ahead of the adult and nobody was biting. Bill was one under and I was five under when he shook my hand on the thirty-fifth hole knowing he'd been beaten. I had won my first championship at the age of fifteen and I felt elated. I wished Grandfather could have seen. But Dad *did* see and I knew how proud he was. I could only see cups and glory ahead.

Was I cock of the walk or what? Not yet sixteen years of age and the 1987 Home Park club champion and playing under par most of the time. I broke the course record twice within three days and strongly felt this was just the beginning. I didn't know it then but not everybody at the club was as happy as I was at my rapid ascent. In that same year I entered the London Junior Open which was a huge tournament with a field of 137 young talents and the final stages were going to be televised. I knew it was going to be a massive challenge but I was determined to win it and my confidence was so high I thought I could and would. We travelled, me and Dad, in his old scrap-metal truck and Mum took the faithful family Ford Cortina, us figuring she'd be less likely to be pulled by the police on the way – the Cortina being the family vehicle that had run out of road tax. We pulled into the car park alongside Mercs, BMWs, Jaguars and even Bentleys and Rolls-Royces. I felt like a Beverly Hillbilly, slightly intimidated, until I reminded myself this was not a posh car show but a golf competition and I was going to win it. I got off to a nice steady start with one birdie and one bogey and I was level after seven, and then the rain started and the game became tougher. Nevertheless, I kept my head down and made eleven straight pars to card my score of seventy. With the rain so heavy we headed home while the other contestants still played and switching the TV on as we walked into the house we were surprised to see coverage of the tournament on the BBC channel.

'And the winner with an excellent round of seventy was Joe Smith of Home Park, Kingston...'

'Dad, Dad, we've won!' We couldn't get back in the car quick enough to race back to Richmond Park for the prize-giving, not wanting to miss any second of glory.

Dennis Thatcher, husband of the then Prime Minister, Margaret, was on the podium waiting to hand out the prizes. His wife may have been somewhere else in the world, possibly sucking up to President Reagan or courting Mr Gorbachev, but Dennis was here, shaking the hand of a scruffy gypsy kid and beaming from ear to ear. I can't remember what he said but it was something nice and encouraging. I held my trophy aloft and photographers knelt and snapped me, like they did in the films, while well-wishers slapped my back and others even asked for my autograph. Some reporters interviewed me quickly and to add to my feelings of celebrity the BBC came round a short time later and made a mini-documentary to be broadcast on a children's television programme. We never had a video recorder then and I do not have a copy to refer to, but if I recall, the angle they took was curiosity at a gypsy boy winning a major junior golf tournament. I lapped up all the attention.

The first British Open I had been to was in 1981. Our family had travelled down to Sandwich, Kent with my Uncle Cliff and his family in our caravans. We set up home in a small car park next to the train station and Dad and Uncle Cliff got into a conversation with Gary Cullen, a leading tour player, and they ended up having a few beers together. In the morning my sister and I got up early and went out looking for dry wood to make a fire with and Mum cooked some egg and bacon. Bernhard Langer was, and still is, my golfing idol and we followed him around all week not missing a single one of his shots. Bernhard nearly clinched it too, finishing second to the American, Bill Rogers. Bernhard was my first golfing hero because a couple of years previous to this British Open my dad had wagered on him in another competition and we had followed him round the course as Dad monitored his investment. I liked his attitude: a determined, dogged fighter who got on with the job and that was it. He didn't go in for any of the flamboyancy that some of his contemporaries were beginning to show and he was a perfect gentleman, always. He won and Dad got a nice few quid. Bernhard became our man. We saw him again in 1985 at Royal St George's in Sandwich in another British Open and this time ten of our families had travelled together and we all managed to get plotted up on the course. It was fantastic, now old enough to get up in the morning and wolf down breakfast on my own and get straight over to the practice range and watch all the players. Then off to first tee, and to watch Bernhard every shot of the round. Exciting stuff and he was leading going into the final round but eventually finished third to Sandy Lyle, the winner, and the runner-up, the much missed Payne Stewart. Payne, who tragically died in a plane crash a few years back, was a real character and once played dressed in garb in the design of America's star-spangled flag. I made a mental note about that.

Two years later in 1987 I was back at Royal St George's in Sandwich, but this time I was playing. After winning the London Junior Open the question was asked: the gypsy kid is good but how will he fare against the country's top amateurs and adults? In an attempt to answer this we entered the Grand Challenge Cup for amateurs. This was certainly a step up in class and, because my handicap was relatively too high, at first I was told I was on the reserve list. I was desperate to get in as it was a prestige event and back in 1959 it had been won by an up-and-coming nineteen-year-old American named Jack Nicklaus, so it had a pedigree. Again I was confident of doing well. I felt I knew the course because besides tracking Bernhard Langer around it I had caddied there for Ian Cummings in the PGA Tournament in 1983. Time was ticking away when my dad confided in me that he had had a dream.

'I saw you, me and Grandfather at Sandwich and you were playing and were walking to the eighteenth fairway and a policeman told the crowd to make way for us...'

'But Dad, did I win the championship?' I needed to get to the crux of the dream.

'The dream did not reveal that,' he replied rather mysteriously. 'But, *he* won't be there...'

Dad's words tailed off as he looked into the distance. 'He' was Grandfather. I looked at my dad and his eyes were clouded with tears. The next day the phone rang and I was no longer a reserve. I was playing the event.

I knew my way around St George's, but nevertheless was overawed when we arrived, recognising faces and seeing the names of all the quality golfers competing. I managed pars over the first few holes but missed a tiny putt of a foot on the twelfth hole but shook this off. Anyone who has competed over this course will verify that pars are your score and birdies are bonuses after shooting seventy-five. Jack Nicklaus won here scoring 149 for two rounds. In the afternoon with head down and Dad on the bag we drilled on. Coming down the eighteenth I needed a par-four for seventy-two which would be an excellent result around this beast of a course. That would be easier said than done. A good drive down the right left me six-iron into the green. I struck well but pulled it left a shade into the little valley where Sandy Lyle had famously taken three to get up and down. This time, at least, I did better chipping it and seeing the ball run into the bank to within four feet and then sank the putt perfectly in the middle of the hole. As I had been a reserve and my handicap was higher than anyone else's I had been in the very last group to play and when finishing I signed my card and asked how I had finished to be told that I had tied first on 147. I waited expectantly to find out when the play-off would take place. I was elated to have jointly won the competition, against all odds, and believed that on this form I would win the play-off. An official approached me smiling broadly. 'Congratulations, young fella. You have won – there's no light to play off and the other chap can't make tomorrow so on count back your second round of seventy-two against his seventy-four means you are our new champion. I think our youngest ever. Top performance, I must say.'

'Thank you, sir.' I looked at Dad and he looked at me and we beamed. In our minds we were both thinking of Rymer. Was he here? Suddenly my thoughts went to other things. I would be expected to make a speech in front of all these people! Shit. Only at this point did my legs turn to jelly.

'Don't worry,' said Dad, 'say anything. Just keep it short and sweet.'

It's all right for you, you bastard, I thought, you haven't got to do it. I even considered just getting up and saying: 'My father would like to say a few words.' I sat down and looked at the floor and rehearsed in my head what I was going to say. Dad and I overheard snatches of conversation: 'Apparently some gypo kid has won it...' was one remark from a man not realising I was the gypo kid standing near him. I was too nervous thinking about my speech and I did not want to let anyone down or confirm any prejudices some of these people had about the general intelligence and courtesy of gypsies.

At this point another committee member approached: 'I do apologise Joe, but there will be no winner's presentation because it has been decided there will have to be a play-off.'

It's funny how these people when they know a decision could be dubious try to distance themselves from it by using language like 'it has been decided' as if some other invisible body had made that decision.

'Fine,' I said, not betraying any emotion. 'What time tomorrow, sir?'

'It is not possible to play tomorrow,' he replied. 'It will take place in six weeks' time.'

'But, I'm ready to play now, sir.' The odour of a rat was beginning to waft around.

'Yes Joe, but your opponent has a job and he can't do it until that time.'

He stressed the word job as if it was a term I could not be expected to understand. Whether that was due to my tender age or me being a gypsy, I do not know. To be honest Dad and I were intimidated by the occasion, by the people and by the surroundings and we accepted the decision even though it was not in my favour. I was in red-hot form as my playing over the last few months had demonstrated – but I could not guarantee that in six weeks' time my momentum would be maintained. I will never know why the decision was made not to present me with the winner's cup there and then *after* telling me that they were going to, but even though my opponent's protests probably played some part I can't help thinking that there were influential people around who did not want a gypsy boy winning that day.

The play-off came and even though I killed my opponent tee to green my putting was off and he won two to one. I was hugely disappointed but accepted defeat gracefully and got on with improving my game. However, the bitterness I felt about the events of the original match came flooding back and intensified when some months later I met a top amateur from Kent.

'You're the kid who played that joker in the play-off for the Grand Challenge Cup?'

'Yes, mate.'

'How disappointed you must be to lose to *him*.'

'Too right. I should have beaten him, but my putting was shit.'

'Did he get up to any of his antics?'

'Antics? What d'you mean?'

'Didn't you know? Didn't anyone tell you? He's a cheat. A convicted cheat. He's served a three-year ban.'

I didn't feel angry. I cannot say whether he cheated in his game against me. I was not looking for that. It had never occurred to me that *anyone* ever cheated in golf. I was deeply upset and hurt though because it was a learning moment for me. I had largely been insulated from prejudice against gypsies. Indeed I felt that some of the prejudice *our* people felt about Gorgios and the outside world was overdone. I had been treated well and fairly up to that point and felt that most people did not have it in for gypsies, as we are sometimes prone to believe. People like Jim Needle, my reading tutor, Joe Taylor, my old trainer at the Epsom and Ewell Boxing Club and countless others had built my faith in people whatever their background, race or religion. But I had to face the probability that the people who ran that club preferred to have a convicted cheat in their sport listed on their winners' board rather than a gypsy kid.

SANDWICHED

My next event was the Basingstoke Junior Open. Back now at junior level I was taking nothing for granted as I had been chastened by the defeat at Sandwich and wanted to get this exciting golfing career back on track before anyone noticed. Straight out the blocks with a first round of seventy on a very tough testing course set me up for victory although I dropped some shots near the end of the round, my lead was huge at one point with a total of 145 for two rounds. I was a comfortable winner when receiving the prize. I had literally walked it and I felt my momentum was recovered. I played so well that day that it wasn't only me that believed that it would not be long before I was competing with the big boys and my name be recorded in the newspapers and on the television. My replenished confidence was soon to be shattered.

Pleased as punch after I had collected my award we began to leave when the bar steward approached and presented Dad with a bill for £4.25 – 'for the sandwiches we ate at lunchtime'. Now, we did eat sandwiches at lunchtime but we had not ordered any, in fact we believed they were for me and my partner as part of the entrance fee, or just complimentary. I remember thinking there were a lot of sarneys and Dad and my brother eight-year-old John (who was growing at a rate of a foot a week at the time) had demolished them. A dispute ensued. 'I didn't order them.'

'You ate them.'

'They were there.'

'You ate them – you pay for them.'

'Don't take that tone with me...'

It descended into a row over these grossly overpriced slices of bread. Finally the steward said that if Dad refused to pay he would be reported to his own club. As Dad didn't have a club he said that was fine and we left not really giving the incident much further thought. What we didn't know was that the

Basingstoke officials were as good as their word and their complaint fell upon some receptive ears at my own club, Home Park, and a chain of events was triggered that almost ruined my life and some of those around me.

I won six Open tournaments that year of 1987. I never had a bad word with any member and represented the club to the highest standard. Due to my success the club was mentioned on national radio and television and in several magazines and newspapers. The complaint about the sandwiches may have been embarrassing for them but surely this didn't outweigh the positives I had generated? At my young age I had not become sufficiently jaded and cynical to realise it may have been *because* of my success that the club reacted to the sandwich scandal in the way they did. But I'm getting ahead of myself.

Over the weekend after Basingstoke I was playing happily at my club when someone mentioned casually that the captain wanted to see me at 2.30pm in his office on the following Tuesday. I didn't ask what it was about – I didn't think to. I assumed it was something to do with an upcoming tournament or the like. Come Tuesday I was helping Dad on a scrap-metal job and misjudged some traffic and arrived at the captain's office half an hour late. The captain was not there but another official was, a man I did not know too well. His face was bright red.

'What time do you call this!' he barked.

'I do apologise sir, but I was caught in traffic.'

'Well, the captain's gone home. Come back at 2.30 on Thursday and don't be late this time.'

This arrogant man was talking to me like a drill sergeant in the army and I was his private who was not carrying his rifle in the correct manner. It worried me. OK, I was a kid but I was not a little kid, and never being rude to anyone I did not expect them to be rude to me. Thursday I was there early so stood outside Mr Len Roberts' pro-shop when my close friend and voluntary coach Grant Harrison ambled past. 'What's wrong with you Joe? You don't look too happy.'

'Grant, I've got to see the captain and I think he's going to throw me out the club.'

'Why, what have you done?'

'Nothing I know of, but there is something up,' and I told him about the business and brusque words on Tuesday.

'Don't be silly. Throw out the London Junior Champion, the Club Champion, the Lullingston Park course record-holder, Grand Challenge Cup runner-up, I don't think so. Relax. See you in five minutes. It'll be nothing, believe me.'

I knocked on the door and entered the captain's office.

'I'm sorry I was late on Tuesday, Captain'

He ignored this and said: 'Joe, we have had a report from Basingstoke Golf Club that your party ordered some sandwiches and then refused to pay for them. Clearly, this does not reflect...'

'But, Captain...'

'Don't speak over me Joe, I haven't finished,' he continued. 'This behaviour does not reflect well on us, at all. Some might say this is stealing. At best it is deception and I'm afraid I'm asking for your resignation.'

Resignation? Resignation? I was sixteen years old. Who did he think I was? Edwina Fucking Currie? I was speechless and breathing heavily.

'We want you to leave the club, Joe, but if you resign rather than us expel you then we may allow you to rejoin at a later date,' he said in a softer voice, as if he was trying to help me. I didn't want the bastard to see me cry so I turned around and left his office without a reply or any pleading. Grant Harrison was hovering outside so perhaps he didn't think it would be as OK as he said it would.

'Well?' he asked.

I burst into tears, big heavy sobs and he tried to comfort me as I blubbed out the story. Grant was furious with the way I had been treated but he told me to go home and that it couldn't be right. Everything would be OK, he said.

It wasn't. A member called Peter Tribe worked hard in my defence but his efforts fell on deaf ears, as for every member who felt that the gypsy kid had been meted out a red raw deal there was another who held that a golf club was no place for a gypsy kid in the first instance. Some of these people were embarrassed to have a boy, and a pikey at that, representing their club. More so getting rid of him would mean getting shot of his family with their trucks and beat-up cars lowering the tone of the car park.

While I waited and hoped that I'd be reinstated an incident occurred that confirmed to me that prejudice lay behind the decision rather than any fall-out from the Abominable Ham Sandwich Affair. Two junior members were caught stealing from Len Roberts's pro-shop at the club. One of the boys was a policeman's son. Now in most clubs the resident professional is the most respected man around, definitely more than the captain, or so was the case here, and nobody would dream of stealing from his shop. These boys were hauled in front of the captain and their memberships were suspended for six months. They get suspended for stealing from the club pro and I am expelled for my father refusing to pay for some sandwiches he disputed ever ordering and never did. Len Roberts himself was struck by the inequity of the decision and he protested. He told the committee that I had always showed the utmost respect to him and would say if I had picked up a tee too many, yet these boys blatantly thieved from him. How come the punishments don't reflect this? I don't know what response he got but Len had a living to make and why should he rock a boat for me that he might end up falling out of?

Prejudice. Up to that point I'd ignored it. It had gone over my head. I had no sympathy with the people who complained of it. It was something they blathered on about on the telly. It didn't affect me. I was getting on with my life and had my dreams and was striving forward to fulfil them – up to that point I hadn't seen any evidence of people trying to stop me or put me down. Of course, I had people call me a dirty thieving gypo and a fucking smelly pikey cunt and make jokes about stealing and littering and cursing people and all that. But then I often heard jokes about black people being lazy and smoking ganga between eating bananas and swinging from trees and Pakistanis smelling and overcharging and Japanese torturing people and Chinese cooking dogs and I thought nothing of it. That was Britain in the 1980s and it had been that way for years. It wasn't meant with genuine malice: we were a name-calling and stereotyping society. That's what we did to each other; few people had any real desire to do harm to those in the other groups or nursed any real hatred for them. I remember as a small kid watching Jimmy Tarbuck on the telly and his side-kick, Kenny Lynch, who is a Barbadian man, waiting in the wings of the stage in this particular sketch and Tarbuck kept throwing him bananas. If that happened now Tarbuck would be forced to apologise tearfully on *Richard And Judy* and Kenny would have to pretend he was deeply traumatised. The truth is they were and are the best of friends (both golfing nuts), adhering to a script. It was nothing to them – it's just now as we apply 21st-century values to the 20th-century way of life that we shudder. The problem, I guess, was that the majority white society did not have similar stereotypical handles to grab hold of: 'You tea-drinking wanker' does not have much of a barb about it so we in retaliation would focus on physical characteristics in the abuse war. Fat cunt, skinny bastard, ginger wanker, cripple, spaz, spotty, tramp etc. So I count none of that as real prejudice, especially in the time context, but what was happening to me in the golf clubs, although dressed up in respectable language and delivered in posh voices by men in nice clothes, *was*.

Looking back on it, I saw more prejudice from my community to the outside world. Then, all gypsies were raised to fundamentally distrust Gorgios and the Gorgio way of life. Ironically we thought they were unhygienic, uncaring and immoral; these being the very traits Gorgios accused us of. The insides of our caravans were spotless and gleaming. Dust would not be allowed to accumulate anywhere. We were fastidious about the cleanliness of food utensils. We would not have animals inside. We never robbed one another. We were highly critical of adultery and it rarely took place. We respected our elders and would not dream of allowing them to go into care. We would not lay in dirty bath-water. We didn't molest children. Many families I grew up with forbade their children from mixing with Gorgios in any way whatsoever. It is no wonder there was such a divide. My family were more tolerant and as a child I sometimes brought Gorgio kids home but even I was under instruction that I was not to enter a Gorgio's house unless we knew them well as a family. No such instruction applied to entering a gypsy caravan or home of a family we did not know.

I loved Home Park. They had helped me to develop as a person and a player. Most of the people were nice to me and encouraging and I had matured fast, learning to mix with people from all walks of life and all ages. Some people in my community had warned me against the Gorgios, saying they'd shit on me at the first opportunity, but I thought different – these were decent people. Office workers, builders, doctors and policemen all rubbed shoulders here and the fact they had all embraced me, judging me on my playing ability alone, gave me a confidence and high level of self-esteem that I would never have had. I waited in the wings hoping that my case would be heard and I'd be reinstated but the silence was deafening. I eventually drifted away from Home Park, firstly destroyed and broken-up, then angry. Fucking angry. For a short while I was incensed with my dad, even. Why didn't he just pay the fucking sandwich bill? He could have done. Why did he make a stand? I was short and snappy with my parents and I regret that, but I was mixed up. Soon though I could see clearly again and could see it *was* prejudice and nothing else why I was kicked out. Those club officials may not have known it (and probably would not have cared), but their decision set me on a road that partially closed and soured my open mind and which would end up nearly killing me and hurting many others along the way.

Should anyone be in any doubt about the institutional racism that existed, and still exists to a lesser degree, against gypsies, take a look at this genuine entry from the *Encyclopaedia Britannica* of 1954:

> The mental age of the average adult Gypsy is thought to be about that of a child of ten. Gypsies have never accomplished anything of great significance in writing, painting, musical composition, science or social organisation. Quarrelsome, quick to anger or laughter, they are unthinkingly but not deliberately cruel. Loving bright colours, they are ostentatious and boastful, but lack bravery.

Good job we couldn't bloody read! If an encyclopaedia salesman came to the caravan door with that, and we had flicked through and alighted on that peach of an entry, he would have left on a stretcher.

PLAYING AROUND

I left Home Park therefore and felt too low to approach another private club and played my golf instead on a course at Hounslow Heath. It was a pay-and-play course with queues of people on the first two bouncy and hard, slow greens. It was not conducive to my development as a golfer. My form remained good in Open events despite the limitations of Hounslow Heath. I only really got excited though about county matches as I was immensely proud to play for Middlesex, my county of birth. This is despite the fact that in some official eyes Middlesex does not exist having been split up and moved about under some bureaucratic reshuffle but people actually from Middlesex have largely ignored this administrative tinkering. Cricket, golf and football clubs and all manner of organisations still thrive all bearing the Middlesex name. I finished second in the Middlesex Under-21s qualifying tournament, losing by one shot to old rival Gary Clark, a great player you didn't mind finishing second to, and who, to this day, is playing some of his best golf in Open tournaments around the world. This performance was more than enough to get me selected for the Middlesex Under-21s full squad in 1988 and I quickly bonded with my new team-mates.

Around this time, and still raging inside about the Home Park business, I had a couple of street fights, the first of which would have reverberations later in my life. It was a Christmas Eve and me and my sisters went out to the Lady Margaret pub in Southall which was packed to the rafters with gypsies. My sisters allowed me to go with them even though I was only sixteen or seventeen and my dad wouldn't have allowed it. Because of my size getting served in a pub had not presented a problem since I was about thirteen. Not that I did it too often. As we entered we said hello and nodded to some young travellers that we recognised. I couldn't believe it but one replied: 'Hello, nancy boy.' I carried on to the bar but asked the girls if he said what I thought he said. Not wanting their Christmas Eve ruined they claimed not to have heard. I dwelt on it and searched out the young boy who said it.

'What's all the nancy boy stuff?'

Before he even answered the adults who were all sitting up against the wall, well oiled and in braces and shirtsleeves, jumped up and started throwing their arms around and yelling. 'You want to fight me, big man,' and all that malarkey. Married men with chunky gold rings and nose hair they were. They should have known better. They were on me and pushing me around. I ripped my shirt off in true Incredible Hulk style and said I'd fight any one of them, one at a time, outside. But by now they were punching me and the force of their aggression was carrying me towards the door. Fists like slabs of meat were raining down. At least four of them were serving me up.

'You call yourself travellers? Give me fair play, for fuck's sake!'

'Joe, run or they will kill you,' screamed my sister, helpfully.

We were outside now and I was trying to take her advice but one of them punched her full on in the face. I was horrified. I turned and kicked out but they had stopped in their tracks, shocked at what they had just done. On the other hand they may have been getting their breath back. We found my other sister in the melee and jumped in the car.

'Hope we got plenty of petrol, bruv,' my sister said when I asked her to drive. We slowed down as we passed by the pub and Sis rolled the window down and shouted over.

'Big mistake you bullying cunts. We're from the Stockin family. We'll be back.'

'Come over here and shake hands. We don't want no trouble...'one replied.

'Yeah, I will, won't I? See you soon,' I called out and to my sister: 'Ealing Hospital.'

Five stitches and three Ibuprofens later, I was back at home nervously telling my father about the fight in the pub. I assured him I wasn't drunk and I hadn't started it. My sisters backed me up. I told him about the four grown men hitting me. He was very calm and collected and believed everything I told him. 'OK, boy, you don't need to say any more. We will sort this out.'

The following morning, Christmas morning, Dad said I could drink in front of him and when Uncle Cliff turned up outside sounding his horn he told me to come along with them. We'd already been to Rymer's grave over in Hanwell as we did and continue to do every Christmas morning, and nothing had been said about the previous night's events until Cliff turned up. There was Dad, his pal Tony Horton, Uncle Cliff, myself and brother Aaron. 'Where are we going?' I asked noticing we were going in the opposite direction of Dad's local pub.

'We're going to find these so-called gentlemen,' Dad said.

I was worried what they might tell Dad. If he thought I had been rude or abusive he would not have approved.

'Look son, I believe you and frankly even if you had been mouthy it's wrong for grown men to bash up young boys, especially three- or four-handed and especially our own. And it is unforgivable for any man to hit your sister however old or however big or small they are.'

He was firm and resolute. I'd never really seen him like this. Not overtly angry, just very strong.

West Drayton gypsy site in the west of London was where we pulled up and climbed out of Uncle Cliff's Ford Transit van. A man approached and Dad pointed at me and said that I was his son and that I had had some trouble with a boy last night.

'Yes, that was my son,' interrupted the man.

'Well my boy is here to fight your boy without anyone else joining in this time.'

First of all he said his son was not around, but then the boy himself appeared from a trailer and walked over. Dad addressed him: 'I hear you wanted to fight my boy last night but it all got a bit messy. Well he's here now so perhaps we can get on with a fair fight?'

'But, I'm only eighteen, Uncle,' pleaded the boy looking sideways at me throbbing at the temples and straining like a dog on a leash.

'Good, even better, my boy is only sixteen,' Dad smiled.

It was strange to be fighting on Christmas Day in the middle of a site and with five fresh stitches in my mouth, but my life was becoming more and more eventful. I held up a nice guard and waited to see what he had, what strategy he may adopt. Immediately, I saw he was aiming squarely for my head figuring an early knockout punch would be his only chance. He came in close taking his headhunting a step too far by throwing his forehead at me and trying to butt me on the stitches. Aaron grabbed him. 'Oi, you know the fucking rules, punching only.' Another boy stepped out of the crowd and whacked Aaron. I pointed at him and said: 'Me and you next, mate.'

The man who said fair play was John Snook and he was best friends with my uncle, John Brazil, and even though the firm we were fighting were connected to his wife's side of his family he was scrupulously fair. He pulled me, Aaron and the boy from the crowd apart before it descended into a complete free-for-all. 'Right, stop this now. You play fair, these people are no mugs, believe me.'

We fought on and my opponent was fighting well and in my enthusiasm to take his head off I had run out of puff which normally spells the end for a fighter, but I pulled him in close and used precious seconds to think. I moved back and away from him pretending to be completely out of steam and his friends and family started shouting: 'Come on, take him, he's finished.'

As he came forward almost in a victory stride I threw a sickening body shot that conveniently shot his head forward for a measured right-hander that sent him landing on the floor in a heap. There was a pretty little blonde girl standing there with her friends and I heard her say: 'When I grow up I want to marry a boy like that.' I smiled at her and nodded. Then the boy who had clumped Aaron stepped forward and my brother put him through a wooden fence with a left-hook to the body, a short right cross and then a big left hook on the jaw. He practically walked through him and through the fence. It left a hole in the shape of a body almost like a *Tom And Jerry* cartoon. Nobody else came forward as we stood there legs apart and adrenalin running riot and the small crowd shuffled backwards and dispersed.

'Come on,' said Dad, 'let's get to the pub.'

'Cheeky fucker tried to put the nut on your stitches,' Aaron commented.

'I forgot about your stitches,' Dad said. 'I should have got Aaron to fight the boy.'

We had a lovely lunchtime drink and then home to roast turkey and trimmings and dollops of Christmas pudding and cream and then afterwards settled down on the sofa to watch *Indiana Jones And The Temple Of Doom*, again. Happy days.

Christmas was a special time for gypsies too. As children we didn't spend weeks anticipating it, and the present giving and receiving was only a small part of it rather than the focus, but we loved it nevertheless. We'd be given a few sweets on Christmas Day and that would be about it as far as gifts. I don't think this was because there was not much money around, it just wasn't what Christmas was about. We loved the snow, the decorations in the towns, the abundance of food, the happy demeanour of all and sundry, and the television. We rarely went to the cinema so a blockbuster film was a real treat and I can remember the whole family transfixed by *Seven Brides For Seven Brothers*, *The Sound Of Music* and *The Great Escape*.

The other fight I referred to was before my first game for Middlesex against Surrey when we were gathered in a bar when a gypsy boy I knew called Bill suddenly approached me and spat out: 'Gorgio dinlow.'

'Gorgio dinlow' was a term of abuse gypsies would often use against non-gypsies. Simply translated it meant 'you non-gypsy simpleton'. It was a strange thing for Bill to say to me.

'What do you mean, Gorgio dinlow?'

'Gorgio dinlow. Yes, sir. No, sir. Three bags full, sir. Oh, yes please! No, thank you...'

He was mimicking me and putting on a posh voice. Taking the piss. Challenging me. He was accusing me of being the equivalent of an Uncle Tom. This was what some black people were saying to Frank Bruno at the time. That he sucked up to whites and was ashamed of his own race and culture. That riled me no end. 'There's nothing wrong with being polite, Bill. And I am not a Gorgio dinlow, OK?'

'Joe, you're a mug, bruv. You're being nice to all these people but they can't stand the likes of us. Can't you see that? When you turn your own self around they laugh at you, mate.'

'There's good and bad in everyone,' I countered and turned away from him. I was determined not to be goaded, but at this point my girlfriend walked into the bar.

'I bet she's a goer. Must be to wear a short skirt like that,' he said, the comment aimed at me, and then to my girlfriend: 'Here love, I dropped a pound on the floor, can you pick it up please?'

Clearly, Bill had drunk too much. Without drink he was not a bad fella but today he was out of line. I too had drunk a couple of beers but even at this young age I could handle my drink, not that I drank to excess. Yet.

'Bill, I think you should learn to respect people more,' I said, turning towards him.

'Maybe you'll respect me more if I knock you spark out and then I'll show your girl a proper fellow.'

'Get outside you cunt. I've had enough of you.'

I wasn't sure what other response I could have had. He tried to punch me as we rushed through the door together but hit the wall. We tore our shirts off, me revealing my trademark layer of fat over my strength and muscle, and him displaying a toned torso with rippling biceps.

'Here, sweetheart,' he called over to my girlfriend, 'you could have someone with a body like this,' and he patted his six-pack and looked over at me and laughed.

This just served to make me angrier and I double jabbed his motor mouth and drew first blood. Shocked he threw a couple of wild shots, but way off target, and I hit him one to the head, one to the body, and then same again, and then third time I punched him straight on the nose. Grandfather had taught me that move; even in death still coaching me. Bill was a big, strong boxer and realising it was going to be a proper fight he organised himself and came at me slamming me with a right hook to the body.

'Good shot,' I said, but bluffed that I was trying to hide being winded. As he came in for the kill, sensing my impairment, I jabbed him nicely in the mouth. 'Try using you brain, Bill,' I taunted.

He had already launched a haymaker and everyone saw it coming except me. Crash. It rocked and jarred me. 'Try using yours,' he said.

'Nice punch,' I nodded, pretending I was not hurt.

Then he caught me across the eye which annoyingly split, but I was composed and began to control the fight jabbing at his face relentlessly.

'I have hurt my hand punching that fucking door,' Bill announced. 'I'll have to finish you off another time.'

'It took eight minutes for you to realise your hand was fucked? Learn some respect, pretty boy. And, by the way, my girlfriend will be going home with a proper man.'

'Don't worry. I'll lay you out next time. When my hand is better.'

He walked away from the fight holding up his damaged hand for all to see. When we met next his hand would have had ample time to recover, but no mention was made of fighting again.

On to the first tee the next day at the West Middlesex Golf Club I must have looked a sight with my close-cropped hair and eye badly cut and swollen. Sean Whiffen, one of my team-mates, asked aloud who on earth I was. 'This is the boy who finished second to Clarky,' said Warren Bennett. Gordon Weir, the team manager, was eyeing me curiously, wondering, I'm sure, if he had done the right thing by selecting me. I partnered Ian West and we lost two and one in a really good game. A foursome can be a very tough format. In the afternoon singles I played number eight anchor man and was in with the Surrey Best Young Player and we came down to the last all square with our match deciding the outcome. I pushed him all the way in an exciting game. I hit my seven-iron to within fourteen feet and pressure forced him to miss the green, but he responded with a good chip to three foot. I putted hole-side. I finally asked him to hole out for half the point, which he did, but under pressure, all considered, I believe I served my new team well. And I was proud to be part of a team which normally read: Warren Bennett, Sean Whiffin, Gary Clark, Ian West, Matt Deal, Alan Johnson, Neil Jenders, Justin Phelps and myself.

After just one match paired with Ian West, the manager decided that Alan Johnson and I should partner each other. We won more rounds than we lost and complemented each other's game and to make it easier he was a very pleasant young man. Alan would hit the ball high naturally and I would hit it low. I liked to drive the ball low, running miles and when the course was hard he would then fly those high iron shots straight at the flag, which would stop quick. One day we got it all together and we were up six after nine holes but hadn't realised it wasn't an eighteen-hole game. We both lost our rhythm and when you are playing foursomes you can't always recover it as you are playing alternate shots. Our lead was disappearing faster than we could count. We eventually lost the game, one down. Gordon Weir was hopping mad when we went in for lunch, demanding to know how we could have lost a six-hole lead. Alan was a quiet lad and could not give an explanation and neither could I, as there was not one. Finally, I said: 'I can't repair what has been done, Mr Weir, but I will win this afternoon I assure you so there is nothing to worry about. Now shall we enjoy our lunch?'

It was an audacious thing to say but I tend to come out with such bluster when I'm stuck for words, even at that young age, and it certainly took the wind out of Mr Weir's sails, or maybe he simply thought I was mad. Thankfully for all concerned, I did win in the afternoon. Phew!

Middlesex continued to play well as a team although we did not manage to become English County Champions which was our goal, and on a personal level I was playing good golf, winning Junior and Men's Opens, but my rapid progress had stalled. I put this down to the lack of practice facilities and a lack of a golfing 'home'. In hindsight I know I should have just gone out and found another private club but I had been damaged by the rejection and scandal of Home Park. I was paranoid and felt that all the various captains would have spoken about me and my family and they would have been warned not to allow me in. The County matches though were hugely enjoyable and I look back on those Middlesex days as among the best golfing ones of my life, and I am happy that so many of my colleagues went on to bigger and better things. Alan Johnson achieved excellence by reaching the English Amateur Final, Warren Bennett won on the European Tour, Matt Deal and Neil Jenders landed good professional posts, Sean Whiffen is playing in major championships including the Open, Justin Phelps remained a top amateur winning the County Championship, and Gary Clark is holding his European Tour card with the very best of them.

My hopes were raised when a chap from the County invited me to join his golf course, Wyke Green. This was ideal as it boasted a decent practice ground and a nice putting green. I knew and relished the course as I had won the Worman Sword, one of the county's biggest Open events there, beating Ealing's highly-rated Rob Goldie in a three-hole play-off. I had also won the Wyke Green Junior Open by six shots which was pleasing as I was playing head-to-head with Gary Clark and Warren Bennett. The invitation was followed by a spate of bad form in the shape of poor County results and a miserable performance in the Jack Kirkham at Sudbury. When I bumped into the club man again I was loading my tools into my old van, which I was using to do garden work which was funding my golf then as a young seventeen- or eighteen-year-old.

'Any news on the membership? I have the money ready.'

'Sorry Joe, all the memberships have gone,' he replied casually.

I suspected another rejection such was my fragile state and the man did not realise that his shrug was like a blow to the solar plexus to me. Then to accelerate my loss of self-belief I had a call from Harry from the County Board and he broke the news that I was being dropped from the Middlesex team.

'You understand Joe you have been brilliant for us... it's only temporary... we want to give a couple of new boys a try out... when your game's a bit sharper, of course...'

He was one-hundred per-cent right and I felt sorry for him having to deliver difficult news, but at that time it felt like the end was drawing near for my golf. I became so introspective that I believed there was a conspiracy to put obstacles in my way.

Even at Hounslow Heath where, with all due respect to the members at the time, I was the best player, course record holder and Club Champion, I was slipping back. A tournament called the Clapham Common would seal my fate. It was a public golf course championship in which I contested every round and we, Hounslow Heath, made it into the final. I had a phone call from our captain who said that the following morning we would be practising on the course where the final was being staged. I told him I could not make that as I was at my sister's in Southend but assured him I would have a practise round where I was. A statement that was perfectly true. Later, the phone rang again and it was the captain.

'Joe, we have decided not to play you in the final.'

It's funny how when people bring you good decisions they say 'I' but when they have bad news to convey they spread the blame around and use 'we'.

'But, I have played in every round.'

'Come and watch, Joe. By all means and, of course, you can still have your trophy.'

I was speechless and cut the call off. It was at that point I decided 'Fuck the golf', I would become the Heavyweight Boxing Champion of the world.

SMASHED

Financially, as a family, we got by. We all did bits and pieces and pooled our money to buy the necessities and kept individually what we had left over. Even Mum went out and grafted. Her and the other womenfolk would go out what we call *monging* – selling lucky heather and charms on the streets or wherever crowds gathered. Obviously, relying on the generosity and superstitions of the general public did not yield good money, but she would never come home completely empty-handed. Years earlier she'd have gone out selling pegs door-to-door but a combination of pegs being sold for almost nothing in the shops once they got made in Hong Kong or China and the colder and colder welcomes received on the doorstep meant the practice died out. Over dinner in the evening we'd tell each other about our day. Someone always had a story, a yarn or an observation.

'We were up on Richmond Green today,' Mum began once, 'and there was this tramp sitting on the bench and I felt sorry for him so I gives him half my sandwich. He was ever so grateful and when he took his hands out his pockets he had fingernails this long.' She gestured with her hands a length that was obviously ridiculous. We laughed. 'He did, I'm telling you.'

We thought no more of it. A couple of weeks later she started again. 'Do you remember that tramp man I told you about? You know the one with the long fingernails? Well we saw him today again up in Richmond and you know what he did? He says let me repay you for your kindness and he only took all four us in the caff and bought us a meal each and teas.'

'He probably fancied one of you,' my brother joked.

'No, it's sad. He used to be a top pop star, you see. Top of the hit parade he was. Been on telly and everything. He told us. He's had plenty of money as well. He said it still comes in now even though he don't want it. He sends it back when it comes. So I says well send it on to me then. He laughed at that. He said he grew his fingernails so he can't play the guitar, said all the guitar has done has brought him grief.'

'Pop star, Mum? What's his name then?' I asked, getting into the swing of it. 'It ain't Mick Jagger, is it? He lives Richmond way.'

'I don't know his name. I never asked. Wouldn't mean nothing to me anyway unless he was Elvis. We just call him Takeithigher.'

'Takeithigher,' Dad repeated, confused.

'Yes, he sang that song to us – go down to, Electric Avenue, then you take it higher – so we calls him Takeithigher.'

'You didn't say he was black, Mum.'

'He ain't black. What you on about?'

'Well "Electric Avenue" was by Eddy Grant and he's black,' Aaron explained.

'Well, I don't know about that but he sang those words to us.'

Dad shook his head. 'Are you sure it wasn't Elvis? Was he wearing a white suit with sequins? Sounds like a nutter to me. You shouldn't go round believing everything a person tells you.'

'I know he's telling the truth and he's not mad. You can tell. Underneath it all he's a real gentleman. I read his hand for him and told him he would rediscover his fame and fortune.'

'I thought he didn't want any more fame and fortune,' I interjected.

'That's a point,' Mum mused.

Dad looked over at me without Mum seeing and raised his eyes into his head. No more was said. Months later, maybe a year or more, I was sitting indoors reading the paper and Mum looked over my shoulder. She could not read or write yet she leant forward and squinted at the story I was only half reading as she polished up some brass.

'That's him!' she exclaimed.

'Him? Who?'

'Takeithigher. The bloke from Richmond. What's he done?'

'Well, it says here he is Peter Green and he's the founder of Fleetwood Mac the pop group. They're massive they are. He's been in a mental home and he's lived like a tramp and now he's getting better and he wants to play music again. Blimey Mum, you were right.'

'Never heard of them,' Mum said, 'but I told you he was a pop star, didn't I? Ah. That's nice he's on the mend. You'll have to get me one of his records, Joe.'

Only Mum could sit on a park bench and end up sharing a sandwich with a rock legend and be none the wiser.

By now I divided my time between living with my parents and in Southend in Essex where I stayed with my sister, Marie. It was here in the seaside town in 1989 where I bumped into a Scottish gypsy fellow named Tommy Gray. He happened to mention to me Johnny Frankham and Les Stevens, who were well-known fighting men among gypsies and beyond. Johnny Frankham, who is a great pal of mine, had scaled the sporting heights when he defeated the late Chris Finnegan in 1975 to take the British Light Heavyweight Championship. Tommy told me that he had been a fighter too and years before he had travelled to the Netherlands with Johnny and Les to participate in a boxing tournament. I later learnt that he had been a good middleweight and had had thirty-three professional fights. 'I should have guessed,' I said, studying Tommy's flattened nose. 'I want to become a pro-boxer. Would you help me?'

'Aye, I may be able to do just that. I'm in the middle of applying for my trainer's licence. But Joe, silly question, can you box?'

I told him about brother Aaron and how I trained in the gym with him and the fights I had there as well as the knuckle fights outside. I told him about my golf and how it had got me down and that I was determined to excel in boxing and how it was a sport more likely to welcome me.

'You're a determined young man, Joe. We'll certainly take a look at you.' He looked down at my tummy. 'I think you better make that your last pint.'

We were in a pub. I knew I had to get into shape. 'Last session?' I smiled, and went on to have another six or seven pints knowing that I would cut the beer out as soon as I went into training.

He took me to his parents' snooker and gambling club and I soon came to know them as Uncle Easor and Aunty Lucy. They were not, of course, related to me, but it is a thing we gypsies do as a mark of respect to our elders. We all have scores of aunties and uncles, not just cousins and brothers. Sometimes we call strangers Uncle just in case they are. Aunt Lucy made a delicious gypsy stew and as she ladled it on to my plate she commented: 'I know you will be a heavyweight boxer, Joe.'

'What makes you say that, Aunt Lucy?' said I, fishing for a compliment.

'Because that's your third bloody helping of stew and you'll end up a heavy weight.'

She was a diamond of a lady and I treasure the memories of her and the kindness she showed me.

Uncle Easor told me that he had made a mistake by signing his lads, Tommy and his brothers, to Terry Downes the former Middleweight Champion of the world. He said good focused management was a key to a boxer's success and he wished he had managed his sons himself. Richard, George and Tommy had all become Scottish champions at one grade or another and had fought at the highest level around the world clocking up seven hundred fights between them as amateurs and pros.

'I'd like to manage you,' he told me, 'but I have some conditions. Firstly we have to speak to your parents as you're not quite eighteen and, secondly, I need to see if you can fight. There's a big black lad at the gym who I would like to see you spar with. Are you ready for that?'

I was, but on the day the black lad was not around so Uncle Easor sent me in the ring with Tommy, who was by now almost forty and past his best. Tommy dictated the pace and soon caught me with a looping left that cut my eye. I was unfazed and this upped the tempo a bit and I felt some licence to start catching him nicely with my left. Easor looked on all the time intently and after a few minutes called time. He examined my eye.

'That's nothing,' I said. 'I've had worse.'

'If you are going to be a pro you have to look after yourself. Not put yourself on offer.'

'Do you think I'm good enough, though?' I pressed, but Uncle Easor did not answer, suggesting only we talk about it over a beer on the seafront. In the pub I was expecting my next rejection, but Tommy broke the silence.

'What do you reckon, Dad? I say he's got the fastest left hand I've seen in a long while.'

'He's good,' and turning to me, 'you're good. But Tommy, you have to train him and I want to see him out on the road every morning. He eats too much and he drinks too much. If you can sort his diet out and get him properly fit he stands a good chance.'

I was delighted and from that very next morning I was determined to prove myself to Tommy and his dad. Each morning I ran down Southend sea-front from Pier Hill, where I was staying, and then back up it. It was a huge bloody hill but within a couple of months I was sprinting to the top with ease. They got me sparring with Darren Humphreys, one of my brother's old opponents, at the Canvey Island Gym who was now number one in England as an amateur, and then with Joss Harding, at the Peacock Gym, who was a heavyweight contender for the British title who they were gently preparing to go pro. It was perfect, measured training and just like with the golf I could see the results myself. My boxing was improving by the day.

Regularly I'd travel from Southend back to Hanworth to see my parents and girlfriend. One night I went round to see my gran. 'Give us a kiss, Gran. Guess what? I'm going to be a boxer, just like Grandfather Rymer. My boxing name is going to be Gypsy Joe Bugner Smith. Like it? I'm going to...'

I was full of myself but noticed that my aunts and sisters were not getting into the spirit and seemed to be troubled. 'What's up with you lot?'

'Nothing.'

'Don't lie. Something's up.'

Further probing revealed that my sister Marie had just had a fight with our cousin, Nugent. They were normally the best of friends but some idiot had stirred something up about Marie wishing harm on Nugent and her husband Champ's son, Clifford Boy. It was nonsense as we all loved Clifford and still do. Vodka, it seems, had been consumed and a fight ensued whereby Marie had fallen to the floor and got knocked out. In the scrum Champ had apparently become very angry and when she had said she would be back the next day someone had said make sure you bring your brothers. I was enraged at all this and said I would take her to fight Nugent and that if her brother or husband said anything I'd fight them. It was silly and getting out of hand before it had even started. It was silly because it was a fight over nothing, borne from booze, and it was even sillier because me and Champ are first cousins and good friends. Champ was the brother of Charlie who I had had all those fights with nearly ten years earlier on the Epsom site.

Before you knew it and as is the way in gypsy life a fight had been arranged between me and Champ and the news spread like wildfire. It was to be a spectacle. A family tiff had been elevated in a matter of hours to a duel, a battle of honour, and an event that would provide entertainment for crowds of people, many of whom who would not even know Champ or myself. The momentum was such that neither of us could have backed out even if we had wanted to. Champ was an accomplished boxer already and had fought professionally while I was more of an unknown quantity: I only *wanted* to be a boxer.

It's a cold November afternoon at the Cranford site and an area has been marked out for the two of us to fight. It's normally a no-go area for anyone other than the residents, their families and friends, but today cars and pick-ups are pulling up and parking untidily where they can and crowds trying not to look like crowds are making their way quietly across the fields and down the lanes. Champ greets me: 'I know why you're here.' I nod. There is no need to say anything. 'My brother's on his way over.'

Creamy, a top heavyweight fighter himself, is to be Champ's fair-play man. 'No problem,' I say, 'Jimmy's going to be my fair-play man.'

Jimmy Stockin is my cousin on my dad's side and like Creamy a renowned bare-knuckle fighter. The two of them command ultimate respect and will ensure that fair play is adhered to, as the name suggests, and prevent side fights or disorder breaking out which is a problem sometimes at these events. They fought in 1981 at Mitcham in a match that is talked about to this day. These bare-knuckle fights while not generally recorded or reported in the press are kept alive by the verbal passing down and around of the people that witnessed them. Creamy was the bigger and stronger man and dished out to Jim a severe beating that somehow he withstood. His face, by all accounts, looked as if a team of surgeons had folded back the skin and were operating on the muscles, tendons and raw flesh beneath yet somehow he caught Creamy with a couple of late rib-breakers that pulled him up. Talk about snatching victory from the jaws of defeat. Sylvester Stallone himself could not have made it up. Perhaps, he could. Uncle Ruffy comes over and offers me and Champ money to forfeit the fight. I want to take it. I don't know if Champ does, but I do. But I won't admit it. God bless Uncle Ruffy, he is a good man.

We get off to a slow and cautious start feeling each other out like it's going to be a fifteen-round contest. No way. This bare-knuckle game is one long round. I break the caution and with a decent left followed swiftly by a right to the head but Champ's defensive skills cause me to narrowly miss. We are moving smoothly around. Champ is at his peak at twenty-five years old and the full implications of my position dawn on me. A left piston-type jab rips through my guard. His bare hands and bony knuckles start to tear me. I must try and block. Block. But I can't just defend because Champ is getting through. I'm bleeding now. I'm getting some counter jabs in but I need the knock-out. I have the weight advantage but he knows I'm plotting for the big one and he's not falling for it. He's in close. Relentless. He's only ever been beaten once and that was against his brother, Creamy. That's no black mark. I try to wind him up, make him make a mistake. 'Good punch but you can do better than that.' He promptly does. Fuck me, I felt that. A right hand has flown in over my guard and opened a cut above my left eye. I feel it go just like unzipping a jacket. It's a beauty of a punch.

'That's better, partner. Well done.' All bravado and he knows it. I want him to know that I'm not going to give up. I need him to know that. If he knows that he will become despondent. I pretend to go for a big head punch and switch and land a crunching body shot. He winces. That's better. There are cuts all over me and my nose is fucking throbbing though I feel I can win but my eyes are the worry. Bare-knuckle fights often end because of the eyes swelling up and the fighter not being able to see. Sometimes it's a race to drop the other man before the eyes completely close. He's caning me on points but points are sweet fuck all in here. He's still focused on my face. Jabbing the fuck out of it but I'm landing the body shots that are hurting him. I know they are. 'Joe, you'll never knock me out,' he says as we come face to face.

'I probably won't. But I won't give up trying,' I revert as I deliver a sharp rib-shaker. Another body shot lands and he lets out a groan and staggers backwards and I'm thinking I'm going to carry on and on and on. My Lonsdale shirt is drenched in blood but I notice now his jaw is hanging a bit. I bet it's dislocated. That side of his face is swelling up. Don't even remember the punch that did that but he's starting to look like Joseph Merrick, the Elephant Man. You can't see them but his ribs must be killing him. He comes in close and then holds out his right hand. 'Joe, I'll give you best. You are prepared to go such lengths to win. I'm not. I want to win, Joe, but not this much.'

'Well, if you give me best, I'll give you a draw.'

'No, mate. You've won. Let's go and have a drink.'

The crowd burst into applause. I should think so, we've just spilt pints and pints of claret for their amusement. Uncle Ruffy comes to tidy us up. 'I think I'll go back to golf after that,' I only half joke.

'Yeah, maybe you should,' said Nugent's brother, Mark who is not looking too happy. Adrenalin still pumping.

'I'll fight you now.' I know my body is calling out for respite, bathing and stitches, but I feel so strong and confident.

'No Joe,' Mark says. 'I never meant it to come out like that. You fought well. I meant golf is a better sport. You won but look at you. Golf is better. That's what I meant. Less fucking painful. Less fucking dangerous. That's what I mean.'

Mark was not being funny with me. What he said was right but I was not listening, intoxicated as I was with my little victory. Mark was a good fighter and I am glad we never battled then or ever. Today we are great friends and close cousins. Champ went straight off to the pub and I was taken to the hospital where they told me my nose was broken and they inserted seventeen stitches into my face. I was keen to get back to the pub where by now a full celebration would be in full swing. Watching two young men nearly kill each other seemed to always provoke a raging thirst in the spectators. As we left the hospital a well-dressed man who I recognised as being near the front of the spectators at the fight stopped and spoke to my sister and me. I learnt later he was a wealthy second-hand car dealer from North London. 'How old are you, Joe?'

'I'm eighteen.'

'Well done. That was an excellent fight. One of the best I've seen and I've seen a few. This is for you. Look after it but don't open it until tomorrow and open it when you're alone. I think you'll do that, won't you?'

'Yes, sir.'

I stuffed the brown envelope which was sealed with thick elastic bands into my back pocket and went to the pub where Champ and I drank happily and basked in the admiring glow of the people around us. As we left together we had to push our way through the crowd to the door as everyone hugged us, slapped us or insisted on shaking our battered hands. My friend Kevin was one of the last to congratulate me and as I bent towards him, he did the same, and Bingo! our heads clashed, my eye opened up and I sprayed him with blood. Back up the hospital for seven more stitches.

With my girlfriend I stayed at a hotel that night and in the morning when we went down for breakfast I could see people staring over and then averting their gaze. The girl on the desk asked if I had been through a windscreen. I didn't mind. I was on cloud nine because I had earlier opened the envelope and found five grand inside with a note saying that my benefactor had taken a 7-1 bet on me and had done 'rather well'. Have you ever seen £5,000? Yes, in your bank account maybe but have you ever seen it and handled it? I hadn't and it was an extraordinary experience for me as I counted it and recounted it and spread it over the bed. Folded it. Rolled it. Fingered it. Holding and folding. Marvellous! It was an enormous amount of money for an eighteen-year-old and an extremely generous gesture from the north Londoner.

'Don't worry about that,' said my cousin Jimmy Stockin later, who was more experienced in these matters. 'If he gave you five large, then you can be sure the man himself won fifty grand.' £50,000! What sort of world was this I was moving in? That was a house or a few Mercedes on the drive. I knew that side-betting was a big part of the bare-knuckle game but I had no idea these sorts of monies were genuinely being won and lost. It made me want to fight again, which I suppose was the general idea.

BAD

Back in Southend I could not wait to find Tommy and tell him my news. I felt like I had a really special present to give to him. I'd won my spurs – that's how I saw it – I was a man now and a proper fighter. I found him at the gym and I bounded up to him like a big old Golden Labrador. 'Hi, Tommy, mate...'

He jumped like he had seen a ghost or a tax inspector.

'Joe, what the fuck have you been doing? Look at the state of you.'

'I had a real good knuckle fight, Tommy. It was a great fight, Tommy. Everyone said it was one of the classics. My opponent has been a pro and I won, Tommy.'

'Did you,' huffed Tommy, puncturing my enthusiasm with his long face, 'and I expect you entertained the bloodthirsty hordes for fuck all? It's not clever, Joe. Your face will take two months to heal so there will be no sparring and no real training. You've put yourself backwards by having a knuckle fight for everyone else's benefit but yours. That's the good news. The bad news is you don't know what damage you might have done. Permanent damage, I mean. Bare-knuckle fighting is like two fucking cavemen standing in a field pummelling each other with clubs. You can't be a pro and prowl around the country having bare-knuckle fights. It's a mug's game.'

'I earned five grand.'

Tommy stepped back and looked at me again as if he had just realised who I was.

'You earned five grand! That's five times more than I got for fighting Pierre Fourie and he was a challenger, a serious fighter, he fought Bob Foster and *he* fought Muhammad Ali. Five grand! I can't believe it. Who the fuck paid you five grand?'

I explained about the car dealer and his big bet and Tommy calmed down a bit and could see I was disappointed with his reaction. He put his arm around my shoulder and squeezed me. 'I've got more bad news, Joe. You see I haven't charged you any training fees and I've been adding them up and it comes to £4,800 so you better take me to the pub and buy me some drinks with the £200 you're going to have left.' Laughing now we set off to Minerva, our bar of choice.

The fight had transformed me. The five grand (or was it four now?) in my bin made me feel strong. I felt valued and powerful. I started thinking I could do one of these a month and earn £60,000 in a year. Even the Prime Minister probably didn't earn that. I'd be up with the whizz kids in the city, except they'd be punching keyboards and I'd be punching chins and noses. Greed consumed me. For the moment I could go anywhere and buy anything I wanted within reason. For the time being at least I did not have to think about graft. Some people I knew barely earned five grand after tax in a year! The confidence a large wad of cash can give you as a teenager is frightening. Secondly, and more scary, I felt I could fight and beat anyone. Nothing and nobody bothered me. However, it was the reaction of others that impacted on me the most. The fight itself had been watched by some four hundred people yet word of it spread around like wildfire and gypsies and non-gypsies alike approached me wherever I went and generally bummed me up. I'd walk into a pub and the old villains would tease me: 'Here he is, Babyface Smith, number one scrapper.'

They were joking but they brought me a drink and another and another. They wanted me to be around them. No longer was I the big, quiet kid in the background with the weird obsession with golf. They were showing me respect; if respect is the correct word. It was an intoxicating thing for an eighteen-year-old to be accepted into the circles of fighters, old lags and gangsters. *Names* we called them. And they knew my name and it was like a spiral because once I started associating with these people others saw me as part of them and I was getting more of what I thought was respect. I could walk into a pub alone and people went quiet and moved away for me to get to the bar. Sometimes when I was served my drink the landlord would wave his hand as I delved in my pocket to pay. 'On the house, Joe.'

It wasn't because of the fight so much that changed the way people reacted to me, it was because of the people I was wrapped around and were wrapped around me. And I started mixing with these people after the fight and when I was flush with money. I had always known them and had drunk in the same places but serious criminals are by necessity a fairly close network and although you can be on nodding and first-name terms they are wary who they allow into their network, or should I say web? After the fight there was a shift in their attitude and I stepped enthusiastically into that circle. I couldn't see it at first, but I had embarked on a criminal career. Of course I had broken the law before this period in my life but breaking the law does not make you a criminal. In my mind you only become a criminal when you indulge in crime as a career choice or for pleasure. The first 'job' I did was doing nothing yet I still got a drink for it. One of the men was discussing collecting a debt and he said: 'Fancy coming with me?'

'What have I got to do?'

'Nothing, just stand behind me.'

And I did. And nothing happened. It was an informal hiring. Was I being asked to do anything or just casually being invited to accompany someone on an errand? The lines are blurred, but I did get a score for it. So it must have been a job. It had all been very civil too. My friend had approached the man who owed the money on neutral territory and had been polite and in my mind not at all threatening. He mentioned the debt as if almost in passing and the man produced a cheque book and scribbled out a cheque. That was that.

Then, not long later, another man asked me to collect a debt alone.

'What do I do?'

'Just go and see the mush. Tell him you're just collecting. Nothing to do with you. You're just collecting. He'll pay, but if he don't, give him a clump. Then he will.'

In this case the man paid without any hint of clumps and when I returned my 'boss' peeled off three twenties and gave it to me for my efforts. It all seemed simple. Easy money. Low risk. Painless. I thought of my dad and other relatives and friends driving here and there, haggling over a piece of metal and then having to sweet-talk some other mush just to make a turn. I thought about my mates out knocking in all weathers and often coming home empty-handed. I thought about other people I knew grafting and struggling all their lives to save up enough dosh to buy their own piece of ground. That's what many gypsies dream of. Not a house. Not a mortgage. Their own piece of ground paid for in banknotes and somewhere they can put their caravan on and where nobody can tell them they should not be there. At this rate I could have my own bit of ground in a year. Maybe quicker. I was in thrall to these new people, their money and lifestyle. I had become Jack The Lad, or more accurately, Joe The Lad.

'Ever handled a shooter?' asked another man, I'll call Tim.

'I've shot pigeons and rabbits.'

'Well, we want you to come with us. We need to have a word with some chaps and they may cut up rough. I want you to produce the shooter from beneath your coat if they do. Worse comes to the worse you'll have to use it. But it won't come to that. If it does, and you have to shoot, aim for the leg. Got all that, Joe? I'll show you how to use it. Don't worry. It's just a catch and a trigger.'

'No problem,' I said.

This was a serious escalation of anything I'd been involved with before. Carrying a firearm let alone using one was a serious offence and to produce one a high-risk strategy in any circumstances. The other side might spot it and decide to get their retaliation in first. But, incredibly, I didn't even swallow hard such was my confidence in my own invincibility and in the status of the firm I was now running around with. We arrived at this drinking club and my crowd went to the bar and the other little mob were sitting around a couple of round tables. Within minutes they had sauntered over to where we stood and were drinking with us, laughing aloud and cuddling like long-lost relatives. I'm standing there smiling like a cunt with a shotgun under my coat not knowing what to do and hoping none of them decide to embrace me. 'Put it in the car,' hissed Tim out of the side of his mouth.

'Why did you get me to bring it in?' I asked him when I came back in.

'It's cushty but I wasn't sure. Have a drink, Joe. Relax. They're pucker this firm. There will not be any trouble.' Pucker? Fucking hell, he was explaining to me twenty minutes earlier how to shoot one of them in the leg! In a matter of months I'd gone from a fresh-faced boy at the gym to carrying a firearm under my coat that I would have used. Ridiculous. Looking back it seems like a film of a life condensed down to ninety minutes, but that's how it happened and I thought nothing of it. This crowd were their own fan club and the more violent and scary a person was the more they referred to him as 'salt of the earth', 'a gentleman' and 'a diamond'. They set great store by 'loyalty' and 'respect' and 'playing fair' and people being 'sound' when in truth they'd stitch each other up and play anything but fair if needs be. I couldn't see this at all. It had not occurred to me that if it had come on top that afternoon in the club it would have been me facing the murder, attempted murder or wounding charge – not them. I actually felt warmth for them for letting me accompany them and allowing me to do these 'little jobs'. Shamefully, I even wished that my dad was like them and not like he was. Unlike some of the hangers-on in these circles I was hanging on because I wanted to, not because I was scared. I was genuinely not frightened of any of them and having seen their methods would have resorted to the same if they had turned on me. I think they knew this.

In the same way I was hanging around the big men and the big names, people started to hang around me. It's amazing how many people are attracted by danger and violence, or the threat of it. People who have no bottle. People who would run a mile from a sharpened lolly stick. They were saying stuff in my ear – 'You're the business'... 'You're my fighter'... 'You could do him'... 'They won't mess with you'... and so on – and it all served to inflate my ego further and reinforce my delusions of indestructibility. At the same time my five grand, although being topped up by my little jobs and other petty crime, was evaporating rapidly. My new admirers may have been hanging on my every word and buttering me up, but they didn't mind buying one drink to my five.

I could trust my brother Aaron, of course, and he was soon on the firm, seduced by the easy money and the excitement of living on the edge. Before we knew it we got to taking protection money from low-key establishments, off our own backs and for ourselves. Southend and training had gone out of the window what seemed like an age ago. In my eyes I was leaning on a few people for a few quid in exchange for keeping the peace and I had taken an important step forward in my career. I had done the equivalent of resigning from the local employer and setting up my own business. I was a man going places. But in reality it was extortion I was getting into and I had taken a step forward into the abyss. The only places I might be going were all establishments beginning with the acronym HMP.

I had become blasé about money and full of myself. On one occasion it was not even my money I was quite literally throwing around. There was a decent old trainer by the name of Eric Hilton and he worked up at the RAF camp at Uxbridge. He said to me once that he had a West Indian fighter at the gym called Mick who he raved about. 'Joe, you couldn't go three rounds with this guy. He's awesome. I'd have big money on him with almost anyone. You should see him Joe...'

Now, old Eric was not trying to goad me, he was not that sort of chap, he was only stating what he believed but his words landed in my brain like poison darts and I got to feeling that a challenge had been thrown down and every day that went by was a glaring example of my inferiority, my cowardice even. My thought processes speak volumes about my state of mind at the time. One day cousin Charlie had entrusted me with £10,000 in readies to go and purchase a motor for him from another family member that he had his eye on. Instead, or before at least, I went to buy the car, I stopped off at the RAF base and marched in to see Eric.

'Where's this Mick?' I boomed.

I tossed the package with the ten grand in onto the canvas of the ring. 'There's ten large in there, Eric. Match that and we'll see if I can't last three rounds.'

Eric shook his head, aghast. Mick was there and standing in the ring. He was clueless. I gloved up and got in with him regardless and reluctantly he fought me. I merely kept out of his way for three rounds. It was easy. I barely landed a punch but he only caught me once or twice and I successfully stopped him opening up on me. When the fourth round began (knowing that I'd won the bet had of Eric taken it) I threw caution to the wind and battered Mick all over the place. I stopped short of knocking the man out as, after all, he knew nothing of what was going on, picked up my wad and stormed out. Eric stood there mouth agape having barely uttered a word. He was in shock, probably. Not at seeing his protégé humbled but more likely by being in the presence of a fully paid-up nutter.

What would I have done if Eric had taken the bet and I had lost? I don't know. Such was my self-belief and arrogance I did not contemplate it. I was a man on a mission and somehow, whatever it took, I would have not lost Charlie's £10,000. It was a dangerous place to be. I was infallible. At that point, in my head I believed there was not a man on earth I would walk away from in a fight. If John Major had asked me to head up Desert Storm and wade unarmed into Iraqi Revolutionary Guard, I'd have done it and congratulated the Prime Minister at the same time for making a shrewd military decision. I was mad.

Around this time in the early 1990s I was at a gypsy horse fair and recognised a man. The fairs were a huge part of gypsy life and for centuries our calendar was planned around them. You could say that's *why* we travelled, especially in the summer months. They were horse fairs rather than amusement fairs although by the time I was growing up the horses, just as they were in human life generally, were playing a smaller and smaller role. What was important was the opportunity to meet up and socialise, to drink and make merry and to tell stories and sing. In those days most gypsies would not be on the telephone and for obvious reasons did not write to one another so the fairs were the perfect and only opportunity for families and friends that did not live or travel together to catch up with one another. There are not two gypsy people in the land who will not know personally someone in common. Also, with the demise of hop-picking the fairs became the main places where males and females could pair off. The main fairs were at Appleby in Cumbria, Horsmonden in Kent and Barnet in Hertfordshire. The latter fair has become immortalised courtesy of rhyming slang: Barnet Fair shortened to Barnet for hair. There was once many more of these horse fairs but over the years they had died off.

Back to the man: he was a big lump in his thirties and it did not take me long to register his face. He was the main instigator the night in the pub four years back when I got battered in front of my sisters. I do not think he was the man who punched my sister nor was he the young lad who suggested I was a homosexual, but he was the man who escalated the whole incident inside the pub and really kicked it all off. Most of all, he was the one they all looked up to and could have told them all to pack it up and stop and he didn't. I could have been killed that night. My sister was struck and the feelings were still raw. I filled up with hate and rage and had to look away from him because I hadn't decided what to do. My sisters were only seventeen and nineteen years that night and did not deserve to have gotten dragged into all that and certainly none of them asked for a punch in the mooey from a man. He was a bully. I was a big boy, given, but I was fifteen years of age for fuck's sake. I hated bullies. Always have and always will. It's good to beat up a bully now and then because you are actually doing a service for others. When a bully gets a hiding he thinks twice about doing it again and therefore you've saved some poor sod a beating. Sadly, because that 'victim' did not actually get the beating from the bully, he, and everyone else, will never be aware of the good work you have done on their behalf. So, it's a thankless task sorting out bullies, most of the time.

The ground was full of mud as usual and hot slippery grass churned up by thousands of people and horses and the first thing I did was swop my leather slip-on shoes for my pal's trainers. Then I walked close to him looking in another direction trying to fool him, but he had clocked me and was half-expecting what happened next. I aimed a vicious right hander at his head but he moved and caught me in the chest and I remember thinking fucking hell there's some power behind that. I was conscious that getting too angry in a fight was not always a good thing and I concentrated and threw a flurry of punches at maximum speed into him and most of them hit the target. There was nothing coming back. Then a fella said we should make a ring and do it proper and my opponent got some respite as the crowd that had appeared from nowhere acted as our ropes and I went back to work.

'What's it all about?' he protested lamely. Like he didn't know, as I buried my fist in his mouth time and time again.

'Fight back, you shitbag,' I screamed.

I pictured his twisted face that day in the pub when I was fifteen years of age and the terrified faces of my sisters when they thought I might get killed. I showed him no mercy and served him up very severely. The people present know what I mean. He lay on the ground bleeding from the mouth and elsewhere and the crowd were silenced by the extreme violence. Shock travelled from him to me to them. I wanted them – these strangers – to know what he had done and why I had just done what I had. I shouted out about the night in the pub when I was fifteen and told him he was fortunate that I had not killed him and then I disappeared into a mass of shuffling bodies now all keen to get as far away from this bloody, animalistic scene as possible.

MADE MAN?

I was nineteen years of age, nearer ten years old than thirty, and I had seriously injured and beaten a man and been quite prepared to kill him, yet I felt no remorse. No fear. No guilt. I was perfectly happy that what I had done was justified. I had boarded an escalator of crime and violence and the stakes became higher by the day. I was brutal and brutalised. In a short period of time I had careered out of control. I have in recent years often puzzled over how quick I transformed from being a courteous, fresh-faced, law-abiding gypsy boy with the world at his feet in to a hard-drinking, violent thug, moving in criminal circles and destined to meet a sticky end.

The first pivotal moment must have been when I was thrown out of Home Park Golf Club. Up to that point the only things that happened to me were good ones. I was Little Joe making my way in a man's world. Making my way in a Gorgio world. My gift for golf at that young age was opening doors and generally people made a fuss of me. I knew in my young mind that I was going to succeed and I relished every new day. Then when the sandwich incident happened everything changed. I lost confidence in myself. I lost my respect for Gorgios and wanted to retreat completely back into the gypsy world where the Gorgio can't hurt you and ruin your dreams. Effectively I came to believe, rightly or wrongly, that my future had been smashed to bits by jealous and prejudiced Gorgios. From there I guess I started seeing rebellious people from my own community as role-models rather than the Bernhard Langers of this world.

The second pivotal moment was the fight with Champ. As I have described, immediately after that people started treating me differently and I was awarded a notoriety (easily confused with fame and respect) that came as a complete surprise to me. It flattered my ego. For the first time since I was a junior golf champion I had self-esteem and those feelings of destiny and being different all came flooding back. I was not about to let that go. Perversely, and without ever articulating it in my head, I decided to forge a career in crime and violence and the business of fear. Looking back on it now, that's how I feel it went.

From wanting to be a golfer and then a boxer I now had ambitions to be a gangster. In the same way that I worked on my abilities in those sports I focused on being a thug and getting good at it. The incident in the pub when I was fifteen led to the vicious fight at the Horse Fair and that led, in a way, to me getting involved indirectly in the protection game. I had now moved to Essex and walked into a pub there one day where members of my outer family were stood drinking. The publican looked at me and almost dropped the glass that he was wiping clean. Apparently he had been present at the fight some months earlier in the mud and slime and been talking about it at that very moment, no doubt saying what a psychopath the blond gypsy fella was to the gyspy lads that regularly drunk in there. They had replied that the gypsy lad was their cousin and he was coming to the area and then like a bad dream, in I walked. Hence his shock. He immediately stood me a drink and then another and another. The landlord who was a big old boy himself showed his fear openly and started to tell his clientele not to mess with me, to watch out for me, don't look at me the wrong way and all that stuff. I had put no pressure on this man whatsoever but he piled it onto himself in spades. Understandably, the regulars who only wanted a quiet life slowly but surely took their custom elsewhere and within weeks what had been the busiest pub in the area resembled a morgue. One night when there was almost just me and him in the bar he said: 'Joe, can I have a word? Don't take this the wrong way but people are frightened. Frightened of you and your crowd. Do you think you could stop coming in...?'

'Are you barring me? Have I ever disrespected you or your customers?'

'No, Joe, slow down. I want to pay you not to come in.'

'What, and then you call in the Old Bill and I'm nicked for demanding money with menaces? I don't think so.'

'Joe, I've never called the Old Bill in my life and I never would.'

We reached a deal whereby I rolled up each Monday and the landlord paid me and I supplied him with a receipt for maintenance on the outside of his pub. I duly moved down the road to drink in the landlord's pal's pub and he too offered me a 'job' and this time I was carrying out 'driving work' on his behalf and I picked up my wages on a Tuesday. Another pub in the town belonged to my uncle and this establishment doubled up as the local nightclub at weekends and they began to bung me to turn up regularly and this prevented the local nutters from smashing the place up. Or that was the idea.

I was on a roll of menace and decided that as the local snooker club was the only likely place left in the immediate vicinity that was not contributing to my fund I would pay a visit to the Italian owner. He said he knew me and he obviously did because he cited an incident where I had broken a man's leg with a bat when I had been fighting him and his pal. That's another story. He told me he was the guy who had tipped my brother-in-law off that the police were getting involved. He was the manager and not the owner and said he was not in a position to pay me money so I said that was fine, but asked him to pretend he was paying me off to keep up appearances. I also suggested my snooker could be free which he agreed and that we'd put up prices to the punters each hour up by 50p – 25p for each of us. I said he should tell the owner if he had a problem he should contact me. Shortly after, the owner did just that but it was not to remonstrate. Instead he told me that another snooker club that he owned in another town was experiencing problems with a little Maltese firm. They had basically taken over the place, not paying for the tables and using it as their base for whatever naughtiness it was they got up to. One of these guys had put a fishing hook through a customer's nose when a row had broken out with another genuine customer and now punters were giving the place a wide berth. He told me the Maltese family owned the barber shop in town and that Fishhook himself worked in there and described him as being in his early twenties with an earring. I strolled downtown and there were a few people sitting in the shop leafing through old copies of car magazines and leaning up against the wall smoking a fag was my man. Now this was before the days of it being a capital offence to be in possession of ten Silk Cut, but to be smoking in a hairdresser's struck me as disgusting. I could not understand why they had customers.

'Excuse me, sir. How long is the wait?'

He lifted his shoulder off the wall and grunted: 'As long as it takes.'

Fucking hell, this bloke was a master at customer care.

'If I pop next door, will I lose my turn?'

'You might. I'm not psychic. Depends if anyone else comes in...'

I went next door to get a paper and then returned and waited patiently for his big red leather chair to become vacant. The rudeness had already provoked a healthy hatred for the disrespectful and surly wanker. Finally, he jerked his head to signal he was ready and I settled down in front of a mirror partly obscured by a little pyramid of dusty and ancient bottles of Hai Karate!

'What you after?'

'Just a neck-shave mate.'

He opened up his cut-throat razor and laid it down on the side and then fetched an ashtray from the station next to him and lit another cigarette.

'Do you mind not smoking while you are shaving me, please?'

I stared at him hard in the mirror and watched his facial muscles tighten.

'Look, this is my shop and I'll smoke if I like,' and to underline the statement he flicked open a silver lighter.

'It's your shop, is it?'

'That's right.'

'Is this your business, then?'

'That's right,' he repeated, inhaling his cigarette.

I leapt out of the chair pulling off the sheet he had tied around me with one hand and grabbing the open-razor with the other. Almost in the same movement one arm was around his neck and with the other hand I held the razor to his throat. 'And that snooker club is my business, you horrible bullying cunt. Got that?' I said. 'Got that?'

'Yes,' he whimpered. I let him go and walked out of the shop, glancing back as I closed the door to see him standing there trembling with a pool of piss forming around his feet.

I was loving all of this. Now a professional criminal and I had not stopped to question it at all. I have tried to analyse it since and throw light on what I really got out of it. Because the money was, for me, only a small part of the buzz. To some extent I got some sort of adrenalin rush from the lifestyle (it beat gardening, I'm afraid), but mainly I enjoyed the pumped-up self-esteem, enjoyed being someone people talked about, enjoyed the 'respect'. Of course, like all thugs and, although it hurts me to say it, bullies, I confused respect with fear. In my head I was waging a war on bullies. This is how people like I was then do what they do. They kid themselves they have right on their side. People shook my hand vigorously when they saw me and suddenly the rest of my family, especially my parents, were getting treated differently. This meant a great deal. Both me and brother Aaron had witnessed people not showing my dad the respect he *really* did deserve. He is a genuine man, an all-round good bloke in all senses of the word and unfortunately in the grimy world we lived in this was often perceived as a weakness. His treatment by others angered Aaron and I. We'd say: 'Dad, why did you let that man speak to you like that?' or 'Dad, you were next on the pool table, don't let him push in front,' and he'd smile and motion us to leave it. Don't get me wrong, he'd always stick up for us if needed and was nobody's pushover, but he believed confrontation was something one only did when one absolutely *had* too. Being young, stupid, and with testosterone coursing around our bodies my brother and I could not see that the way he carried himself was strength to be admired above anything physical. Now people were calling my mum and dad 'Mr' and 'Mrs' and they were having drinks bought for them. I was made up about this and felt proud that I was making something of myself and that this was rubbing off on them.

What I didn't like about the gangster business was when I encountered abject fear. I must have still had a conscience because it would twist me up if I saw an innocent person with terror in their eyes. Some of the types I knocked around with got off on that but I honestly never did and I tried not to get involved in anything where I considered the 'target' to be honest and innocent. In my role as a debt collector and enforcer I would always investigate in detail the task in hand. This was not only for altruistic reasons but also to save my own skin. The last thing I wanted was to go knocking on someone's door to collect £10,000 only to find out it was a member of one of the leading London criminal families, for example. It happens. You had to be careful. Most of the work I took on was for small businessmen who had been knocked for debts by customers and who themselves had exhausted all conventional and lawful methods of collection. You would be surprised how established and large this business is – a debt moves from invoice to reminder letters to legal letter to court proceedings to bailiffs and finally in extreme cases to people like me. Very often the businessman (or woman) has written off the debt and is therefore happy to pay 30% or more of the invoice value because it has become something they think has no value. In some cases certain organisations and unscrupulous individuals prey on small companies, running up debts they have no intention of paying and they don't realise or care about the damage being done to the person's business and personal life. This sort of situation gave me that 'right on my side' frame of mind to execute my work professionally.

Although the youngest person on the enforcement team I promoted myself to General. This was not because I had gone completely ego-mad but because I *was* the General. I liked to plan everything meticulously down to the last detail and it was me that invariably was the front man. It was me also who planned the surveillance, me who dealt with the customer, me who sorted out whatever reward deal there was and me who interpreted the client's wishes. I couldn't believe how slipshod others could be in this game, whether it would be putting pressure on the wrong person, using violence when not necessary, going on jobs drunk or drugged, and much worse. It is an industry desperately in need of a good regulatory framework and a strong level of standards. We were good and word soon got around about our efficiency and results and all sorts of people started to approach us. Unfortunately many of these offers were from people wanting us to collect debts incurred in the drug trade and I am glad to say I rejected all of these. Drugs are a fucking curse and I detest them. The gypsy community managed to resist their insidious hold a good deal longer than mainstream society, but I am afraid to say the habits have now filtered through and it's appalling when you see it. It used to be unheard of for Romany people to rob one another, but now it does happen and you can guarantee when it does drugs are behind it. Like most young people (and it *is* most young people regardless of colour and class) I tried them out but they were not for me. They were and are all around us yet I would never seek to earn a living from them, in any way. Even then in my dark days I believed in Christ. I didn't go to church though we were brought up with basic Christian beliefs and they never completely left me. I tried not to scrutinise too much what I was doing against Christian values but as I said I always felt that although what I did was *legally* wrong it was not *morally* wrong. Nevertheless, in the back of my mind Christ was a nagging presence.

Once I was approached by a man who had all but written off a £250,000 debt owed to his company by another and he said we would receive 30% of whatever we recovered plus some expenses up front. We immediately set up surveillance on the three directors of the knocking company and there was no question that these men were in a position to pay my client. The first man lived in a large mock-Tudor house, with electric gates and well over £100,000 spread across three cars on his drive. The second man had a more modest property but it was set in the middle of a farm with acres of grazing land around him. The final director had converted the village school and ripped up the playground to plant two swimming pools. They seeped wealth and luxury while my client was worried sick and in imminent danger of going out of business. I was happy to go to work on his behalf. I took great pride in my surveillance and thoroughness. I needed to know as much about them as possible. It always made the job easier. They went to their place of work each day and worked long hours but on a Friday they all packed up at noon and went to their respective homes. Electric Gates liked to go to the gym, Farmer Giles would get on his horse and canter around his land and the Headmaster was straight up the golf course. I decided it was time to strike. Splitting the team into three pairs I told them to approach their targets and put the severe frighteners on but not to resort to any violence at all. I was going for Electric Gates, my brother was taking the Headmaster and my cousin was dealing with Farmer Giles. My aim was to catch all three at exactly the same time so they could not warn each other of the experience or be prepared in any way. I needed them to be equally traumatised at roughly the same time. The scale, timing and style of the operation needed to shock them sideways.

John, my brother, and his partner dressed in golfing garb and waited in the trees for the Headmaster to hit one into the copse as I was sure he would. As he stepped into the undergrowth to retrieve his ball John, who was so tall his head almost emerged from the top of the trees, was standing there smiling. 'Is this your ball, mate?'

'Yes, thank you.'

'Well, before I give it back to you, Mr Wealthy Businessman, you need to make arrangements to pay back that quarter of a million quid you owe. You know what I'm talking about. Don't look confused,' he leant down into him and glared, 'if it does not get paid, the next time you walk into the trees I'll take your driver from your hand and split you in fucking two. Don't ever say you weren't warned.' The man stood there speechless, his mouth literally hanging open. John called me on the mobile a few seconds later and said simply: 'Job done.'

Almost a hundred miles away at the same time my cousin was driving slowly down a country lane that ran parallel to the track that Farmer Giles rode his horse along knowing that shortly he would dismount to close one of the gates behind him.

'Hello sir, how is your wife, Anna?' said my cousin cheerily.

'I beg your pardon?'

'You owe a quarter of a mill to someone. Do you realise how vulnerable you are? I know everything about you. I even know that you had chicken for dinner last night. Don't annoy me any more. Just pay up, OK?'

'I will sort it out straightaway.'

My cousin said even the horse was trembling.

This news had been called through to me straight away, but I knew that once the moment of shock and fear has passed that people grow in confidence and start thinking about the police, protection or even disappearing, and that I had to hit mine, the managing director, the hardest. He was in the gym training on his treadmill and I was bang next to him, with a woolly hat on, having brought a day pass. I was going to talk to him there but too many people were around and I didn't want to risk it. I followed him down to the changing rooms and perfectly for me he headed straight for the steam room. I followed and sat down on the bench next to him. Soon the only other chap in there went and we were left alone, although visibility was down to about six inches. I slid along the bench next to him.

'I wonder if it's OK to shave in here,' I said, producing an open razor from under my towel. Then I grabbed him by his hair and jerked his head right back. 'I haven't decided whether to kill you or not.'

Mr Electric Gates was gurgling and clearly had no idea what it was all about and thought maybe I had just absconded from Broadmoor which was not a million miles away.

'It's my friend that you have knocked for a quarter of a million large, you evil cunt. His business is going down the pan and his wife wants to leave him. And here you are swanning around living the good life. See how easy I can kill you? Pay the bill.'

I strolled out the steam room as if I had all the time in the world, not looking over my shoulder, but as I went through the double doors of the changing rooms I threw my joggers and a vest on, grabbed my bag and ran out to my right-hand man who had the motor running in the car park.

Within the hour my client had had his first call from this debtor company in fourteen months. 'What are you doing to us?'... 'We could have been killed'... 'You could go to prison'... My client responded exactly as I had told him to: 'Lovely to hear from you at last'... 'I don't know what you're talking about'... I told him to be even more careful when the next call came because you couldn't be sure that the police would not be listening in on that one. My client turned his phone off and let them sweat. Listening to their ever more frenzied messages they were leaving on his answer-phone they certainly were sweating, asking that if they paid now would we be out of their lives for good. One of the team became excited and suggested we go for more. I told him not to be stupid because then they would think there was no end to it and they had nothing to lose by going to the Old Bill. I told my customer not to reply to any of the calls fearing the police may have anyway been contacted. Instead I sent one of the boys into their plush offices dressed in a Parcelforce uniform where he delivered a note to the Managing Director stating that a gift to my client's wife of 250 red roses (one for every thousand of the debt) and immediate settlement of the debt would end the matter for good. Interflora fulfilled their very bulky order and so did our knockers.

When cleared funds had refloated my client's bank account he called me and suggested we met at a hotel bar.

'How much do I owe you?' he asked.

Silly fucking question, I thought. He knows.

'We agreed. You owe me £83,333,' I said, trying to not get cross.

He sighed in relief. 'Is that it?'

'What, did you think that I was going to ask for more?'

'Yes, I thought you might want most of it.'

I was insulted.

'Look, sir. I'm a businessman. We cut a deal. I don't know how people carry on in your world but I'm not like that and I'm offended you think I am.'

And it was moments like that when I did not like what I did. My customer thought I would renege on the deal. He feared that because there was nothing he could do about it if I did, and because I could, I would clean him out. We had a drink together and it gave me pleasure to see a weight being lifted from a man's shoulders as we socialised. I advised him to continue to do business with the guys and lay out a payment plan. A few months later I saw my client and his three 'customers' together in a sushi bar knocking back wine and laughing and joking like the best of friends. I looked through the window at them as they back-slapped each other and toasted one another. It's a funny old world.

DICING WITH DEATH

Nearly a hundred grand in my bin for that piece of work and for the life of me I cannot say where it went. There were five other people to pay and there were other expenses incurred yet I was still left with a lump of dosh that could have bought me a flat but instead it slid through my fingers like a bar of soap. As far as I was concerned it was legitimate money and properly earned and it could have set me up. If I had invested it in property in 1991 it would be worth well over a third of a million by now but I did not think in those terms then, unfortunately. It went on hard living, horses and thin air. It burnt a hole in my pocket and the pockets of plenty of others too. Also I laboured under the illusion that there was plenty more where that came from. I was eating well and drinking like it was an Olympic sport and so were my entourage, which some days could be as many as ten strong. The ironic thing was that it was muscle or the threat of it that underpinned my endeavours yet because of the lifestyle I was leading I was in the worst condition to have a fight – a proper fight – than I ever had been. I could still knock people out but these were people in bars who were drunk, often drunker than me, and they are not fights. They are mini-explosions of violence committed by the standing comatose on one another. If I had been called to fight in a ring or a field by anyone half-decent, I would have lost, and because of my refusal to submit my body would have soaked up ridiculous punishment. I wasn't aware of this or didn't care. I was a big, tough criminal striking fear into suburban barber shops, remember. A big fish in a small pond, though soon I was to witness my first shooting. Point blank. Close up.

My cousin Fred had got himself mixed up with and then into some bother with a firm from Belfast who were over here and he called me and my older cousin Jimmy Stockin to help him out. Jimmy and I have always been close although he is thirteen years my senior. We share the same birthday. He was a brave fighter in the ring, always displaying superhuman stamina and a bravery that many thought bordered on insanity. Yet, he was a family man who always carried himself with a quiet dignity that I admired. He was and is trusting and trusted. Fred had told us that the Irishmen told the family to bring their best to a meet where their dispute would be settled once and for all. The showdown had been arranged at an old warehouse over in North London. Jimmy and I drove there in his Land Rover not sure what to expect but pretty sure one way or another we'd be called upon to hold our hands up and fight. 'They're no mugs,' Fred had told us ominously.

Jimmy and I jumped out of the car and with nobody around took our shirts off and started to warm up, hopping around and shadow boxing the air. Jim was in his thirties, lean and rippling with understated muscle, while I was still a young man but with a beer belly tumbling over my jogging bottoms. I felt self-conscious. 'I'm out of shape, Jim,' I said. 'But I will fight to the end.'

'I know you will, cuz,' replied Jim, always economic with words.

By now Fred and some more cousins had arrived on the hard standing, screeching in like Starsky and Hutch and one said: 'Fellas, there will be fighting. This little firm are liberty taking cunts, believe me.' He grinned and his eyes sparkled as he pulled from his waistband a Colt 45.

Then his brother chirped in: 'And I have the twelve-bore repeater shotgun and John here has a small handgun,' as if he was a door-to-door salesman spreading out a cutlery set for a vaguely interested housewife. John took his firearm from his pocket and held it aloft like an auctioneer. Another shotgun with its butt sticking out of a Sainsbury bag lay on the back seat of their car.

'Me and Jim will have to be fast if this is the type of ammo we're dealing with,' I said, only half-joking. 'Do you have shooters for us? Fucking hell, you could have briefed us up a bit better.'

The enormity of the situation hit me and I could see Jim's eyes had widened at the scenario that was unfolding but before we could decide on a course of action two cars came careering towards us brakes squealing and sending clouds of dust into the air. It was like *The Sweeney* without any police. Before the Irish firm could apply their handbrakes my lot had started firing with no further ado. *Gunfight At The OK Corral* had broken out but there was no return of fire. It was very one-sided and I will never know whether the Irish firm had the same armed intentions. My cousins reckoned it was shoot or be shot but I caught the look on one of the drivers' faces and I have rarely seen such a look of abject horror as bullets tore into the bodywork of his car. They reversed away at high speed, spun around and retreated and who could blame them? I looked around, my stomach upended and my hands shaking to see Fred literally blowing smoke from the nozzle of his Colt 45 and with a slim Panatella (he was trying to give up smoking) clutched in the side of his mouth. He was as cool as a cucumber, thought at that second he was Clint Eastwood and I have no doubt he was shooting to kill. We heard later that nobody had been murdered and miraculously only a few grazes had been sustained, thank God. What the body-shop boys thought when they took their cars in for repair, I can only guess.

I thought I was a hard man but that little episode terrified me. I don't recommend it. I didn't even know the Irish mob and therefore felt no real hate for them despite knowing that they had threatened and bullied some members of my family. It seemed ridiculous that without realising it I had put myself and Jim in a position where we may have killed, been killed and/or banged up for life. There is living life on the edge and there is out and out stupidity. This was fucking stupid. In the gypsy world families stick together and this has always been the way. If one member is wronged then the wronger will have the whole wrath of his or her family to contend with. Occasionally and tragically these feuds can end in bloodshed and loss of life and these are the incidents you read about in the paper or hear on the TV, but actually it is, in a way, self-regulating. Rows are most often nipped in the bud because both parties know where it can lead, or it is extinguished at the first level with a bare-knuckle fight. Gypsies, as a rule, do not involve the police or the authorities in their affairs and without a statute book and a justice system we do police and punish within our own community. I have a large family, probably the biggest gypsy family of all, and you would think that incidents like the above unsavoury episode would be commonplace but they are not. There are wankers and troublemakers amongst the Smiths (like any family) and they soon get worked out. The wider family will not necessarily be there for them in their hour of need. Now Fred who did the Dirty Harry impersonation is one of the good ones. He was not one to get into fights for no reason. He didn't throw his weight around and is one of the funniest blokes around. If you saw him in a pub you'd not be intimidated and you'd like him. He'd chat to you at the bar and crack the corniest jokes. That's why when he said he had trouble me and Jim did not hesitate to come to his aid. We had no idea he was envisaging a gun-fight to the death.

A hail of bullets and the whiff or cordite was not enough though for me to change my ways and move in different circles and not long after the shoot-out I got involved in a row where I could easily have lost my life. To be fair I was no innocent party in this chain of events and it was probably the closest I came to getting topped. It started with brother Aaron getting into a fight with a local geezer who was known for his readiness to chiv you up and had a fearsome reputation. The guy had tried to smash Aaron's face in with a house brick and I decided I would sort him out and broadcast the fact. A few days later I was invited to a party by a local girl who had stupidly invited this man and his friend as well as me. This is the sort of error even the most inexperienced party planner should avoid. As I walked in they spotted me and I spotted them. I went into the lounge trying to act relaxed and they went to the kitchen and then came back into the same room as me and sat on the settee. I watched them in the mirror and clearly saw that each had pulled a cushion close to them and that they had their hands rested underneath. I guessed they had taken knives from the kitchen and were ready to use them. I was thinking fast. I'd had a good drink but not too much to know that the alcohol would impair my chances. If I didn't spark them within seconds of it going off I would be really and truly carved up. Turning towards them I acted as if I had only just registered their presence.

'Hello mate,' I said to the bigger one, who had tried to clump Aaron with the brick. I held my hand towards him and he took it and looked up at me. His other hand had not emerged from beneath the cushion.

'Look, that row you had with my brother. Let's forget it. We've all grown up in the same area. We shouldn't be rucking with one another. It was one of those things. I've forgotten it, anyway' I said.

'Yeah, Joe. Spot on,' and he shook my hand like he meant it.

The other one remained quiet fixing me in his sights.

'What about you, mate? Don't you think us West London boys should stick together?'

He nodded.

'Let's have a drink then,' I said, and we went to the kitchen together and drank and smoked and chatted. Then they left. The party was full of people we knew and the two men would have seen that as a victory. Joe Smith had backed down. Even grovelled. Walking back into the front room I confronted the bird whose party it was.

'What the fuck are you doing inviting those cunts?' I demanded.

'They're nice blokes, Joe. They were doing no harm.'

'No harm? You dopey cunt. They could have stabbed me up and you knew I was going to be here.'

'They wouldn't do that. They wouldn't be carrying knives.'

'You stupid whore. They had your knives.'

I lifted the cushions and took the two nasty looking blades from her kitchen set and held them to her face. I was fuming and threw her out the flat even though her mother owned it. Two nights later I saw the smaller of the two in a local takeaway. This time there was just the two of us who would be fighting and I attacked him with a glass ashtray that lay on the counter. I am afraid his form of taxi home that night was an ambulance.

The following evening I was in my local when a mutual friend came in. Word had got around about what I had done the previous night in the takeaway.

'Joe, it's bad. They're going to fill you up with lead.'

He was shaking his head and worried. I invited him to stay for a drink but he obviously felt that sitting in a pub with me at this precise time was a high-risk affair. When threats like that are made you have to take them seriously and I felt that I had no choice but to act very decisively. I had raised the stakes and anything else would be seen as a weakness. I rounded up six close pals, all of whom were related to me, and they all knew what needed to be done. We decided to strike the following Sunday morning when the ambience of the day tends to catch people off their guard. They're thinking mint sauce and buried in the *News Of The World*. We set off in a Transit with an array of weapons on our person and more rolling around in the back of the van. Our targets were not in their normal local so we moved on and tried three or four more pubs but to no avail. About to give up I decided to pop my head in a final one – a pub I would not have expected this firm to use – where the most lively thing to happen on a Sunday lunchtime would be someone being accused of taking too much cheese from the dish on the bar. The big one was sitting around the corner from the door and I lunged straight at him before he could me. As I punched him he reacted by jabbing me in the face with his glass. Cutting me in the side of the nose and under and over my eye he also managed to stab me in the shoulder. Fair play to the man, he knew he had to stop me. His mates tipped the table up grabbing their glasses and bottles and were ready to serve me up good and proper. But my trusty cousin was behind me and as cool as ice he produced a bottle of ammonia from his pocket and squirted all five of them directly into their eyes. Ammonia, or squirt as it is sometimes affectionately known, is not nice stuff. It blinds. It stings. It stuns. It hurts. They're thrashing around fingers pressed in their eyes and I ran out of the pub and roared across to the others 'They're in here. Let's do the cunts.'

We scrambled for the weapons we had in the van. These included a machete, a baseball bat and assorted golf clubs. The blood was pissing out of my wounds and I was up for finishing each and every one of them off. I started up a chainsaw and strode purposefully across the road. Hearing the purr of the power tool they slammed the door shut and bolted it. I was ready to cut through the door. I'd seen such behaviour in the film *Scarface* (or was it *The Shining*?) and was beginning to enjoy myself. Luckily for all concerned a marked police car drove by the pub, the driver doing a double-take as it dawned on him we could not be workmen before stopping up the road and reversing back by which time we had thrown the weapons back in the car and had torn off with the police Rover soon in hot pursuit. We had no chance, but every time we turned a corner and for a second or two were not in the gavvers' vision, a weapon was discarded straight into someone's garden. At least one West London resident benefited from a free chainsaw. Then me and my pals, Alfie and Kevin, leapt from the van's side-loading door and legged it. The police car had a choice whether to chase us or the van. They stuck with the van. Knowing we were away and I was the one who would have the most explaining to do brother Aaron innocently pulled up. 'Is there a problem, officer?'

'You know there is a fucking problem, what is going on here? Get out the van.'

On the policeman's radio a message crackled: '... three white males last seen in St Mary's Road. One is bleeding heavily with face and head injuries.'

Meanwhile Kevin had veered off and Alfie and myself ran into John and Golly Pidgeley's house which happened to be nearby. Aunt Golly cleaned me up but she said the wounds were deep and that I needed to go to Casualty at the local hospital. I couldn't do that as I'd be collared just as soon as I joined the three-hour queue. Aunt Golly did a great job and I would let my wounds heal, but she was really concerned. Her eight-year-old son Lenny looked up at me as his mum went to work with cotton wool and cream. It could not have been a nice sight for someone so young and hopefully it was that that spurred him into becoming a footballer not a fighter. That's what I like to think because Lenny went on to become a fine goalkeeper for Chelsea Football Club, among others.

The others were all taken to the police station. They were asked to turn out their pockets and the top to the Vick's Nasal Spray bottle where the ammonia had been stored was taken away for forensic tests. Bollocks! It was the only thing we forgot to jettison on the way. The five men we fought had also been questioned, some in hospital, and credit where credit is due they did not say a word or finger anyone. It was the first respect I had given them. Nobody saw anything, nobody remembered anything, and nobody wanted to press charges against anybody. The police decided to let everyone go and although they had a Vick's bottle-top their forensics did not pick this up. I hope a policeman didn't keep it for personal use when he next had a cold because he'd have got some fucking shock if he sniffed heavily on that ammonia-sodden top.

The problem now was where do we go from here? The other mob were not going to get caught like that a second time. I'd been glassed and they'd been ashtrayed. They saw how far we were prepared to go and knew that they'd need to go further if they wanted to come out on top. It was a hairy few days. It's not nice knowing that there are several people living in the close vicinity who may be nursing thoughts about how to kill you. Alfie Sommers, my pal, had strong underworld connections, and it was he who brokered a peace. He had bumped into the man that glassed me and they had talked. Alfie told him how much we respected the fact that they had not bubbled to the police and had made the point that if the police car had not turned up that Sunday lunchtime someone would certainly have died. Alfie negotiated cleverly – so nobody felt they had lost face and that the violence could stop. And it did. Years later I discovered that the man in the takeaway was a good friend of my pal Jason Marriner, and we have met since from time to time and always get on. There are no hard feelings now, both of us realising, perhaps, that we were casualties of the violent playground of wayward youth.

Jason Marriner, by the way, is a good lad. Loves his Chelsea Football Club and has been a bit of a herbert in his time but no way did he deserve the demonization that was heaped upon him when a journalist called Donal Macintyre did an investigative documentary on football hooligans. Macintyre would argue that he is a serious investigative journalist addressing crucial issues. The last time I saw him on television was as the subject of *Cash In The Celebrity Attic* which vied with *The Alan Titchmarsh Show* for afternoon viewers. Enough said.

OFF THE HEAD

The next seriously violent episode I recall did make me stop and think because I thought I may have really killed someone and realised that far from being the cool, intelligent hard man that I liked to think I was – I wasn't. In fact I was out of control. I had been out with my girlfriend and this chap was a boyfriend to one of her friends and during the course of the evening we had ended up giving them a lift from pub to pub. Thrown together we did not like one another and an aggressive mood floated between us. A couple of snide remarks on either side led to us having a full-on slanging match and then I offered him outside foolishly marching out of the pub door first. He followed and as I turned around I saw he was brandishing a blade in one hand and clutching a small bar stool in the other. He lashed out and not prepared for this extreme attack I ran off with him in hot pursuit.

'Fucking coward!' he screamed at me. 'Call yourself a man? Leaving your girlfriend sitting in there. Fucking poof!'

I ran faster than him but to be fair I was not laden with pub furniture and he eventually stopped and shook his head at my cowardice and barged back into the pub, his shoulders swinging the gait of a bolstered man with adrenalin coursing around his bloodstream. I guess he said to the girls something like: 'That's dealt with him – the tosspot's on his way to Brighton by now.'

I didn't much mind the name-calling but the blade worried me and I was not going to risk getting plunged if I didn't have to. I've seen and heard of many people getting knifed by absolute idiots over the years and did not want that to be my fate. My car was outside and I leant in and picked up a piece of cut-off steel scaffold bar that I kept behind my seat for 'road rage' emergencies though I doubt if the term had been coined then. I slipped the bar up my sleeve. Now feeling emboldened myself I opened the door and let forth a volley of abuse to him.

My opponent seemed genuinely pleased that I had returned and grinned from ear to ear which was disconcerting and replied: 'Well, well. You've built up some courage.'

His stool and his knife were back in a hand each so he must have been half expecting me back and he came outside the pub again. He swung the stool at my head but I grabbed it mid-air with my left hand and let the bar slide down my sleeve and into the palm of my right hand and struck him an almighty blow across the shoulder which I thought would leave him in a heap on the deck. But his shoulder merely dropped and he was roaring forward with the knife an extension of his fist. I stepped back and with sickening precision brought the bar down again, this time clean over his head. I had not held back and the noise of shattering bone and the speed with which he fell made me close my eyes and cringe. The few people watching fell silent and then probably only five seconds later, though it seemed like five minutes, he got up. 'Ok mate, you've done me with your tools. Let's have a straightener. Can't you have a row without a tool, you mother's cunt?'

I thought that was a bit rich considering it was he that had introduced a stool and a knife into the equation so I hit him with a massive punch and he went down again. Twice afterwards he got back up for me to lay him out again. I learnt later that he had collapsed again elsewhere and had to have an ambulance ferry him to the hospital where he had over fifty stitches to his head wound and I felt bad about it all. The blow with the bar was something I never thought I'd do and its sheer viciousness worried me. Many of us keep blunt instruments in our cars and in our homes for protection but none of us think we will ever use them. However, a few split seconds can change it from being a comfort blanket to a murder weapon. I reflected on the incident. I could have murdered him and equally it could have been me that my parents were identifying up the mortuary and what the hell over? We didn't take to each other when we were thrown together in a pub. We put each other's backs up. Testosterone-fuelled rivalry. Absolute shit.

I soon heard that the guy and his pals were 'after' me and planning revenge. As is often the case in these quarrels some heavy names were thrown in. He's a pal of so and so – that type of thing. Whatsisname is not too happy. Youknowwho is on the case. Much of the time it is showboating and most of these 'names' have no idea that their reputations are being used as pawns in a low-life violent slanging match. But sometimes you make the error of getting tied up with a real firm or a high-level criminal family. All you can do is show no fear and ensure that the man who has escalated the row or is threatening to escalate it knows that whatever happens *he* will pay the price if anything bad happens.

One day I received a phone call at the pub I was drinking in and I went behind the bar to take it. 'Hello Joe,' said the calm, assured voice on the other end. 'Do you know me? I'm ***********.'

'Yes, I have heard of your name.'

'Well Joe, you've overstepped the mark old son. I think you know what I mean. I'm afraid you're going to get done. I think you might know that.'

I tried to remain calm, anger and fear jostling for the emotional dominance inside me.

'Look, listen, your mate. The man you are avenging. The wanker you are sticking up for. Well, he deserved everything he got. Ask anyone who was there. He pulled weapons out on me first. I defended myself. Most people would have done the same.'

There was quiet at the other end of the line so I continued: 'I'll tell you what. Come down now and do me. I'm in The Oxford Arms as you know, you've just rung it. I'll wait outside for that grey Merc you're driving.'

'How do you know what car I'm driving?'

'I have my people as well. You remember the girl whose eye you threatened to take out? She told me, actually. I know quite a lot about you. Where you eat, drink and live. Because, I need too, because, I've been hearing for a few weeks now that you're going to do me. I'd be stupid, wouldn't I, not to do my homework? You're going to have to kill me. Because I will come back and back and back. Just watch. And I'm a fair man and I'm telling you come down now but bring a few with you because I have some friends with me.' I slammed the phone down and looked over at the manager who'd been listening wiping glasses as my voice rose. He looked alarmed, and not surprisingly, as we were the only two people in the pub.

'Calm down, calm down,' I said in my best Scouse accent, but he wasn't laughing. The pregnant silence was broken by the phone ringing again, this time I answered it.

'OK, Joe. This is the situation. I am willing to let this go. Only because I've had it confirmed that the other man started the row. But, I don't want you to think anyone's backing down or anyone's worried. Right?'

'I never said anyone was, mate.'

'Good. That's understood. End of matter, then?'

'End of, yes. But, one thing, tell that mouthy cunt to learn some respect and how to behave when he goes out.' There was no immediate reply and I thought I could hear teeth grinding. 'Can you hear me?'

'I'll do that, Joe. Goodbye.'

Now, this little story comes with a health warning: Do not attempt this at home. I fronted a name. A known and seasoned villain and I got away with it. It could have just have easily gone the other way and me and the totally innocent publican could have been battered near to death in that lonely, empty bar.

The aftermath of this whole business was not entirely over, though. My opponent had been true to the criminal code and when the police questioned him after he recovered consciousness in hospital he said he had no idea who attacked him and that he had no memory of the entire evening. Because of the severity of his head injuries the police were inclined to believe him and they only went and stuck up one of those yellow triangular boards outside the pub appealing for information. Decent law-abiding citizens may come forward. They also had my car registration number although it had never been registered to me. It was time to dump the motor and time to disappear.

Southend, for the second time, was where I pitched up, but instead of keeping my head down I got involved in a load more skulduggery and before long I had been charged, along with a few other lads, with a very serious offence. I was remanded in custody and because the prisons were bursting at the seams and the prison officers had been taking some industrial action I was doing my time on remand awaiting trial in a succession of police stations. I don't know whether doing time in police cells is worse than conventional prison or not, but I sure had time to think as there was no real routine, no exercise period, no recreation periods, no TV, no real visitors and so on. Hour after hour, day after day and week after week were mainly spent lying on my bed with my hands behind my head reading and re-reading the wall graffiti and thinking. With no distractions, no alcohol, no mates that was all I could do. Think. Think. Think. My body and mind began to detox. My five-year relationship with my girlfriend had ended before I had been banged up and I played that over in my mind and for the first time could see with some clarity the turning points in our time together. I thought about my parents and how I had been an utter disappointment to them and a source of grinding worry and fear. Despairing looks on both Mum and Dad's faces at various times came back to me and I hadn't even realised I had registered them at the time. To while away the hours I read and re-read golfing magazines that had been brought in for me and each time I saw the name of one of my former contemporaries playing in or winning some tournament or other it was like a knife going into me. They were leading the life that I should have been. They were out on the rolling greens in the open air, swinging their clubs, immaculately dressed and doing what they enjoy most while I was lying in a cell with only the drama of hearing drunks wanting to fight the world being thrown next door and then hearing them in the morning being discharged all meek and humble to break up my day and night. I was engulfed with self-pity. It didn't help when my brief told me that if I was found guilty I was looking at three or four years at best.

I managed to do the time in the run-up to my trial by keeping myself to myself and relaxing. My life had been like one massive bender the last few years and having the time to merely relax and think was a novelty and a luxury. Unbelievably, and now I cannot say how, my days started to go reasonably quickly and painlessly, though when an opportunity arose for me to get bail I jumped at it. My two sisters were now married and comfortably off and they turned up at court and offered to stand bail for me. They were prepared to go to whatever level the judge decided. I was so grateful for this gesture and also to their husbands, who are not blood, yet they supported their wives in their efforts to help this errant brother. I felt overjoyed to be bailed awaiting trial yet unworthy of their trust and support. A condition of bail was that I lived at one of my sister's address and this I did, though I chose to stay in a caravan nearby rather than impose myself on them in the house.

Writing this now I can see that the lowest point of my life was living in that caravan. It was worse than being in prison or a police cell. At least in those circumstances there was an end-game, be it a prison sentence or release. Here in the caravan I was truly alone. I was now in my early twenties and not a kid. I owned nothing, the car having been my only possession of any value. I had no visitors and nobody to visit. No money. No phone. I began to drink. Not that I didn't drink before but when you're out on the town with all your mates the drinking is merely the background and not the purpose. When you're alone in a caravan drinking bottles of vodka there's no two ways: you're drinking because you need to. My transformation from hard-drinking young man to fully-fledged alcoholic was a sickeningly fast process. There are few things worse we humans can inflict on ourselves than getting paralytic alone and waking up not remembering anything that happened and then realising nothing could have happened because nothing ever did. The violence had drained out of me. The swagger had turned into a head-down slouch and my self-esteem had evaporated. With a few pounds each day I'd go down to the local snooker club where I could get a cheap meal and a few pints before taking a bottle or two of spirits home with me. The new owners were kind to me and it was a salutary lesson that not so long ago I minded this club and now it was minding me. Sadly, a member of the local CID became a member and then I thought it was best to stop using the place. Walking around town pretending I had somewhere to go was another dose of reality because when I'd run into my pals, my so-called pals, and asked them to lend me a tenner anyone would think I'd asked them for the crown jewels. These were the same people who I had been lushing up for years. Paying for their drinks and meals and often protecting them. Fighting their battles. I didn't argue. Just stored it up. I vowed from then on that I'd always help a mate genuinely down on his luck but, more importantly, never allow people to ponce off me. They knew I was a drunk. I was not down and out but they saw me tumbling and it was no longer a plus, in their minds, to be seen with me. The humiliation – when I'd see a mate coming towards me in his car and I'd raise my arm in a big wave and they looked the other way, or pretended to be doing something with the gears, pretending they hadn't seen – stays with me to this day. And I had kidded myself *I* was the clever one. I was a pisshead, with jack shit in my sky rocket and about to be birded off for a few years and they all knew it.

Sometimes back in my tiny, dingy caravan I'd pull open a drawer and find a ten-pound note and in my inebriated normal state I'd firstly think what a stroke of luck but slowly it dawned on me that someone was putting them there. Visitors to my caravan were thin on the ground and I soon worked out that it was my Uncle John who was leaving them around. He wanted to help me but did not want to embarrass me or himself by just giving me money, and he also knew that my pride would not have allowed me to take cash off family. It made me cry that it had come to this. Living in a metal box that would never again cruise the roads and had no lighting or heat and reduced to living off handouts from caring relatives. Time had become my enemy. I'd look forward to going to bed because it signalled the end of another empty day, but when I got into bed (unless I was nearly comatose through drink) I could not go to sleep and lay there staring at nothing, listening to the hiss of the crickets and squeaking of bats outside. My natural state is optimism and I'd wake in the morning and grab a bar of soap and wash under the freezing tap outside, but slowly my situation would catch up with me and by the time I was clothed and ready for the day I'd sunk into a depression.

The people I loved were torturing me too though they knew nothing of it. My parents came to me in my dreams, and when I was awake, just looking at me, their faces betraying despair. I kept thinking of Rymer too and the conversations we had had together and how he had told me to keep away from trouble and play golf. It was almost like his ghost was there in the caravan with me. Not to chide me or tell me off, he was just there and the only way I could get him and Mum and Dad to go was by banishing them with alcohol.

Not eating much and drinking spirits rather than beer caused the weight to drop off and some people assumed I was in some sort of self-imposed exile and on a rigid fitness programme to get myself in shape for an upcoming fight. When this was put to me I did not correct them (better they thought that than admit the pathetic truth) and before I knew it there was a full-blown rumour going around that I was going to be fighting Bobby Frankham in a bare-knuckle challenge. It was nonsense. Bobby and I were good friends. He had been on course for a cruiserweight title when he sparked the referee in a big professional fight with Billy Sim at Wembley that led him to being banned from the sport. Some years later Bobby became friends with Brad Pitt after they worked together on the film *Snatch*. If there had of been a fight then whether I'd lost weight or not I'd have had problems. In drink, even between sessions, your nerves are shot to pieces and you are weak. Mental strength is just as important as physical strength to fight effectively and if you are wrapped up with alcohol, mental strength is one thing you definitely do not possess.

This meagre, pathetic existence continued up until my court case came around. I did not want my family to attend court because I was convinced that I was in for a lengthy sentence and I did not want them to see it. I had to eat my porridge all on my own. And I really was on my own because my two co-defendants, who had also managed to get bail, had sourced a couple of dodgy passports and had made it to Rio di Janeiro in exotic Brazil where undoubtedly they were sunning themselves on a beach. Why they suddenly decided to do this, I'm not sure, but it wouldn't have surprised me if it was a spur-of-the-moment thing after watching Phil Collins in the film *Buster*. Losing two of the defendants seemed to knock the prosecuting counsel off balance and my defence barrister found a loophole in their case. What everyone believed would be a two-week trial folded on its first day. I can still remember the South African judge's crisp and measured words: 'I appreciate the attendance here today of everyone in this court, not least the jurors and witnesses but due to a major inconsistency of evidence, namely that the defendant who stands before us – Joseph Smith – was the first man to get out of the car and that this man had been watched by the witness for two months and he is described as 5ft 4in with brown hair and slightly built...' he nodded over at me and all the court's eyes were looking at my blond hair and six-feet-plus frame, 'well, this glaring inconsistency is completely unacceptable in my court and I will not allow the case to proceed.' He turned to me and said: 'Joseph Smith, there is no case to answer. You are free to leave this court forthwith.'

ROAD TO RECOVERY

A weight had dropped off of my shoulders, but as is the way, then I started to worry about the next thing and that was the matter of the assault with an iron bar in West London. I needed to discover if I was being sought in connection with that before I could show my face around there again. Being impressed by and eternally grateful to my brief I asked her if she could make discreet enquiries of the police on my behalf. 'Yes,' she said, 'I'll make an appointment and we can go and meet them together.'

'Do you mind going without me?' I asked, smiling weakly.

She did and came back confident that they had no interest in me for any outstanding offences and that was another huge relief. I started to feel a degree of control over my destiny once more. I phoned my dad and he informed me that one of my old friends from Home Park Golf Club had called round to the house and said that he was going to Sweden to turn pro at golf. Dad suggested that I could try the same thing. Brush up on my game. He said he would fund me.

I was choking up on the phone. Dad still there. Worried sick. Felt that by getting me out to Sweden he might reignite my passion for golf but more importantly remove me from the environment that I was in. For the first time in several months I travelled back from Southend to see them. Dad and I went to the pub and we skirted around talking about me, my past and my future. We basked in the pleasure of being in one another's company and then at closing we went back to the house where for the first time in years we sat together alone. Me, my dear mum, and my lovely wise old man. The conversation was gently switched around to me and my misdemeanours. They told me that night how disappointed they were in me. Ashamed, even. How they could not believe some of things I had done that they had heard about. How lucky I was to not have been killed or to have killed another. That there was no glory in violence. I sat there listening

Joe and Mary, my wonderful grandparents in the early 1960s. God bless them.

What a man! And a lovely little woman too. Grandfather Rymer and Granny Ria. God bless them also.

Above: My great-grandmother, Anda, with Granny Ria and Aunt Phyllis among the hops in Kent.

Right: Me in the caravan dangerously close to the cut glass.

Opposite, clockwise from top left:
The kids leaning against Uncle Neville's 'Roller'; I'm on my brother's lap.
Dad, Aaron and me up against the caravan.
Meet the Smiths. Hampton site circa 1973.
Grandfather Joe with Mum and Dad showing off baby Aaron.
Aaron in his favourite tank top leads the Smith fashion parade.

PRIVATE CAR PARK

Above: Inside the vardo. I'm starting to like the camera.
Below: Pollution-free transport. My cousins and me circa 1974.

Below: Me shaping up at a very young age.

Right: Me in the gym sparring at ten years old.

Right: Uncle Neville enjoying life. Sadly, he died at just thirty-five.

News Tel: 01-942 2484 Display Tel:01-891 1211   Classified 646 4355   Richmond Series, Thursday, December 1, 1983 Page 3

A convoy of limousines leaves the campsite

Hundreds honour the 'Gipsy King'

HUNDREDS of gipsies from all over the country came to Hanworth last Tuesday to pay their last respects to one of the most respected characters in the gipsy world.

Jack Smith, who died suddenly two weeks ago, had lived on a small campsite in Green Lane, Hanworth, for more than 40 years.

His son Wally described him as a "king among gipsies."

Passers-by, seeing the hundreds of wreathes and convoy of limousines, could have been forgiven for thinking it was a state funeral.

Local people watched conies. Nobody had a bad word to say about Jack.

"He was a very good man," said one resident, "we never had any trouble with him."

The campsite where Jack Smith had lived with his wife and two daughters was ablaze with flowers for the funeral.

Wreathes in the shape of boxing gloves and a boxing ring were the only reminders of Jack's former days as a fighter.

For four nights before the funeral male relatives and family friends kept an all-night vigil at the camp.

Hughie Smith, President of the National Gipsy Council, said: "Well-respected gipsy people are always given a good send-off.

"Jack was a true-born gipsy, respected by all the gipsy community."

Gipsies unable to attend the service marked Jack's death in their own way. There was even a ceremony on the Isle of Wight.

The crowd fell silent as the coffin was carried out to the waiting hearse.

"Great fighter" murmured one gipsy as the procession of limousines slowly moved off.

Above: Rymer's funeral makes the papers, 1983.

Right: Mixing in high circles. Denis Thatcher presents me with the London Junior Open trophy, 1987.

London Junior Open winner Joe Smith receives his trophy and prizes from Denis Thatcher

JOE Smith, aged 16, from Home Park Golf Club is the 1987 London Junior Open Golf Champion. The competition was held at Richmond Park Golf Courses on Wednesday July 29 with 135 12-17 year old junior golfers taking part. Joe Smith won the championship with an excellent round of 70 and in addition to his other prizes Joe was presented with the London Junior Open Trophy , valued at £1,000, by Denis Thatcher.

Mr. Thatcher, himself a keen amateur golfer, attended throughout the afternoon watching the play and talking with competitors.

Later, he presented 23 prizes to the various winners commending all the players on their efforts especially in light of the appalling weather conditions which prevailed for much of the day.

Despite the heavy rain the standard of play was extremely high and several excellent performances were recorded.

Adam Musikant from Potters Bar Golf Club won the 15-17 age group handicap division with a superb net score of 60, whilst 13-year-old Anthony Wall from Royal Ascot Golf Club took the 12-14 age group winner's prize and trophy.

For the second year running the girl's division was won by Susan Little of Hindhead Golf Club. There was double the entry of girls this year and it is hoped this will encourage even more for 1988.

Perhaps the highlight of the day was the Holiday Prize Draw which was held at the end of the presentation ceremony.

Royal and Ancient regulations relating to amateur status prevented the award of this prize to the winner but the competition sponsor, Clive Hamilton Mudge, representing Hamilton Insurance Managers, was keen to reward the parents for their support of junior golf and so decided to offer the holiday in the form of a draw.

Darren Walpole, aged 16, from Stevenage Golf Club was the lucky winner and was able to thank his parents by presenting them with a one week Mediterranean holiday to be enjoyed later this year.

JOE MAKES 'EM CROSS

Haircut sparks golf row

By ANDREW DILLON

STARE CASE . . . Joe doesn't look like a typical golfer

JOE SMITH does not exactly fit golf's stuffy image.

But, at 6ft 2in and 18st, the former bare-knuckle fighter has trouble squeezing into anything.

And, with fingers like sausages and a stare that could bend a five iron, the British pro hopeful is used to raising a few eyebrows as he stomps round the fairways of Hounslow Heath golf club, west London.

But his latest fashion-statement is a step too far for the brass-hats at the PGA. Patriotic Smith has infuriated golf bigwigs by having a George Cross shaved into the back of his head.

PGA tournament chief Iain Burns even threatened to boot him off the UK Tour unless he covered up, when he was spotted during practice at Princes course at Sandwich in Kent.

The proud Brit, 27, said: "I was stunned. There is nothing in the rules about what sort of haircut you are allowed to play golf.

"I just wanted to add a bit of colour and character to golf. It needs it. I'm not racist, I just love my country. I love England. I enjoy being different but I do not set out to cause trouble.

"Fifty years ago, ordinary people couldn't afford to join their local courses. Now it is a game for the people. Even the local builder can play and people like me can become pros. I've earned my right to be on the Tour. It's 1999 and I think the people who run golf should be more modern.

"I don't know what's said behind my back but the other pros seem to accept me. I'm just the same as them, out there trying to make a living and make it on to a bigger tour."

PGA chief Burns admitted: "There is nothing in the rule book to cover it but I have the power to do as I see fit.

"It's a question of standards. Joe's a nice guy but showing off a haircut like that is not the image we want to project."

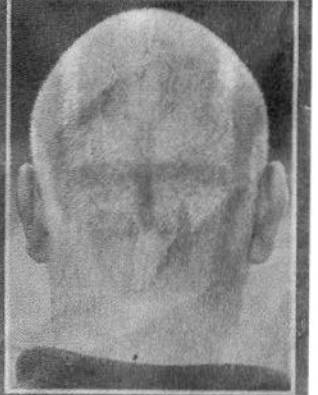

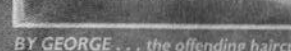

BY GEORGE . . . the offending haircut

Above top: Bad Hair Day. The *Sun* reports on the George Cross scandal.

Above middle: Ready for action. Waiting for my opponent to arrive for a bare-knuckle fight.

Left: Bang! Take that. Straight down the middle.

Left: Sometimes I forget whether I'm boxing or golfing.

Below: Whose phone is ringing while I'm trying to take a shot?

Above: Aaron, Big John, Jimmy Stockin, Jimmy Dean, Paul, Dad, me and Rymer.

Left: Mr and Mrs Smith and young Rymer with gold medallist Terry Spinks and British Light Heavyweight Champion Johnny Frankham.

Above: On the attack.
York Hall, Bethnal Green.

Opposite top: Me and my
lovely wife on our wedding day.

Opposite bottom:
Meeting my hero, Bernhard Langer.

Following pages
Left top: All the kids at baby Joseph's
christening with cousin Katie.

Left bottom: Me, Rymer and the girls.

Right: Two old battlers.
Esteban Toldeo and me with our sons.

PLAYERS
& CADDIES
ONLY

CRAZY
DAVE'S
Golf Store

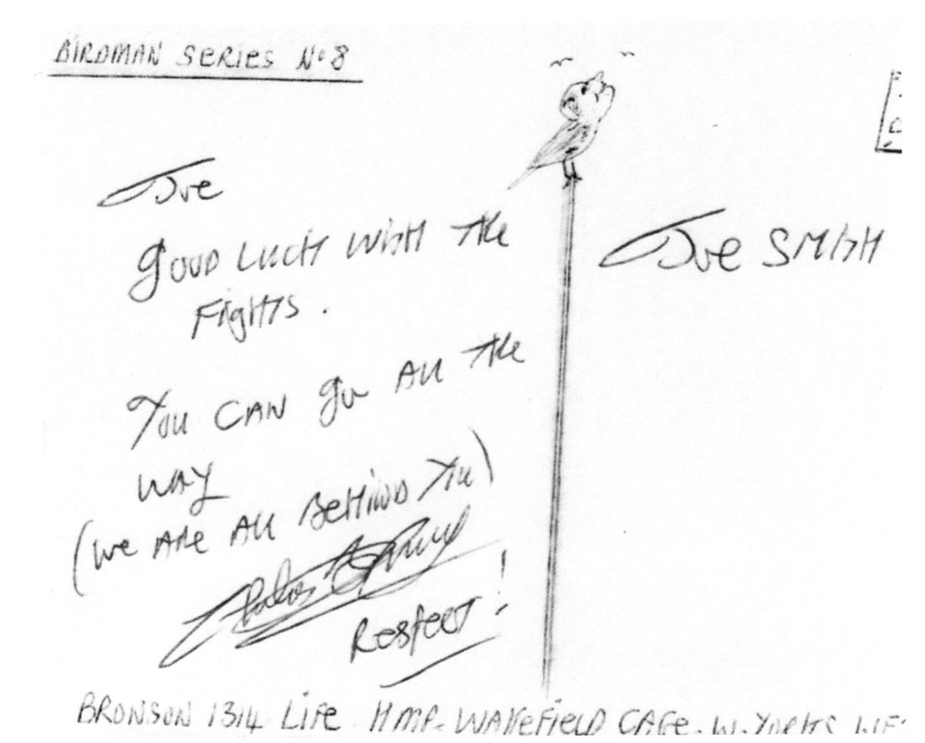
BIRDMAN SERIES No 8

Joe

Good Luck with the Fights.

You can go all the way

(we are all behind you)

Respect!

Joe Smith

BRONSON 1314 LIFE HMP- WAKEFIELD CAGE. W. YORKS

Charles Bronson was kind enough to send me his own special brand of encouragement from prison.

Above: You can get knocked about a bit in football too. Young Rymer after a very competitive match.
Below: All about me – golf, boxing and scrap metal.

Above: Mum and Dad. God rest.
Below: Muhammad Ali. He probably *was* the greatest.

to these home truths from two quietly-spoken, dignified people and my head fell forward in shame and I cried buckets of tears. All the tears that I should have shed over the previous five years came out and the doors opened to my conscience. At the end of it I stood up and walked to my room, the room that was always there for me, feeling like a seven-year-old child who had done something naughty. Very naughty. I lay in my bed, a warm comfortable bed like a cocoon, and marvelled at the calm words of wisdom that had been spoken in the privacy of my home. They had not reprimanded me. Merely painted a picture and opened up their hearts so I could look in and see their pain and their pain was all about me. Not them. That hour or two did more than any beating or any prison sentence could or would have done. I slipped off into an exhausted sleep extraordinarily peaceful and happy. I knew that I would no longer be a criminal. When I woke up the next morning Mum and Dad said nothing. Everything was back to normal and the talk from last night was private and between us. Emotions that had flowed around the room like an oil slick the previous night had all been safely returned to their barrels. Adrenalin bubbled inside me and all I said was: 'Mum and Dad, I'm going to practise my golf. I will go to Sweden and turn pro. And I've finished with all the other stuff. You haven't got to worry.'

There was a fee involved to participate in the Swedish tournament although you had to have attained a specific level of golf to be able to pay the fee and because it was competing in a competition for prize money this meant I was a professional golfer. That is how it works. Alan Jarrett, an old friend, and myself flew from Heathrow to Copenhagen and then ferried to Malmo where the golf course where we would become professionals was situated. I knew and my dad knew that my golf, even with some hurried practice, was not good, but going to Sweden and knuckling down was the best course of action for me. I watched my step and unashamedly did everything I could for my fellow professionals so that my shortcomings would not irk them too much. I congratulated and encouraged their games, retrieving their balls and raking the bunkers. I would have wiped their arses if they had asked me. My confidence and self-esteem were still at an all-time low. I felt like an imposter. The night before my big pro event I dreamt that I would miss the ball altogether on the first tee and I nearly bloody did. It was a nightmare. I could not hit one decent shot all the way around. It was a pathetic, embarrassing performance and my scores in Sweden were ninety-four and eighty-seven. But I put my card in and took it on the chin.

Someone should have said to me: 'Look Joe, your game is in a mess. Go back and play as an amateur where the pressure is a lot less. Build up your confidence and when your game is on the up then turn pro.' Nobody did and I probably would not have listened. Instead others who thought they were being cruel to be kind, advised me to pack up golf for good. 'You are never going to make it,' they said. 'You have to face up to it.' To me that was like waving a red flag to a bull. Why should I? I was still young. Nobody had any doubt that I had the talent when I was a teenager. That must still be there somewhere. I wanted to tell those people that preached doom to fuck off. Some of them wanted me back where I was. When you're swimming in shit there is a perverse comfort in the fact that your friends are in the cesspit with you. If someone climbs out the cesspit, or tries to, it unsettles everyone. Plus I would not consider throwing the clubs in because I had promised Dad and he had reminded me that I had promised my grandfather too. Rymer's name alone being mentioned had been enough to provoke the tears that night at my parents' and I was thinking about him more and more. I had promised I would become a professional and until I had taken a cheque from a golf tournament I knew I could not claim to have genuinely achieved that.

My stroke average of eighty-seven for my first year as a pro-golfer after returning from Sweden was nothing to jump up and down about. Mum and Dad were always there to watch and encourage me but they must have thought what had happened to their boy who would bestride the fairways with such confidence and play with that cheeky panache? They would see me twitching and often trembling and know that I was still shot to pieces and that my return to normality was going to be a long haul. I was attempting to come off drink and although I had only been an alcoholic for a short time it was very difficult. One day another pro – one who deserved to be where he was – asked me how come I was a professional? I looked at him knowing that three or four years ago he could not have held a candle to me on the course and only a few months ago I would have wrapped the club I was holding around his fucking head. I bit my lip and shrugged my shoulders resisting the temptation to nut him or something because I knew that it would all be over if I did. It was my first test. On the surface it was something quite insignificant but in my head it was quite major. Not only were my parents behind me and supporting me, they were funding me also and to fall at the first hurdle would have been such a failure.

To do my bit and also to put some much-needed cash in my pocket I started to do garden work. Me and Mum would get up in the morning and jump into the family estate car. I'd drop her off into the nearest town where she'd hawk her lucky heather and then I'd park up in a quiet residential road and go knocking. I took to it quite easily. I felt that being on my own was a distinct advantage. Even though I was big and a gypsy to boot, because I was alone it didn't make potential customers so initially wary. I was always very polite and never pushy. If they said 'No' I'd say 'Thank you for your time' and walk away down the path and then sometimes then they'd call after me and say 'Actually, I could do with that hedge being trimmed.'

I enjoyed the work even though gardening can be the most deceptively hard graft there is. You can spend hours weeding and at the end of it the customer (and yourself) can hardly notice the difference. But it is also rewarding. Many a time I've cut an old person's lawn who would have been unable to get it done for months and they are genuinely over the moon and it's a nice feeling. Customers started asking me to come back and others told neighbours. When I'd finished I'd pick Mum up and we'd compare notes. She'd have made a few pounds and I'd have a fair day's wages. They were happy times again and soon I'd saved enough to buy a small van which added to my credibility as a gardener and allowed me to carry more tools around. After eighteen months my golf was edging forward and I broke eighty, but I was still on seventy-nine on a par-seventy. It was barely progress.

Soon there was progress on another front. Since breaking up with my long-term girlfriend I had been out with a few girls but had no interest in or was in no fit state to pursue a serious relationship. Now I was feeling like I wanted a girlfriend. A partner. Someone to share my life with. I craved female company as opposed to men's. I wanted to meet a nice gypsy girl and in my mind had a mental image of who that could be. She was pretty, slim and bubbly. A no-nonsense, switched-on girl. I was on the look-out but the lady of my dreams never seemed to come along. I started thinking about lowering my sights (I was hardly a great catch, after all) when one night I was in a pub with my cousins and she walked in. The girl from my dreams.

'Who the fuck is that?' I said to my cousin Charlie.

'That's John Snook's youngest.'

'They're all married aren't they?'

'No, she ain't. Not yet anyway. Though someone will snap her up soon, cuz. She's my old woman's cousin.'

I pleaded with Charlie to get his wife Cilla to fix me up for a date and he said he would. The feedback when it finally came was not good. She had heard I was a bad man. A waster. I was trouble, so thanks but no thanks. Well at least it wasn't Fuck Off You Animal. That was enough encouragement for me and I was persistent in my efforts to meet this beauty. Christine was her name. Still is. Finally she relented to meet me and I sat her down and told her my life story. I told her where I had been and where I was going. It was easy and I felt like I had known her all my life. She knew it wasn't old flannel and at the end of it she agreed that we would be boyfriend and girlfriend and I almost skipped home doing the Morecambe and Wise dance. Now it was time for me to go and meet her father and ask his permission to date his daughter. Make it official, like. In our culture this is expected. It is the height of disrespect to date a man's daughter without seeking his permission and declaring it. Nothing fazes me much but I was as nervous as hell and when John Snook handed me a cup of tea it was obvious to him too as the cup practically did an Irish jig on the saucer.

'I will look after your daughter,' I opened with, solemnly. 'I will not put her in any danger and I will comply with your rules. Whatever time you say she should be in then I will have her back by then. I respect...'

John flicked his hand, faintly embarrassed by my seriousness. 'OK mate. No problem.'

Well that was easier than I thought, but her mum who was hovering in the background decided it was time to intervene. 'Another Stockin or Smith – whatever you lot call yourselves – in the family. I've already got a son-in-law and a daughter-in-law from your family...'

'But it is me she is dating, Mrs Snook with all respect. No offence intended, but please judge me by me and not by others.'

'Don't worry, boy. Your word is good enough for us,' intervened John. And that was that.

On the 26th June 1993 I walked my beautiful Christine down the aisle and I was the proudest man in Britain. They all say that, I know, but it was true. She was nearly nineteen and I was about to become twenty-two. We were only young but I felt I'd already had one life. My old pals were saying we never thought we'd see you get married. What did they think, I wonder? I was only twenty-two for Christ's sake. Some people who go to university, for example, have not even started grafting at that age. In America you can't get served in a bar until you are a year younger than I was. I know what they thought. They thought: 'Joe, we never thought we'd see the day you got married because really we thought you'd be dead or lifed off in prison somewhere.'

The wedding was attended by hundreds and even my old trainer Tommy Gray flew over from Spain for the celebrations. Uncles, aunties, grans, chavvies from all branches of the family were there enjoying themselves and the jellied eels slid down lubricated by copious amounts of beer. It was a vintage gypsy wedding and in the middle were Mum and Dad looking on me like I was one of their daughters being wed. The relief and pleasure on their faces was plain to see. Finally, after the umpteenth playing of 'All That She Wants' the Ace Of Base hit by the DJ, I gathered up my new bride and took her back to our new home – a caravan that I had saved like mad to buy. That night she told me that many years earlier she'd seen me fight as a little girl on the caravan site and that she had said to her playmates that when she grew up she wanted to marry a man like me. I remembered then the little girl when I fought the man that Christmas Day, years back. More destiny.

Even though I enjoyed the gardening there was a limit to how much I could earn and that limit was on how many hours I put in. To support my golf I needed more money to allow me to spend more hours practising and not pulling weeds. To that end I went into scrap-metal, a business I knew through Dad and Grandfather and a business where now and then there was the opportunity to make a good turn on your money. Having said that, it was now much harder to make the day-to-day regular living at the scrap-metal game, times had moved on. For a start there was now far fewer establishments in the south of England using metal as their raw material and those that were now put up tall security gates and you spent countless hours talking into intercoms to faceless dopey birds doing everything in their power to stop you seeing the guvnor. One of the problems was that by now these factories were being besieged almost by eastern Europeans who had muscled in on our old scrap-metal customers and who would call constantly. They put the barriers up and we all suffered. This is not a racist statement. It is a fact.

I had a good relationship with one customer over in south London and one day I pulled up the truck and went into see my friend who was an Italian gentleman with a prosperous little metal-works on an industrial estate. After a nice chat and a cup of tea I said goodbye and walked out of the yard promising to return when they had finished a big job they were on.

'Oi you. Move that fucking truck.'

A man of about fifty years was walking over to me from an office block across the road. My truck was probably impeding the access to his place slightly but his tone immediately riled me.

'What are you – an idiot? I have deliveries coming in and out all day. Go on, away with you.' He waved his hand imperiously, dismissing me like a piece of shit.

'Do you want me to knock your fucking teeth down your fucking gullet, you useless cunt?'

Suddenly he was walking backwards as I stepped towards him.

'Don't you threaten me. That would be a silly thing to do...' he shouted over his shoulder toward his yard.

'I just did.'

He shouted again, this time louder, shitting himself. A big man came running out and took one look at me and ran back inside. I smiled at the other man triumphantly and decided I would give him a real scare by pretending I was going to hit him but had no intention of doing so. I rolled up my sleeves in an exaggerated fashion, but as I did this the younger man reappeared this time brandishing a sledgehammer. This time I backed off to the truck and opened the door and pulled out a piece of lead piping. The situation was escalating rapidly. They approached me and instinctively I threw the bar low at them and it went like a boomerang seemingly gaining speed as it flew. It hit the older man in his leg and he crumpled to the floor and I climbed into the truck and drove away. A week or so later I called my Italian customer.

'Joe,' he said. 'You better not come any more. You broke the man's leg, Joe. I have had the police over here asking questions about you. I said I didn't know you. Please don't come, Joe.'

It was a stupid, stupid instance. I lost a good customer and nearly got myself nicked in the bargain. Over what? Nothing. It was a relapse into past ways and I could not understand how it had happened. I knew that I had to overcome my temper if I was ever to make myself a better person and I vowed to redouble my efforts in that area.

Christine was supportive of my golf and the dreams I was nurturing and she endured my poor performances witnessing me block the balls in the trees and even topping and doffing. It must have crossed her mind that I was deluded. It wasn't all work and golf though because after eighteen months of enjoyable trying we were overjoyed to discover that we were to become parents. Around this time I also nipped over to America to play some golf out there and recapture my form and momentum.

On my return and lifted by the USA break I entered a tournament on the British Professional Golf Tour at Colintree Park in Northampton. Christine was my caddy although now eight and a half weeks pregnant, but I did treat to her a stay at the local Jarvis Hotel and a Chinese meal – so it was a fair deal. There was a gale force wind blowing but this bolstered my confidence as I am heavily built and a naturally low hitter of the ball. However, growing confidence was one thing – playing well in a field that included some Tour and Ryder Cup winners was another. I started well and continued to do so, working the ball well in the wind and putting effectively. With a field of 144 competitors, I was lying in fourteenth position. The press got wind of my progress and Lewin Mier from the *Daily Telegraph* mentioned me in dispatches. Could this be the match where I gained my first cheque as a pro? This would be the measure that me, Dad and Grandfather Rymer would accept as having made it as a professional golfer.

In the second round I started off slow and nervous but managed to settle down and play into a rhythm until, coming down the stretch, the old twitch factor kicked in. I fluffed two short putts in a row as the nerves clanged inside me. Then I regained control and hit a glorious two-iron on my penultimate hole. That set me up for par. The eighteenth was straight into the wind and I hit two good shots about 130 yards short of the green. This very testing par-five was still no walk in the park, with dangerous water circling the green. I struck an eight-iron a tiny bit thin and watched with my heart in my mouth as it just looped over the water to sit on the front of the green. Then I putted past the hole by about four feet – not a good stroke – but what was important was that it went in the left side of the hole – a huge sigh of relief. One of my playing partners, Alan Lovelace, and a well-respected professional shook my hand vigorously. 'Joe, you have turned your game around,' he said 'that was a brilliant round. Well done.' That was good to hear from someone I respected. I recorded my score and went home.

I told Dad I'd done well and he took me to the pub to celebrate me playing a better game. He asked if I thought I'd won any money and I said I wasn't sure. From the pub I rang Randy Fox (his middle name is not 'Old' by the way) who was the tournament director. He confirmed I had indeed won some money. Just on the button. I tied forty-third with seven other guys and the top placed fifty got paid out. It was not a huge amount but it was the first time I had won money as a professional from a recognised tournament and therefore I had achieved my, Dad's and Rymer's dream for me. I was a real pro-golfer at last.

I ordered champagne as I put the phone down and Dad knew it was good news and he summonsed my wife and my brother Aaron to the pub to celebrate. Considering I couldn't break eighty not so long before it was a massive step forward and with the champagne bubbles dancing on my tonsils I lifted my glass and said: 'Dad, I am now aiming to qualify for the British Open Championship because that's what you said to me once was *your* dream.'

Dad sat there grinning from ear to ear as pleased as punch. Prison, police cells, visiting orders and crown courts and all that goes with them seemed a million miles away.

Granny Ria was always dear to me and during my wife's pregnancy she asked what we would name the baby and I told her that Christine and I had made a deal whereby if we have a boy then I pick the name and if it was a girl she would. 'Granny Ria, I think you know that if it is a boy I'm going to call him Rymer after Grandfather.'

She smiled and replied: 'I thought so, Joe. In that case I am going to start a money box for the little boy Rymer and buy him a nice present when he is born.'

'What about if it's a girl?'

'Then we take the money and put it on the first favourite to run after the birth. But Joe, this baby is a boy. I'm a gypsy, remember? We know these things,' and we all laughed. A happy family once again.

Sadly Granny Ria did not live to see whether her prediction would come true or not. On 17th December 1994 in the early hours she was rushed to hospital and died there from heart failure. Everybody was at the bedside except me. My family had tried to get hold of me but I was out of contact. That fresh, cold morning I was in a scrapyard in North West London where I regularly did business. There was a phone call in the yard and my friend said that my sister Marie was on the line. In the pit of my stomach I knew something was wrong. It was early and my sister had never contacted me at work. Afterwards I realised that my brothers or my dad could not face making that call to me as they knew how badly I would take it. 'It's Granny Ria,' was all she said and that was all she needed to as we both dissolved into tears at either end of the telephone.

I could not believe that Granny Ria was dead. Because she'd always been there and in my child's eyes had always been old, I expected her to live forever. Now, I appreciate everyone out there loves their old gran but I just can't see how anyone could have loved their gran as much as we loved ours. She was kind, generous, funny, warm, wise – I could go on forever. I never heard her run anyone down. She saw good in everyone and often in people others couldn't. People loved her where ever she went and this was demonstrated when we brought Granny back to our own yard where we all sat with her, among lighted candles and welcomed a procession of mourners for three days. One of those days sticks in my mind because firstly a big black guy who was about to go to court to have seven years served up by the judge stopped by to pay his respects. I didn't even know Granny knew him that well and for him to come when that was hanging over him was special. Then an Indian guy arrived who I didn't know, but he explained he knew Granny from the betting shop and he stood there sobbing. 'We will all miss her terribly, Joe,' he said.

Following on the chap who ran the local Chinese fish and chip shop turned up and then a cousin, Mick, who in some moment of madness in his youth had had NF crudely tattooed on his head appeared. 'Wild horses wouldn't have kept me away,' he said, head bowed. They all stood around the fire, shaking hands, laughing and remembering Ria, and I felt the warm glow of pride as I watched them. Granny Ria in death bringing people together like that.

That was Ria, yet I felt angry remembering that this soft, old lady had once served a six-month prison sentence for selling flowers. Well, she had been innocently doing that but the lady with her had chored some money and as far as the police were concerned Granny Ria must have been part of it and nothing she or the other lady said would convince them otherwise. The only thing my gran was guilty of was keeping bad company and since when has that been an offence? They didn't lock Tony and Cherie Blair up when they were consorting with the fraudster, Peter Foster, did they? I mean if keeping bad company is an offence then the scores of people that went to Jeffrey Archer's pie-and-mash parties should be doing porridge, shouldn't they? Anyway, that was in the past and now on the day of the funeral you could not see daylight as we drove along the streets where she lived due to the amount of people that were lining the way, and that was the real testament to her life. Oh, I wish she could have seen it. She'd have been shocked to the very core.

My aunts Lou, Phyllis and Ruth (who was Ria's sister) took over the money box and on the 14th May 1995 Christine gave birth to a beautiful baby boy. OK, let's be honest here, he wasn't beautiful at all coming out looking the spitting image of my fucking old man. Anyway, he weighed in at 61b 4oz and looked as fit as a butcher's dog. Dad, at least, was pleased with how the baby looked and he winked at me and took us for a beer. In the pub his eyes were moist. 'The old girl was right, then.'

'Yes, she certainly was.'

'I knew it was going to be a boy too.'

'How come?'

'Well, your grandfather Rymer's favourite number was fourteen because he was released from prison on the 14th of the month. Young Rymer is his fourteenth great-grandchild and I had my first son on the 14th May. Putting it together with what Gran said it could not have been any other way.' And I couldn't argue. Not only was old Rymer looking down on us – he was interfering.

ON THE HEATH

I was glowing with pride at being a father and wanted to spend every waking moment in the bosom of my new family. I had already entered a tournament in Sandwich, Kent on the very tough links course, Princess. Christine urged me to go saying that now I had found some form I should ride it, but I could not leave them at this point and wanted to treasure these first days of a newborn. He had been due on my Grandfather Rymer's birthday, 23rd May, but Christine's caddying had possibly hurried things along and he arrived nine days early. Young Rymer was not to have a caravan as his first home like most of his ancestors, but instead would go home to his maternal grandparents' two-bedroomed flat in Hayes, Middlesex. Soon after the council were to give us a house to complete the new family unit. I was the most settled I had been since I was a kid at home nestled under the protective wings of Mum and Dad.

I rejoined my old course, Hounslow Heath, as a member and would later be invited to become the club professional. The area where the course had been laid was reputedly once a regular haunt for highwaymen. It is, perhaps, Hounslow Heath's main claim to fame. Dick Turpin the fabled highwayman had conducted his dodgy business there but the most notorious criminal with Heath connections was Claud Duvall who allegedly danced on the heath with an aristocrat lady he was robbing. Duvall ended up being hung at Tyburn, already a legend. His ghost is said to haunt the course. Who said that I have no idea. But it is said it is said. Four hundred years on and the Heath still seemed to hold its reputation for slumming it. The fourteenth hole known as the dog leg is bent around a caravan site full of gypsies and showmen, their pro (me) would be a bare-knuckle fighting gypsy who was 'known to the police' and one of the captains was an unashamed rogue. Maybe the ghost of Duvall was influencing the committee members into recruiting members, pros and even captains from the margins.

Strange things happened to me there. Once, back in my amateur days, I was contacted by a former boxer, now a trainer/manager and recognised by the British Boxing Board of Control, and he asked me to meet with a good boxer from the Fen country named David Lynn.

'Why does he want to meet me?' I asked.

'To fight you, but it's a long story.'

I was intrigued. The trainer explained in detail. David Lynn was a good boxer – an amateur with prospects of turning professional – but he had got into an argument with a gypsy man from Newmarket over his girlfriend and had agreed to a bare-knuckle fight. Believing the two ways of fighting to be vastly different he wanted to learn as much as he could as quickly as he could and the boxer and his manager believed the best way to do this was to fight a seasoned bare-knuckle man but under sensible and measured conditions.

'He wants to spar with you as he has heard you are one of the best and he will pay you £500 for the experience,' said the manager.

'You can't really spar in bare-knuckle,' I explained. 'But we can fight for £500 for sure. I know exactly the spot where we can do the business in private and without being disturbed.'

'Where's that?'

'Go to Hounslow Heath golf course at 7am tomorrow morning and meet me on the fourteenth green.'

Sure enough they were there in the morning. The dew was still on the grass and a couple of magpies hopped around the green. David Lynn, who seemed ever such a nice chap, was with his trainer/manager and a fair-play man and I had one with me too. We squared up and I suggested we step off the green as I thought we should not churn it up or damage it for the golfers, but my fair-play man dismissed me.

'Fuck the green and get on with it.'

David started the fight negatively and defensively.

'David,' I said, 'fight as if you were boxing. Don't fanny around. Imagine you *are* wearing gloves and steam in.'

In he came, feinting a jab and catching me on the nose. Blood trickled from a nostril.

'Sorry, Joe. Sorry.'

'Don't say sorry. Go for it.'

Then we had a proper fight and exchanged crunching body shots. The short bout ended when I smashed him with a left hook which unzipped him above the left eye. With his 'real' fight coming up it made sense to stop there.

'Thanks, Joe,' he enthused shaking my hand.

Any onlooker would have been puzzled to see this scene of a man thanking me for opening up his brow and then paying me money for the privilege. He then asked me if he could buy me breakfast and pick up a few tips.

In the caff with hot mugs of tea in front of us and awaiting a welcome fry-up to be delivered to the table he asked: 'Joe, you won't give me duff information, will you? What with the other fella being a gypsy and all that.'

'David,' I said firmly. 'One, you have paid me well for my time. Two, you are man enough to fight this chap and therefore you are worthy opponents, and three, why would you imagine that because someone is a gypsy I would automatically favour them? Do you favour every other Englishman or every other Fenman? No, of course not. I take people as I find, whatever or whoever they are. My advice is simple: Fight as if you were boxing but when you see blood – yours or his – don't panic. It's all about who wants it the most in bare-knuckle. I'm sure you'll win and I don't know the other man but I'd be surprised if he has your commitment and has planned like you have. In fact I'm so confident here's £250 of the money you just paid me. If you can get an even-money bet on yourself, put it on, and pay the winnings to your manager here and he'll get it to me.'

My vote of confidence seemed to lift him and sure enough, I soon heard, he won it in style, battering the gypsy lad. The very next morning on the fourteenth green I putted through our dark bloodstains. I shot a sixty-eight, which was a new course record, beating my old friend Pat Moriaty in the Club Championship. Of course, I did not mention the events of the previous morning.

The rogue at the club I referred to earlier was a guy called Tony Palmart and he was our captain. I liked him and enjoyed his company although I did not mix with him outside of the golf club. I particularly liked to beat him as he was highly competitive and was obviously used to getting his own way. The rage inside him would build at each hole and I thought he would explode and this amused me. Sadly and very mysteriously Tony encountered a masked gunman who shot him once in the head and twice in the chest. He paid, it appeared, the ultimate price for living that lifestyle. I was relieved I was off that particular ladder. However, it was not so easy to shake off a whole way of life and just because I was aware of the decisions I had made others would not be. One sunny afternoon at the pro-shop at the club a smartly dressed man walked in and asked Tessa, my friend and the lady on the till, if Joe Smith, the club professional was around. I was practising my chipping just through the fire exit and outside the shop. Tessa called me in.

'Afternoon sir, how can I help you?'

'You have been recommended to me and I would like to take some lessons. Is it possible for you to walk me around the facility?'

No sooner had we walked out of the shop and were together alone the prosperous looking gentleman laid his cards on the table. 'Look Joe I am here about an incident involving my wife. I understand you may be able to help me.'

I knew what he was leading up to and when he mentioned a pal who had put my name up I knew he was kosher. As we walked around the club he explained that a well-known golfer – a Ryder Cup player – had been at a party and had disrespected his wife and him. He had said things like 'what are you doing with this tosser? Come back with me and I'll show you my balls...' that type of infantile crap. The man who had now also revealed he was a millionaire suggested that for a sum of money I might quite like to smash the man's hands so severely he would not be able to play golf again. I said very little and he sensed my wariness. I was thinking that the punishment he was proposing was well out of proportion to the crime. He had also mentioned serious sums of money that sadly tempted me and I was thinking if there was a way of protecting this man and still earning a few quid. Before I responded he went on to say that if I didn't want to do it could I put him in touch with so and so and so and so. That worried me because the two names he pulled up were animals. They loved their work to a sickening degree and would inflict horrendous damage and then bury the golfer alive on the eighteenth green at St Andrews if asked, believe me. I said I'd think about it and get back to him through our mutual contact.

The more I thought about the golfer and that he had no idea what may lay ahead for him the more I became concerned. I had no doubt where my 'client' was going next if I turned the job down. It made me cross because now I was embroiled in something I had no wish to be. If the hand-smashing (and I was imagining worse with Laurel and Hardy on the case) went ahead then it would be all over the papers and I would not be able to live with the burden that I had advance knowledge and did nothing. I went back to our go-between and said I would deal with the job. What I proposed was that I gave him a hiding and made sure he knew why. I said the smashing of the hands was too dramatic and would attract press, police and insurance-company attention. It was not a good idea. He agreed but still wanted me to deliver a 'thorough' hiding. My plan was to confront the pro and let him know what might have happened to him and how lucky he was that the 'job' had been given to me. If he did not take my words and warning seriously I was prepared to lay one on him. That was all. I was upset with him as well for unwittingly dragging me back into this world. I had also told the 'client' that I was not interested in any payment.

I enlisted my brother to help me and we were to plot up outside the golfer's local club and call him on the telephone to come outside, but before we did this the millionaire rang us the worse for wear through drink. 'Joe,' he announced in a drunken drawl, 'the old whore has left me for my nephew. Have you done the golfer yet? Forget him. Do my wife and my nephew instead. Take those two cunts out.'

'Let's meet tomorrow when you are sober.'

The following day he was in a right state but the bravado had gone and some common sense had returned. He told me that his wife had been having an affair with his nephew before they had even married. He confessed that he had been having severe marital problems for some time. It occurred to me then that she may well have been flirting with the golfing pro all along. Thank God nothing had been done by anyone. It goes to show how dangerously things can escalate and how lethal men with money can be when they feel they have been slighted or scammed. He said forget the whole thing and asked how much did he owe me? He wanted to pay me for the time and hassle. I told him that I had already stated that I wanted no money. 'Let's leave it that one day you may be able to do me a favour.' I have never called that favour in. I should have got him to sponsor my golf.

As you can see, even though I was trying to leave my life of crime and violence behind it was unrealistic to think I could be one man one day and another man the next. I cannot complain. Just because I had resolved to change my life that did not mean others had to respect or even know that. I had not placed an advertisement in the local paper stating that Joe Smith is no longer available to collect debts and wishes not to fight anyone anymore.

Even if I had done so, Mickey Harrison would have taken not a blind bit of notice.

Mickey was a well-known hard case around Hayes in Middlesex. He could handle himself and had once beaten the rated boxer Roy Gumms. He was older than me but still commanded a reputation on the streets and in the pubs of West London. I knew him and liked him. One day he approached me and said in a very friendly manner. 'All right, Joe? Fancy a fight for a hundred pounds?'

I was taken aback. 'No thanks, Mickey.'

'I love a fight, I do,' he said, smiling from ear to ear.

'Not tonight, Mickey. If you don't mind.'

He didn't mind and he went off. There was no animosity. No threat even and it was a strange encounter. Next time I saw him, some months later, he was in a pub with a bunch of his mates and he asked me again. It was still very polite and gentlemanly. I declined again, equally courteously and remembered saying I didn't have time. I thought maybe his crowd were laughing and I didn't like it much. Then, some time on, Mickey had a dispute with a local greengrocer and seemed to think that I was somehow siding with this other chap and he offered me out again. For a third time I said no, but now I felt it had gone beyond a joke.

A short time later I was driving to my local for a quiet Sunday lunchtime drink and Mickey Harrison was the last thing on my mind. As I passed The Cat And Fiddle pub in West Drayton I saw him waiting outside for it to open with a group of friends and without thinking just slammed my handbrake on and jumped out of the car.

'Get on the fucking green, now!'

We took our shirts off and squared up. A typical Sunday afternoon in England. On village greens in the more civilised areas of the country people nodded off to the gentle thudding of willow cricket bats hitting balls towards the pavilion, but here in West Drayton a small crowd of reprobates delighted in watching two big lumps hit lumps out of one another. I don't think Mickey realised that I could box as well as serve him up brute force and I watched the confidence visibly drain out of him as the situation dawned on him.

'Shall we call it an honourable draw, Mickey?' I offered.

'Yes, Joe.'

And we did.

Mickey and I became great friends after that and he started to come to the gym with me. On one occasion my cousin Billy sparred with him and blacked his eyes up before he knew it. Mickey shook his head and said: 'You boys know how to have a row.'

'I don't know about that Mickey. We've got at least ten years on you. If we'd fought you when you were at your peak mate it may well have been a different story.' Billy agreed and we both meant it. Mickey Harrison is a fine, old-school warrior.

I met him again recently at Kevin Finnegan's funeral. Kevin was the brother of Chris Finnegan and they had both been top boxers in their time. Kevin had won the British Middleweight Title from Tony Sibson in 1979 as well as losing to 'Marvellous' Marvin Hagler twice and Chris had beaten and lost to Johnny Frankham in British Light Heavyweight titles in 1975 and lost to John Conteh twice. It was a sad day because Kevin was too young to go and appeared to have been alone in his final days. Mickey Harrison and I reminisced at the wake afterwards and he reminded me of when just a few years back I had arranged a tournament in which Mickey and my cousin Jimmy Stockin were making comeback fights against younger men and it was their first time inside a ring for many, many years. Jim would have been at least forty-five years of age and Mickey not too far behind. Mickey said they were sitting outside the hall in a tiny aluminium working-man's hut in their vests and shorts waiting to be called in to the ring. The rain was hammering down so hard on the metal the noise made them feel they were already under attack. Both sat there silently with their thoughts when Mickey looked over at Jim and smiled: 'It doesn't get any easier does it, old mate?'

OPENING UP

My golfing confidence was now at a level that I felt able to apply to enter the British Open Championship. When the letter came through my door with the R&A crest on it I sat down and opened it slowly. I knew that in seconds I was either going to be elated or deflated. The R&A takes its name from The Royal And Ancient Golf Club of St Andrews and organises and stages the Open Championship each year. This time I was deflated; they did not believe that my scores justified a place and that I had not reached the required standard. Straight away the paranoia that had been with me since I was a kid crept back. Was it because I was a gypsy? It clearly wasn't – the R&A were being scrupulously fair and would know nothing of my background, but sometimes when I did not want to accept my failings I would fall back on this. Soon I would pull myself together and get back to grafting. I was determined to play in the Open and only God was going to stop me.

The next year Randy Fox sent a letter to the R&A saying that I had rediscovered some of my old form and in his opinion had comfortably attained the standards that were required. I proved he was not exaggerating in my first attempt at trying to qualify through the regional stages, losing by just one shot. I failed in my next attempt at the regional stages by five shots and then again the next year by a distant seven. By 1998, although I had improved my form in regular tournaments (normally the important ones), I was falling short of the mark. There was an undeniable question mark over my ability to finish off rounds. I was playing good golf for fourteen or fifteen holes, but that counts for nothing if you have a bad start or finish.

Arriving at Hankley Common Golf Club, the venue for my regional qualifying for the Open, my dad says: 'Will you do it today, boy?'

'I don't know Dad. If I hole out from four feet and I don't have any bad bouncers, I will qualify on the first tee.'

With my brother John on the bag, a very good player himself and a former Middlesex junior captain, we are a good team together. Some players on the first tee are hitting irons for safety, but not me, a narrow drive off the first with the smoothest first top swing you can ask for, straight down the middle. I just miss the green with my second shot. I chip the ball within four feet of the hole. The very distance that is causing me problems with the green. Fourteen on the Stent metre, if you are unsure of what it means I can tell you that the greens are nothing short of lightning and your nerves are pushed to the limits and tweaks or twitches will show up tenfold over most normal greens. Over my four-footer I feel an unusual feeling of calm. My putt goes in perfectly – I am set up for the round. I continue to play beautifully without any dropped shots. I birdie the par-five eighth and the par-five thirteenth, now standing at two under par on the very testing difficult set up at Hankley Common. I am well on my way to qualifying but there is still a big question to be asked. Can I hold my nerve this time and get the job done? On the fourteenth hole I hit two lovely shots on to the green but my nerves are rattling and I leave myself a small three-footer from my first putt of about twenty feet and miss. I am under the cosh to say the least. On the short fifteenth I hit two nice shots to about seven feet, just coasting the ball hole-side then on the short par-three sixteenth a nice eight-iron shot leaves me twenty feet from the hole. A good lag putt hole-side follows; one more down, two to go on the tough seventeenth. I hit a cracking drive leaving me 140 yards from the flag. I strike a pitching wedge straight at the flag. It drifts about one yard to the right as the pin is at the back of the green. This one yard of drift has my ball on the border line of the flag and the bunker. When it lands, my ball jumps about six inches towards the flag and finishes within eight foot of the hole. I barely get my ball in motion, just missing the hole on the left-side rolling with no speed it seemed, but the ball continues to trundle on past the hole and finishes a good five feet beyond. I dig deep to hold my nerve and put my ball straight in the middle of the hole, one under par. With one to play, the eighteenth is a very tough par-four of 453 yards. I boom a drive down the right-hand side of the fairway. I strike my seven-iron up the face of the club a bit and that is my first imperfect strike of the day. It stops short in a deep ravine, my ball coming to rest on a good lie but my task ahead is still not easy. I decide not to go for the flag. I deliberately lob my ball past it – it comes to rest fifteen feet away leaving me a terrifying downhill putt and just to pile the pressure on my dad walks past and says: 'I have checked the scoreboard and two putts will do it.' My mum, wife and Uncle Mick (who yesterday has given me intense coaching in chipping) are all standing around clutching lucky heather they have brought. Dad is puffing away on an Old Holborn roll-up like it was a Havana cigar and my brother John has my ear, dispensing valuable advice and second opinions. 'It will move from left to right when near the hole,' he whispers, calmly, 'it is very fast.' I roll my putt well but about four foot from the hole the ball starts turning right to left but then straightens its course and stops as if I have a remote sensor on the lip of the hole. John punches the air. 'I think I can manage that one,' I grin, and tap the shortest shot of my life. I have qualified in seventh place overall out of 128 players. I have played superbly and although this is only the regional qualifying round for the Open it is the furthest I have ever made and Dad and I hug one another.

For the first time in my professional career I would be mixing with some of the biggest names in the world of golf. My letter from the R&A told me that my final qualifying venue was Hillside, a truly fabulous course fifteen miles north-west of Liverpool, and that my playing partners were to be US tour player Dave Ogrin and the European Ryder Cup player, the Swedish Pierre Fulke. Before our party set off for Hillside I received a phone call from the *News Of The World* who said they'd like to do a story on me. They thought that taking the line of a Romany gypsy and former bare-knuckle fighter on the verge of qualifying for the Open would make interesting fare for their readers. I was not about to disagree. Our base up north was to be the Pontins holiday camp in Southport and myself, family and band of friends and supporters settled in nicely and I went off to suss out this course which was renowned for being quite difficult, yet after two practice rounds I felt relaxed about it and had an early night with my head full of excitement about the following day.

On the first I introduced myself to Pierre Fulke and to a nice lad from Northampton named Stuart Reynolds who had replaced Dave Ogrin, who had recently pulled out. There were hundreds of spectators around the first tee and some nerves broke cover when I heard 'and on the tee from West London is Joe Smith' crackling out of the loudspeaker. I struck my driver well and the ball finished on the left side of the fairway in an old unprepared divot. I hit a four-iron cleanly but a bit to the left. Now, quite nervous, I thinned my chip across the green. I putted down within four foot and it was a double-bogey start. Not ideal, but I knew I needed to keep calm, wipe my mouth and dig deep on the next hole. I hit my drive with the bottom of the club but it went straight on the par-five hole. I played a three-iron for safety and then a six-iron approach to the green which finished just six feet away from the hole. I putted to the left of it, still a par, but now I was trembling. I had left myself a very testing four-and-a-half-footer with the wind playing games with us. It was no formality but I made it and settled down a tiny bit on the next tee when we had to wait for the group that included the world-class South African, David Frost. The crowds were gathering in big numbers to watch the likes of Fulke and Frost and the word was spreading around the crowd that a gypsy bare-knuckle fighter was in Match 19. My brother John and I could hear them talking and pointing and they could hear us discussing tactics. We had 211 yards to the pin straight into a very strong wind.

'Do you fancy driver or three-wood?' asked my brother.

'It's such a difficult hole, bruv. If we get it on to the front of the green we're doing well, but I think if I kill it and keep it down I could even get the ball all the way to the flag with my three-iron.'

'If you see it bruv, play it.'

I lined it up and killed it dead perfect, getting the ball pin high to eight feet. The crowd gave a real loud clap of applause, not only for the result of the shot but because they'd heard me pre-plan it too. I made the birdie putt and got back to just one over in now the most extreme conditions ever witnessed in an Open qualifying event. I was settled in for the task ahead. I continued to play the conditions and after nine holes I was three over and I felt that other than the nervous first hole, I had played well. I had realised that my playing partner Stuart Reynolds was one behind me, not that it mattered, but I couldn't help realising that my other playing partner, Pierre Fulke, was six ahead of me on three under par. I thought maybe this is what tour players of this standard are all about, then I thought, hold on a minute, I have been watching the best players in the world since I was a kid and I have never seen golf like this in these conditions, not even from my idol Bernhard Langer – who was second to none in extreme conditions. Whatever, I had to dig deep, keep on plodding and score what I scored and signed for. A huge gallery were waiting at the par-three tenth – well, at least a huge gallery compared to what I was used to – about four hundred people around the green. I struck a six-iron to the middle of the green about thirty feet from the pin, followed by a decent putt which finished twelve inches from the cup. Decent applause greeted my par and I was really enjoying playing on the bigger stage. On the par-four twelfth I was in trouble from the tee and played my second shot which finished in a bunker about fifty yards short of the pin. I played a more delofted club than the normal sand-wedge from what seemed like a near impossible position to get within six inches of the flag, at which point Pierre said to me it was the best bunker shot he'd ever seen. The sixteenth was a long par-three of 224 yards with the green running at an angle from the tee. With Pierre to play first, he chose an eight-iron and played to the front part of the green which left a putt up the slope of about eighty feet. I chose to hit a five-iron and aimed twenty yards left of the green and put a big deliberate slice on the shot, shaping the ball to come in at a side angle from the tee to match the angle of the green. It was a near-perfect shot which ran all the way up the green and rested only four feet from the flag. Again Pierre praised my shot, saying: 'Joe, you are a complete magician. I couldn't believe it when you chose a four iron. I told my caddie you'd be thirty yards too long with that club, then you chop the legs off the ball and make it travel sideways! Excellent shot.'

These were uplifting words to hear from a Ryder Cup player but anyone who knows me will tell you that my shot-making from trouble is one of my real assets. After completing my first round of seventy-seven at this level you will naturally think you are miles out of contention but I can tell you different. With thirteen players qualifying, the leader was Pierre Fulke on one under par seventy-one. So being just six shots behind my playing partner, my target was to shoot lower than him on round two and see if I had made up enough ground to do the business.

Our practice ground was used for car parking for the actual Open, which was at Birkdale right next door to Hillside so all qualifiers from Hillside were to share the practice ground at Birkdale. Standing next to me during practice was young Tiger Woods. He said to Mark O' Meara who was with him: 'With this wind it will be one hell of a fight this week.'

I turned around to my brother and said out of the side of my mouth 'If this really was a fight then it would be me lifting the Claret Jug and not him,' and we passed the pair laughing to ourselves.

The Scottish Open had finished on the Saturday as opposed to the normal Sunday so all the players outside the Top 50 in the world after the Scottish Open could then try and qualify on Sunday and Monday – the final qualifying stage. This also gave the world's best players more time to prepare for the world's biggest golf event. Before we went off to practise on Sunday I wanted to have a look at the article that the *News Of The World* had said they would run. It exceeded all my expectations when I saw it covering a full page with the headline GYPSY BARE-KNUCKLE FIGHTER REACHES FINAL QUALIFYING ROUND and then in a sub-headline my quote: 'I Lost Over Two Pints of Blood in Fight.' I don't quite remember saying it like that although after my fight with Champ I remember pulling my Lonsdale T-shirt over my battered head and wringing it out on the floor and blood seeping out of it and turning my black boots red. I would not have been surprised if that shirt had absorbed two pints of claret. The *News Of The World* laid it on a bit thick, but I was nevertheless thrilled to see the article.

Within minutes I was to witness the full power of the press. I had gone to bed as Joe Smith and had woken up as Gypsy Joe Smith The Bare-Knuckle Fighting Golfer because as I arrived at the practice ground there was a large crowd, which was not unusual in itself as many of them would be autograph-hunters hoping to collar the big names from Birkdale, but they must have read the paper too and were soon clamouring around me – 'Joe can you sign my hat', 'Can we have a photo, Joe?' 'Sign my ball, Joe.' I looked around to see if Jeremy Beadle was lurking anywhere but readily got into the spirit of it all. As the alumni of golf turned up for their practice they looked over at the huddle around me, wondering what all the fuss was about.

Tiger Woods, Ernie Els, Goosen, Garcia, Mickelson, Faldo and many others had assembled to practise. We were all firing directly into the fierce wind and were dumbstruck at how short our shots were finishing in comparison to normal blustery conditions. The wind was like a brick wall. Tiger started hitting full seven irons and they were finishing only thirty yards in front of him. It was such a strong, silly wind that grown men were shooting like children. It was equal to a snow-storm in the desert and to think we had just competed in it only hours before just next door. Myself and Constantino Rocca were having our fun on the practice ground, seeing who could keep their drives the lowest and not even the Italian Ryder Cup star could match me in that department. As I stood over one shot and prepared to hit it, my brother whispered: 'You better make this a good 'un bruv, yer man's here!'

I knew exactly who he meant. Shaking a bit, I made a good swing and struck the ball nicely then turned around and sure enough my hero Bernhard

Langer put his practice balls down on the ground right beside me. 'Hello Bernhard,' I mumbled.

'Hello, Joe,' he replied.

I was flattered he remembered me and knew my name. Golf-wise Bernhard was my hero and had been almost since I first picked up a golf-club and I first met him and spoke to him in 1979 at the RAC club. I suppose an eight-year-old gypsy kid quizzing you up on golf technique might stick in your mind, especially if he waylays you at regular intervals after. He had won the Masters in 1985 and again in 1993. He carried himself with dignity and I identified with him as he suffered with what he called 'the yips'. These were involuntary spasms or twitches that could afflict him during putting. I had my own yips too. I'd even written to him once when I was twelve years of age with questionable spelling and while I didn't get a reply I put this down to me addressing the letter to *Bernard* Langer, *Germany* and probably not putting a stamp on it. I dreamt about meeting him and chatting and one day playing golf with him, and here we were and he just called me by name.

'What are you doing here, Joe?'

'I'm playing next door at Hillside, Bernhard, trying to qualify.'

'What did you shoot?'

'Seventy-seven.'

'Seventy-seven? That's a fine score, Joe, in this wind. A fine score.'

I was made up. Beaming like a little boy. I looked over to Mum and Dad and they gave me the thumbs up knowing how much this meant to me. I wanted to pull Bernhard towards me and give him a big cuddle but thought it might alarm him. I thanked him for his comments and allowed him to get on with his practice. As we left the ground the crowds had swelled even more and my brother John remarked: 'Don't get carried away bruv, they're here for him.' He jerked his head sideways to where Tiger Woods was following us out. He was wrong, the crowd split, one lot circling Tiger and the other me. Tiger didn't hang around too long but I lingered and signed every last autograph and answered all their questions. I was still standing there, pen in hand, an hour after the crowd had dispersed. This was new to me, if not to Tiger, and I lapped it up and was going to milk every last drop. So having rubbed shoulders with my idol, and perhaps the best player ever to walk the fairways, it was back to Pontins in Southport for a couple of beers, bingo and a good night's sleep to get ready for battle in the morning.

On the first, a good tee shot set me up nicely for a par-four and I was off and running. I settled down and was really up for the conditions which were even worse than the first day. After battling away, I was in control of my three-ball and more importantly I was ahead of Pierre Fulke, the overnight leader. Making some ground on him was important but there was a lot of work to be done and after turning through the front nine in the thirties and making par on holes ten and eleven, unbeknown to me I needed to make par on the remaining seven holes to qualify for the Open. Although I played well, tee to green, I missed a few short putts – my Achilles heel – and sadly for me they made all the difference. I didn't qualify.

It was hugely disappointing to fall at the last hurdle yet I was not as crushed as I thought I would be. It had been an incredible week: I had met my idol, I had led the field, most of the time I played top golf and I had enjoyed my fifteen minutes of fame. Now I could settle back and finish my holiday by watching The Open and getting into the swing of it all at the Pontins Holiday Camp.

One night Mum and Dad had turned in and this left me and Christine, brother John, Uncle Cliff, sister Lou and my cousin Jim. We chatted to the two guys who ran the security up there because we knew one of them, John Green, who happened to come out of West London and the other man was Scottish and for some reason known as Jock. Now it seemed that while I had not been around over the previous few days playing golf and going to bed early a big blond fella had taken a shine to my wife and had been coming on to her. She had not wanted to say anything to me, not wishing to upset my equilibrium while competing, but had complained to Jock. He had assumed I knew all about it and said: 'Look, Joe, I've told this bloke not to try and chat up your missus and that you're not a man to be messed with. But he doesn't seem to listen...'

Christine then told me that he had asked her continually to dance, even when I was at the bar, and she had told him to go away and that I would not take kindly to his attention. I told Jock not to worry about it and did not take the matter too seriously. Christine was (still is, always will be) a very pretty girl and I could not blame the man if he thought she was alone and now he had seen me around a bit I assumed he would stop. Later that night I was at the bar again, daydreaming probably about what might have been on the course, and I saw Christine storming off the dance floor, yelling and waving her hands about. When I calmed her down she told me that the blond man had been standing behind me and had gone to strike me with a bottle but Jock had restrained him. I had been oblivious to the whole incident.

I went outside to hear the story again away from the music just to make sure I understood the situation correctly. It was right. I stormed back into the bar determined to damage this disrespectful, first-class wanker. Uncle Cliff was shouting to John Green that if his lads didn't stop me they'd have a murder on their hands. I careered across the floor towards Blondie who tried to escape via the fire exit but I managed to smash a massive right hand into the back of his head which pulled him up short. My left hand grasped his shirt and I pulled him back towards me. Smash! Smash! Two crunching blows left him crumpled on the floor. He was finished but I wasn't. Cheeky cunt tried to pull my wife and then to showboat was going to do me from behind with a light ale bottle. I was going to sit on him and pummel his face but John Green and another of the security men had locked around my ankles with their arms like two Jack Russells and although I was walking towards him as he tried to slide across the floor away from me I was moving like an Egyptian mummy dragging the two bouncers across the floor with me and my sluggish progress allowed my target to get to the door and to safety.

The next afternoon I spotted the fool about fifty yards away. He'd been frightened but not frightened enough to cut his holiday short. 'I take it you won't be in the club tonight?' I called out. 'Just as well my wife didn't dance with you – she'd never had kept up with the speed you move at.' I didn't clap eyes on him again. The next day another holidaymaker passed me a paper and I read the headline GYPSY GOLFER IN PONTINS PUNCH-UP. The article named me, referred to the earlier *News Of The World* article, and had some eyewitness reports from 'terrified' campers. This time though, and much to my relief, the article was carried in the *Southport Gazette* and not Britain's best-selling Sunday newspaper.

Around this time we travelled together, maybe twelve families and the same amount of caravans, down to the British Open at Sandwich in Kent. We loved going and had been a few times in the 1980s and had drunk in the atmosphere. We had never experienced any problems and had always pulled up as near as we could to the course, enjoyed the tournament and then when it was over headed off again. This year we alighted on some land near the course close to where we had settled before and waited in anticipation for the tournament to begin. In a pub that evening somebody mentioned that there had been an item on the local television news about our arrival which I thought was strange, but I did not take too much notice. In the morning somebody bought a national newspaper and there inside was a picture of our caravans under the headline GYPSIES INVADE OPEN. Here we go again. We could not understand why a fuss had been kicked up and by whom. A representative of the R&A was soon amongst us.

'This is Royal and Ancient land, I'm afraid. You will have to move.'

'But we've stayed here before. We're not in anyone's way. We have not caused any trouble. We've only just got here,' I reasoned politely.

'But you do not have permission.'

'Please can we stay on your land, sir?'

'No, I am not able to give permission.'

'Who can?'

'Only the R&A?'

'But you said you were from the R&A.'

It went on. I offered to pay rent. I offered to lodge a deposit in case we left a stain on the grass. He said he would get an order from the local magistrates to have us moved and we told him to go ahead and get it.

We all loved golf. Some of us played it and we were not peddling or getting in anyone's way. We were on a small piece of wasteland that was barely visible. It was obvious that we were spectators and had no intention of setting up permanent home – many of us had house addresses. It was silly. The order from Folkestone Magistrates Court arrived later that day and in the morning I was elected our spokesman at the court and I went into full *Rumpole Of The Bailey* mode. I told the three magistrates about previous visits in 1981, 1983 and 1985, detailing along the way names of the winners and runners-up and other notable occurrences during those tournaments. I outlined my own golf career and told them about my ambitions. I asked them if they thought that if we were a group of holiday-making members of *The Caravan Club* we'd be standing here now in the local magistrates' court. I stopped short of striding around the court room, my thumbs under my jacket lapels, and asking them to search their consciences – but it was close. The magistrates said they were going to confer and shuffled off the bench. When they returned they said they had considered the case carefully. The land belonged to the R&A and therefore we had no right to be on there and they ordered us off by midday.

However, they regretted that a compromise had not been reached and said that a local councillor would find a suitable piece of land nearby that we could park up on and from where we would be allowed to spectate at the tournament. It was a fair compromise and a very nice councillor took us out in his motor and showed us a few bits of land and when we found one we felt was suitable we shook hands and moved on to it. A smaller article appeared in one of the newspapers the following day that quoted the local police inspector saying that the gypsies had been no trouble and that we left the land clean and tidy. Nice of him to admit the truth, but I find these remarks a bit patronising and insulting. Do they really think we'd be hanging dirty nappies from the tree branches and wiping our arses along the grass verges?

Next season I won my playing card for the British Mastercard Tour after pre-qualifying and making the top 120 in the final qualifying round over seventy-two holes at the Royal North Devon and Saunton – a decent start. One of my favourite tournaments was the Prince's, also at Sandwich, and me and my family decided to go and stay in our caravans for the event. Just before the finish I decided to change my appearance. My shoulder-length, blond curly locks no longer seemed right now that my forehead was spreading. One day I looked in the mirror and a member of some ageing rock band like Def Leppard looked back so I went out and got my head shaved leaving only white lines going down to the back of my neck and a white bleached square on my crown. Then I went to Tesco and purchased a bottle of red food dye and designed a very fetching Cross Of St George on my barnet. I intended to crack my mates up and leave it in a few days. They dared me to go to the tournament with the flag still painted on my head, so I did.

On the range at Prince's shortly before I was due to make my way to the first tee, Ian Burns, the tournament director, pulled alongside me in his buggy. Burns, unsurprisingly a Scotsman, was high up in the PGA based at their headquarters at The Belfry. He did not beat around the bush: 'Joe, you are not playing in this tournament.'

'I beg your pardon?'

'You are not playing, Joe. I cannot allow it with that haircut.'

It was a bit of fun and although I respected Ian I was not going to roll over so easily.

'There's no harm in it, Ian. Surely, people see it as a joke?'

'I don't care what people think. This is a televised event and I'm not having a competitor walking around with a St George's Cross painted in his hair.'

The irony of what I thought he was getting at did not escape me. Years before, I believe, they got rid of me out of Home Park because I was a gypsy and now they wanted me out because I was parading my Englishness.

'You cannot be serious?' I asked, trying not to sound like John McEnroe.

'Joe, I am absolutely serious. You cannot play. Full stop.'

'Under what rule are you stopping me from playing?'

'Dress and etiquette rules.'

'And does it say anything in there about haircuts?'

He stumbled a bit but not for long.

'I have the power invested in me to declare you are not fit and proper to play.'

'I think you are making up the rules as you go along with all due respect, Ian. My family and I have all sacrificed time and money to come here for this tournament and you have taken it upon yourself to interpret a rule in a specific way. I have to ask you Ian if this was the Scottish flag here on my bonce would you be reacting in the same way?'

It must have been fears of political correctness that had prompted him to challenge me and now my final comment had pulled him up.

'Not at all. Not at all... Joe, of course, if you wear headgear then we have no problem.'

'Headgear?'

I thought he meant a crash-helmet or something.

'A cap, Joe.'

He turned the steering wheel and buggied off.

I nipped away and bought a traditional Dunn And Co flat cap and put it on back to front as a final protest. I looked like a cross between Norman Wisdom and Benny Hill. After completing my round Bill Elliott, a renowned golf journalist, conducted an interview with me and I guess that he had pushed the story around a bit because as we drove home to my friend's caravan where we were staying an item came up on Radio Kent saying that Joe Smith, the bare-knuckle fighter turned pro-golfer, put a bad-hair day behind him and made two late birdies to stay in contention at Prince's Golf Club, Sandwich. The next day the *Sun* newspaper turned up and a Sky News team filmed me as I went round. Millions of viewers worldwide watched that day and at the urging of the film crew I just had to remove my cap every now and then to mop my sweating brow and the following day the St George's Cross was on the sports pages of the *Sun* in all its colourful glory. I missed qualifying by three shots but the newspaper coverage generated another fifteen minutes of fame, making thirty and defying Andy Warhol's golden rule.

Granted, it was a frivolous stunt, but I don't see why golf cannot be fun now and then. One day I intend to play dressed in a sequined ball-gown. The authorities probably would not raise an objection to that as paralysed by politically-correct fear they might worry they'd receive a backlash from the British Association Of Cross Dressers. More seriously, how has it become deemed offensive to celebrate Englishness? The Scots celebrate Burns Night and the Irish make a meal out of St Patrick's Day – and why not? – but if the English unfurl a St George's flag it is interpreted as a signal of violent or racially abusive intent. How come a nation once so proud and resolute has allowed an invisible bunch of activists to destroy and muddy our national identity is beyond me.

After losing my card on the Mastercard Tour I regained it in 2000, now playing much more steadily and at a far higher standard than when I had resumed the game seven years earlier. Yet, I was still missing too many half-way cuts by one or two shots and now I had a second child to support – my wonderful daughter, Christina Maria, following young Rymer. Money was tight as usual and I wondered if I was neglecting my responsibilities by only working part of the time and financing my golf, forever chasing my dreams, and if truth be told not earning nearly enough from it. I had fulfilled my pledge to Grandfather Rymer and had been playing professionally for seven years now but I had to face up to facts. I hadn't qualified for the Open, although I had got pretty close. I had a family to support. I could not solve my weakness at not being able to finish off rounds better under pressure. I decided not to quit, but I was going to take a break from golf. It was a hard decision because in golf if you lose momentum and scale back on practice the chances of returning to your previous standards are slim. My family and friends were not altogether surprised about my decision but they were surprised when I told them what I planned to do next. I told them I was twenty-nine years old and that I was going to shed three and a half stones and have one final pop at a career in the boxing ring. History was repeating itself.

Month after month I felt mentally stronger and in control of my destiny.

Those dark alcohol-sodden days alone in a caravan in a field were comfortably in the past but every now and then reminders of that other life came along and slapped me full on in the face. I was sitting in my favourite West London caff when in walked Levi. We had known each other reasonably well over the years – coming from the same manor – and had even done bits of work together, but we were not close friends. I was on crutches and they were propped up next to my table. I was suffering with gout and the double egg, chips, treble sausage and beans was probably not what the doctor ordered.

'Hello Joe,' he said as he passed my table.

'Hello mate,' I replied as I scooped baked beans into my mouth.

'I'm the guvnor round here,' he announced to all and sundry.

It was a strange thing to declare in a barely full caff in the early hours of a week-day morning. Builders, gas fitters and scaffolders exchanged baffled looks and he said it again. I guessed it was for my benefit.

'What?' I asked, bemused.

'I'm the guvnor around here. This is my patch.' I had no desire to be 'the guvnor', but he was getting on my fucking nerves now.

'Who says?'

'I do.'

I put my knife and fork together, wiped my mouth, got up on one crutch, hopped forward and launched him across the caff. He fell into a heap of bucket chairs and Formica tables and made no attempt to get up and I hopped out.

His full name was Levi Bellfield and in 2007 he was convicted of the murders of Amélie Delagrange and Marsha McDonnell and in 2011 for the killing of Millie Dowler, the tragic young girl who was abducted in 2002. Police think he may have attacked many more. When I think about him now, it makes me tremble with rage. He liked young, blonde girls and stalked them, running one down in his car and hitting others with a hammer from behind. My girls are blonde and my wife is blonde and they lived in the same streets as this nonce and he would have driven past them in his van countless times. It makes me shudder. I can put my hand on my heart and say that I wish I had killed him that day in the caff: that when he fell he hit his head fatally on the side of a table. I would have happily done the bird that the judge dished out if it had meant sparing the lives and the terror of Amelie and Marsha and the others.

BOXING CLEVER

I threw myself into a strict boxing regime, including an excruciating diet and road work in the mornings when the only things about are the paper boys, juddering milk floats and scavenging foxes. My first intention was to fight in the unlicensed market where there were decent purses to be had and if you were good enough could be a stepping stone to much more. The unlicensed scene was gloved boxing with referees and rules but outside the remit of the British Boxing Board Of Control. Because the rules were not so strict and the competitors were often not trying to build a career, or protect one, the fights were usually more explosive and entertaining. The crowds love it and venues can sell thousands of tickets. It is legal and definitely *not* bare-knuckle fighting, although you will find famous bare-knuckle fighters in unlicensed bouts along with well-known former professional boxers. It is a bridge between the two sports being the rougher end of boxing and the smoother front of bare-knuckle. Some of the greats of unlicensed boxing include Lenny 'The Guvnor' McLean, Donny 'The Bull' Adams and Roy 'Pretty Boy' Shaw, and these men's fame is arguably as great as many former pro-boxing champions. An industry has sprung up around them with hundreds of thousands of books and videos of their fights being shifted over the years.

The scene came to national prominence when the media got wind of a bare-knuckle fight between Donny Adams and Roy Shaw back in 1975. The police intervened and the two men were then forced to fight in gloves in a match organised by Joey Pyle, who also gave Roy the nickname Pretty Boy for good measure. Roy's first-round knockout victory generated huge publicity and this led to a couple of legendary title fights with Lenny McLean. These matches became underground video and later DVD bestsellers and I hear they get more hits on You Tube than anything else, whatever that is. Lenny became arguably the most celebrated unlicensed boxer of recent times and he even appeared in the cult Guy Ritchie gangster film *Lock, Stock And Two Smoking Barrels*. The appetite from the public for unlicensed boxing is insatiable.

The weight came off me and I was amazed that even at my age how abstinence from beer and fast foods could take effect. I was soon in good enough condition to spar with an old friend of mine, Gypsy George Carmen. George is a veteran of more than eighty fights and had gone head-to-head with former world champions Glen McCrory and Johnny Nelson. McCrory had fought Lennox Lewis in his time and Nelson was WBO Cruiserweight Champion. George had fought for no fewer than eight titles himself and what he did not know in a boxing ring was not worth knowing. On a cold winter's evening at Slough Boxing Club we went for the spar with a small crowd gathered to watch. We touched gloves and away we went ping, pong, pop, pop, bang. George was boxing my head off. I remember thinking – Silly Bollocks, you've done it again. You can't live in the ring with a real fighter. I could still absorb the punches as George was seeing, but all my hand speed had deserted me. George was the United States of America and I was his Baghdad. He was still mullering me, and I was bent backwards over the ropes and I bounced off them and caught George with a wicked right hand. But that was it. George was polite about it and said: 'Joe, I boxed a former world heavyweight title challenger called Scott Welch and he never hit me that hard.' That comment was some consolation as I knew of Welch because he had fought my namesake, Joe Bugner, but George had exposed my limitations.

I made contact with Alan Mortlock who is to the unlicensed scene what Barry Hearn is to snooker. He is an interesting man. He had an epiphany one night and became a committed Christian. He decided that being born again was better than dying once and who can argue with that? He is passionate about Jesus and the sport of unlicensed boxing. We negotiated a purse for a fight at the Epping Forest Country Club. I was preparing well and felt fit and strong but still aware that my hand speed was deficient so I phoned my great-uncle, Freddy French, and told him about my problem.

'Have you been punching the bag hard Joe?'

'Yes, Uncle Fred.'

'Right, that's your problem. Go and hit the bag lightly on the end of your glove.'

And he was bang on. The speed came back. Uncle Fred was the best boxer and knuckle man of his time that came out of the Kent Medway towns and he had resolved my issue in a quick phone call. Now I had more of a package.

On the night of the fight expectation was high and I had a big army of supporters in the house, but we found out at the last minute that my Geordie opponent had pulled out. Alan hastily arranged an exhibition fight with a lovely man called Mark Patrick who had a hundred or more fights under his belt, but he was smaller than me, only making Middleweight division. That was why Alan quickly billed it as 'exhibition'. This is boxing talk for 'they are not going to really hurt each other.' However, I was new to the scene and Mark's people did not know my character. Tel Currie was in my corner and a gentleman hard-man on the unlicensed scene, Carl Bywise, was in Mark's. He approached me. 'Joe, you are much too strong for Mark. Would you take it easy?'

'Carl, don't worry.'

I used all my punches without applying any power and we had a good bout which the crowd enjoyed. I got my few guineas and a good time was had by all.

A fight was scheduled in The Circus Tavern in Purfleet, the home of the BDO World Darts Championship and this was on the manor of some old family enemies. They were enemies which I had not made, but they surrounded members of my family over that part of the country. I had entered the feud when I was sixteen years old when I said 'Hello mate' to a bloke which he took as an insult and a fight ensued in which I came off best. The dispute had festered and ebbed and flowed between the two clans ever since. Mark Sommerfield was to be my opponent and he could box as well as having a huge bare-knuckle reputation up in the Sheffield and Rotherham areas. Four-hundred tickets were quickly sold in the thousand-capacity venue. This was my first real gloved fight and the pressure was really on and I didn't need the added worry about this other mob turning up and ruining the party. In a disproportionate security measure I escorted a piece down with me that contained four bullets. If they started it I was going to end it. Myself, Tel Boy, my trainer and a pal from the gym approached the door of The Circus Tavern, which was being protected by three or four huge fellas in their suits and dickie-bow ties. I told them who I was and they ushered us inside. All hell would have been let loose had they had known what was in Tel's kitbag. Tel, himself, would have had a seizure if *he* had known what was in his kitbag.

Our dressing room was barely bigger than a converted lavatory cubicle and this added to my rising blood pressure. On top of this I had a restaurant booked for after the fight to celebrate my victory and also Valentine's night, and following the meal I was booked on to a plane for a short golfing holiday in Spain. Alan Mortlock had kindly accommodated all this and put me first on the bill. However, the veins in my neck started to pulsate when I was brought the news that my opponent was stuck in gridlock on the M1 motorway.

Soon the time for the meal passed and the clock was ticking on whether I'd make my plane for the holiday. I was fuming. Eventually word came through that Mark had arrived and I went out ringside in my trunks to hurry things along but I was like a bomb ready to explode. The place was heaving with a now capacity crowd all loosened up with alcohol from the bars that lined the perimeter of the venue. Garry Bedford was the referee and he had a reputation as a fair and unassuming man. I danced on the spot and as the bell sounded I charged over to Mark, arms swinging like a madman. He proceeded to wrap me in a big bear hug, literally squeezing the power out of me and, frustrated, I put the nut on him and cut his eye.

'Joe,' shouted the referee, 'that is out of order!'

'Then tell the cunt not to keep on holding me.'

We squared up again following angry words from Garry, but straight away he pinned my arms to my side by grabbing me. Mark was a former professional rugby player and maybe he was confusing the two sports. I headbutted him a second time. The fight was a mess. The crowd were going mad, ignited by the flurry of violence before them. Garry separated us again.

'Last chance,' he panted, looking worried.

This time I advanced and sent in a flurry of punches while not getting close in enough for him to embrace me again. He tried to lunge at me but slipped and I followed him to the canvas pounding my falling target. Garry again separated us and allowed Mark back on his feet and this time he was growling and puffing like a lunatic and he rushed me, trying to steamroller me to the floor. Garry attempted to come in the middle of us but, almost comically, the three of us went to the floor. Now the referee had lost it. 'You northern cunt. Stop fucking holding,' he roared.

I reached for the big brass bell at the ringside and tried to hit him with that (Mark not Garry), but we were rolling about in a twisted tangle of flailing arms and legs. Amazingly Garry, our upstanding referee, started to rain punches on Mark and shouted: 'You are disqualified, you idiot. This is the fourth time I've reffed you and you never learn...'

All this happened in less than a minute and before we knew it the ring had filled with people. Looking up I could see they were my family and friends, even the women. It was a free-for-all. I pulled my gloves off and shouted at Mark to fight me bare-knuckle. With seventy supporters in the ring all shouting the odds he was not about to do that. Fortunately there was no riot and this was down to the fact that Mark did not have an entourage with him and I am glad now of that. The flashpoint passed and the referee announced his disqualification. My arm was raised, the crowd dispersed back to their tables, and I shot off to the airport where I made my plane.

My next fight was at the York Hall, Bethnal Green in East London, a venue synonymous with London boxing for decades. My opponent was called Tony Louie, who I heard was well-known among followers of Tottenham Hotspur football club, and from all accounts Spurs had one of the most scary hooligan followings. I don't know much about these things as at my beloved Brentford Football Club we don't go in for all that. The only rucking we do is the fighting back of tears.

In fact the only trouble I have witnessed at football has been with parents watching their kids in Saturday-morning park matches. What comes over sane parents when their beloved children set foot on a pitch is beyond me. I've seen well-dressed and poshly spoken women watch a game with one eye on the match and the other on their 4x4 BMW parked in the car park suddenly shout out: 'Referee. You're a cunt!'

Others I've seen march on to the pitch and attack a young boy who they think have fouled their sons.

I am guilty of it myself. Rymer was playing in a game where the opposing team had the best player in the league. His name was Ryan. I told my boy to man-mark Ryan and take him out of the game. I said that if he could do that he would have contributed more than anybody else in the team. Rymer was spot on. He did not leave Ryan alone. The kid could not move without Rymer breathing down his neck. This infuriated the opposition's manager, Dave Nugent. He became more and more animated.

'Shake him off, Ryan...' 'you're better than him...' 'lose him...' 'come on Ryan he's no match for you...' 'he's fucking useless...' 'he's got a bent foot...'

That was it. I threw my coat off and walked around the pitch to Dave Nugent. Grabbing him by the throat and lifting him off the ground, I nutted him. Fortunately for him I pulled back to lessen the impact and left my head resting threateningly on the bridge of his nose.

'How about I knock you out cold. Shout and encourage the boys by all means, but don't fucking insult them. My kid or not. You're meant to be a fucking adult.'

I placed him back on the grass and he was very apologetic. Dave later became my son's team manager.

Back on the boxing bill that same Saturday night was also a hardened West Ham fan and to make matters worse Spurs and West Ham had played in a London derby that day and the two firms were still chasing each other around the backstreets and getting on and off the Underground in an effort to ambush each other. When we arrived we were greeted by an orchestra of police sirens, screeching vans and the air of general disorder. Knots of men stood around waiting to be moved on by police and then re-appearing a few yards away. Having just come from the relative tranquillity of Griffin Park, where we had been playing our gentlemanly neighbours Queen's Park Rangers, this was an eye-opener.

East London is part of the same metropolis as West London but they might as well be a continent apart. It is not as if one is wealthy and one is not, or one has a high Asian population and one doesn't, they just feel totally different and the architecture, the smell, the way the people look, talk and walk are all subtly different. I couldn't live there as I'm sure an East Londoner could not settle in sunny Hounslow or Hanwell.

In the dressing room all such feelings were banished when I found I was sharing with Marty Cox, who is a son of Hanworth, home to my family for seventy-odd years. His father is Doug, known as The Fish Shop Man (to us, not Marty), and has supplied our family with fish-and-chip suppers as far back as I can remember. Marty was with a young lad called Darren Bowman, who was also fighting on the bill. I had two of my brothers and Tel Currie in my corner and when four uniformed policemen came to the dressing room to escort me to the ring we were all speechless. They said it was for my own safety and that the crowd were very volatile and looking for an excuse to kick off.

'I support Brentford,' I told them, thinking that would explain everything.

'They don't care who you support. You're not from round here and that is enough for these idiots to start a riot.'

I thought the police were over-reacting to the trouble that had been raging during the day and outside, but apparently the West Ham boys had a history of following boxing and starting battles among the spectators. I explained that I would rather take the risk of some argy-bargy than be known as the boxer who has a police entourage and they shrugged and went away. Forgetting this backdrop I steamed out from the corner throwing punches around like confetti in an effort to finish Tony early, but when he absorbed the flak I settled down into a more measured approach and dominated in rounds one and two. In the third I stepped up a gear and pressed my advantage. I cornered him off with double jabs and then bang, bang, a left, a right to the head and bingo, he's out. I win by a knockout. We didn't hang around to bask in the victory. It didn't seem sensible.

The next fight was arranged by Bobby Frankham, who was now promoting unlicensed fights. He rang me and said he'd lined me up with a Russian fighter with the unlikely name of Griddleas Gredliars. Just like in every other walk of life, boxing had seen an influx of people from Eastern Europe and some of them were handy to say the least. The venue was a disused factory in Milton Keynes, which was cleared out like a fucking great aircraft hangar, and when I walked in the place was heaving and cigar smoke was the dominant odour. As I walked through the throng I had never seen so many velvet-collared Crombie coats, chunky jewellery and cheroots poking from sides of mouths. I recognised some of the faces from Channel 4 television documentaries and could put names to many of them. As they say, if the Devil could have cast his net...

Dave Courtenay stepped in front of me and said with that mischievous twinkle in his eye: 'Are you feeling good tonight, Joe?' He was asking me if I thought I would win.

'I've been training hard, Dave. That's all I can say.'

'That will do for me. My dough is on you.'

Thanks, Dave. No pressure. No pressure at all, especially when I saw the monster in the opposite corner. He weighed in at sixteen stone and was put together better than Iron Mike Tyson. I have rarely seen such a frightening-looking physical specimen. I was grateful that along with Tel Currie in my corner I had Johnny Bloomfield, who was generally considered the best pad man in the business. He trained and padded Frank Bruno for his legendary fight with the aforementioned Mr Tyson. We had worked hard on keeping tight with my guard and firing back with my jab and then the rest of combinations would follow naturally.

The Russian comes straight at me, square on. Crunch! A piston-like jab with razor-sharp speed goes straight through his guard. I move back, he comes at me, crunch, crunch, two more jabs with the same effect. Still on me. He closes me down on the ropes. We touch for the first time and I can feel his physical strength. As quickly as I feel it, a left, right, left hook combination and I move, leaving him facing the rope. He turns only to face a double jab, right upper cut. He's rocked, then I whip a left hook round the corner to his jaw. Then crunch, crunch, crunch, I see him looking totally in trouble. I move in with a long left, right and left to the head and he's down but not out. I go to a neutral corner and wait to move back in for the finish. Looking over at the Russian, I notice he's waving his gloves, he can't continue after just fifty-three seconds.

I was the winner, every punch I threw I caught him with good affect without getting hit myself. This was a good performance by anyone's standards, but I was still a bit puzzled why this renowned warrior had not tried getting up and continuing. When we shook hands after the announcement, I noticed that both his eyes were closed shut. There's an old saying 'if I can't see you I can't fight you.'

Not very long after this fight Johnny Bloomfield died from a heart attack at the young age of fifty-seven in 2004. John was a fine man, greatly respected in the world of boxing, who taught me a great deal about the sport and life generally. He took everyone as he found them and was as honest as they come. I still miss him today. I could have done with him around when I heard that my next fight was to be against a man they called The Battersea Banger, Hughy Robinson. The match was to be over ten rounds at the York Halls in Bethnal Green again and was for the unlicensed British Heavyweight Title, confirming that my fights this far had not gone unnoticed. I was handed some film footage of Hughy and could see his game plan was to take out his opponents as soon as possible. He was a first-round explosion in shorts. I sensed that he lacked stamina and the ability to move well and take hard punches so I planned to avoid him a bit and then jab him up steadily, wear him down and frustrate him and then take control. I felt confident about going into the fight with a plan.

However, I had a niggling problem with my right arm that I noticed in training though more noticeably in golf, where I could not straighten the arm to its full extent. On visiting a sports injury specialist he X-rayed me and delivered the bombshell that over the years I had worn the bone away where my elbow-joint was and that bare-knuckle fighting and golf were the win double that had caused it. He concluded that I would have to stop sport or have surgery, and if I decided to have surgery then I should stop sport until I underwent the surgery. It was not the news I wanted to hear so I ignored it. We kept it quiet and went into training focusing on using the left arm as much as possible. The fight with Hughy – the big one for me – was not to be, as a fortnight before the fight Hughy ran into some trouble with a naughty little firm and sustained head injuries courtesy of a hammer. He was in a bad way and had no option but to pull out. I used the opportunity to book in for the surgery and spent four-and-a-half-hours under the knife. I came out with the surgeons telling me that the operation had been successful, but with my arm in plaster for a month and then ten weeks of physiotherapy and I had not appreciated how long a job it was going to be. The physiotherapy was the worst pain I had ever endured. I yelped like a baby every time the nice lady gently tried to straighten my arm. I've been battered black and blue and hit with blunt and sharp instruments but I'd go for that any day over thirty minutes of physio on my stubborn elbow. It was not repairing and my progress was compared with a chap who had the same procedure as me and was already back on the squash court, so in desperation the doctor gave me a series of steroid injections and within a few days I was hunky-dory. I said to my doctor: 'Why didn't you do that in the fucking first place?' and he gave me a funny look over his half-moon glasses.

CHAMPION

The first thing I did was to go out on the course and hit some soft seven-irons. How good did that feel? My British title chance had come and gone for the time being and I was lined up for a fight with Dennis Bjorn from Denmark. I did not know anything much about the guy, but prepared thoroughly by sparring with the likes of former world amateur champion Roman Greenberg, who was still only a youngster going places, and also Jamie Hearn, Johnny Frankham Junior, Rocky Frankham, Les Stevens, Johnny Lee Ryan, Kevin Phelan and Barry Smith. All these fighters are or were serious players and challenged me more and more. I was down to 15 stone 81bs which was six pounds under my previous best boxing weight and in tremendous shape. I should have guessed it but Dennis pulled out on the night and this was becoming a trend. They put Tony Louie, the Spurs man, in instead of him. I felt like a bully but had to show I was on an improving curve so I wanted to dispose of him more quickly than the three rounds it had taken last time. I floored him five times in the first round and the last one he did not get up from. A first-round knockout. I wanted the powers that be in the unlicensed scene to give me another crack at having a crack at the Heavyweight title.

Though my focus was now boxing I again entered the Regional Stage for the British Open at Hindhead, Surrey in 2003, but did not entertain any serious chances as I had only played eighteen holes of competition golf that season and had had precious little practice. I was out for a stroll. One of my playing partners was a very young, very talented Sam Osborne from Wentworth. He was hitting the ball seventy or eighty yards beyond me and I could see that my young caddy was shocked at how far he could hit the ball compared to me. My caddy was Rymer, who also doubled up as my son, and the two of us plodded around the delightful course which boasts lightning-quick greens, drive after drive, admiring young Sam's flair. On the fourteenth hole my three-wood finished down the right side of the fairway. I was blocked out by the hanging branch of pine tree so sent my second shot left of the branch and faded it back towards the flag where it finished only three feet away. I made the birdie putt. Now my stroll was no such thing because I knew I had to be somewhere near the mark and the pressure kicked in. I made four regulation pars to finish my round with a score of seventy-one. In the recording tent I noticed that I had out-scored both my playing partners. I told my son to check out Match 11 on the main scoreboard to see who had hit the lowest round. He came back excited. 'Dad, Dad you beat both of them. They were great big long-hitters and you beat them.'

'Well, son, now there's a lesson for the future. Length does not mean everything.'

I laughed to myself at the unintentional *Carry On Golfing* joke but was proud he was proud of his dad. All we had to do now was wait and see if my seventy-one score was enough to go through to the main qualifier for the 2005 British Open.

Several hours later I discovered I was in a nine-man play-off for four reserve spots. It was to start on the tenth hole which was a good 183 yards and a par-three. A difficult hole. I was the last to play and all the others had found the green, but with nerves jangling I hit the middle of the green also and made a two-putt par. On the eleventh I struck a good drive and a good wedge two putts. For my par-four we moved on to the par-three, fifteenth. About to strike, a mobile phone rang and I turned around to the crowd with the blood racing to my head to see a woman shrugging her shoulders and mouthing 'Sorry.' If it hadn't been my mother I'd have wrapped the club around her fucking head.

Unbelievably, when I composed myself to shoot again it went off a second time. I knew she did not know how to switch the fucking thing off. Mobile phones and old-school gypsies do not go well together, and I said to her in front of the gaggle of spectators watching: 'Mum, you should stick to what us gypsies have always done – making smoke signals.'

This raised a laugh and I struck my third attempt well to within about twenty feet of the hole and was then faced with a lightning-fast putt that my son and I had deliberated on. At nine-years-old he was a valuable sidekick because he could already read putts so very well. We watched with rising euphoria as the ball rolled along the green ever so slowly, but was surely swallowed by the hole. Eureka! I had achieved the third best ever reserve spot from this venue and was now officially one of the four reserves for the main qualifier for the Open.

Always one to decide the glass if half-full and even overflowing, young Rymer and I set off for Royal St George's venue for the 2003 Open Championship where we met up with two pals, Ryan Fenwick and Dave Clark, who had gone through regional qualifying successfully. We played practice rounds at the Princess Golf Club, which was one of the four qualifying venues and the one ideally I would like to play should I get that chance. Reserves are not normally allowed to play practice rounds but I am friends with the McQuirk family who own the club and also know the head pro, Derek Barbour, and they let me play with Ryan and Clarky. During the round I had a call from the R&A which told me I was to be first reserve at North Forland, not far from Margate. After a quick word with Darren Paris, who was one of the young pros there, I heard from the R&A again and they told me that Joe Robert Gomez, a US tour player, had been spotted on TV still playing in the Milwaukee Open, so unless he owned his own Concorde I would be taking his spot at 12.05 the next day.

I duly arrived at the tee with my family mingling among the scores of spectators who were there. Graham Lyle and David Gleeson were introduced and then after the regulatory five-minute wait for Mr Gomez, so was I. No excuses, I did not play well and went round in a not good enough seventy-seven. The next day I scored seventy-one. I knew it was not enough to qualify and it wasn't. If, by now, you're getting weary of me continually *nearly* qualifying for the British Open imagine how I fucking felt.

Ross Biddiscombe, the leading sports journalist, in his book *Golf On The Edge: Triumphs & Tragedies of Q School*, Ultimate Sports Publications, 2008, wrote about my efforts at Qualifying School and provides an outside view of my efforts and prospects. What he says about me is charming though I disagree with his conclusion on my long-term chances of Open success:

> The most remarkable First Stage Qualifying School tale is that of Joe Smith; a Romany gypsy, former bare-knuckle fighter and one of the most likeable guys in the whole tournament. In reality, the odds of him progressing to Second Stage were huge, his chances of a Tour Card simply astronomical, but Joe is undaunted because he sees Q school as a romantic quest.

Joe's story is neither sad nor desperate because of his love of golf and his ambition is unquenchable. At Q School, he is like a child in a sweet shop; his every action, every conversation, every shot is filled with a joy of life. Joe has none of the airs and graces of so many pro-sportsmen of the modern era who live in a gilded cage of privilege. From him, there are no complaints about the bad weather, his lack of smart clothes and new clubs from a fancy sponsor or whether the greens are too slow and the bunkers too full. Joe is just happy to be alive and to be playing a game he adores. His Q School story – even if ultimate failure is almost inevitable – has the emotional arc of a movie script.

Refreshingly, Joe's ethnic background – unusual for almost any professional sportsmen – is not something he hides from; his golf balls are logo'd with the words 'Gypsy Joe'. In addition, he is proud of his past as a bare knuckle (and later licensed pro) fighter and even the fact that for long periods in his life he never touched a golf club.

At 36 years old, Joe is no spring chicken, yet he has a genuine, appealing naivety. His enthusiasm to speak expansively about his game, to question other pros around him, to investigate his chances with the most unlikely stranger – it all provides for a charming counterpoint to the rash of cookie-cutter young golfers he is battling against. Joe is what we sportswriters commonly refer to simply as 'a character'.

From the age of seven, Joe's chosen sport was bare-knuckle fighting until his mid-teens, that is, when he took up golf. His family roamed around London and its outskirts, so Joe was able to join a club, Home Park (nowadays with new owners and re-invented as Hampton Court Palace GC). With just his natural talent and limited amounts of coaching he won several prestigious events at the club as well as the London Junior title back in the mid-80s. But out of nowhere, his life as a gypsy caught up with him. A surreal row over some sandwiches led to Joe being asked to resign from the club. He believes now that it was racism and the incident remains a bad memory. He was forced to go on to a public course where the practice facilities were not very good and it had a bad effect on him. His game duly suffered and although he turned pro at 20 and tried to make his way in low-level mini tour events, Joe's heart was not in it and he felt more like a Sunday morning hacker than a professional golfer.

By the age of 29, it was time to put down the clubs for a while. He was nagged by the thought that he would never know how good a boxer he could be unless he tried, so he joined the IBA ranks and had 12 fights. And 12 wins. Joe won the London heavyweight title in 2003 and won back his self-respect. His commitment to golf also returned and the Q School dream began.

Joe has come to Q School for the last four years but has yet to make it past First Stage. He is at St Anne's to test himself (his regular tournament golf these days is over two rounds on the Jamega Tour) and hopes for a fairy tale week; even making the third-round cut would be a major result for Joe. He opens with a 1 under par 71, but crashes to a 78 on day two, leaving him tied 67th. For Joe to survive into day four now means everything; for some Q School success is more immediate than a Tour Card.

Joe shoots 75 on day three and is one of the earlier finishers; he has to wait for several hours to see how the rest of the field performs. He nervously practices putting below the tournament office, regularly sending his children – one his caddie, the other a ball spotter – up the metal staircase to check the scores. As it turns out, his eight over par score is right on the mark and he makes the final day. The smile on his round, almost cherubic face is priceless.

The next day Joe would need to shoot 63 to reach Second Stage and, in such unhelpful, cold conditions that would be a world class round by anyone's standards. So his chance are, at best, remote, but his enthusiasm is undimmed.

For his final 18 holes, Joe sets off in hope and his driving and approach work are both solid. He is hitting plenty of greens in regulation and there are birdie chances, but he is not taking them. Golfing miracles are very rare, mainly because when most of your game is in good order, a single part will fail you. So it is today with Joe; it is his putting. He keeps his poise and tries his hardest, but it is not to be. He walks off the 18th green with a 3 over par 75, still smiling.

By the time Joe finishes, sunset is less than 20 minutes away. On the other side of the course, the leaders are being urged on in near darkness by worried tournament officials; no one wants to come back tomorrow to finish a couple of holes.

Finally, at dusk under the purple clouds, Walker Cup star David Horsey completes a round of 68 to win him the event. Somehow, the officials have brought home the last group with about ten minutes to spare and despite the huge delays caused by the bad weather. First Stage is over for another year. While David checks his card in the scorer's office, Joe Smith is already on his way to Blackpool Pleasure Beach with his two sons. He has played his heart out over the whole four days, finished tied eighty-first out of 121 golfers and earned himself a good time among the autumn holidaymakers. Even at the First Stage of Q School, some losers are winners.

I was not disappointed because I had not built my hopes up or made any silly promises to myself and the next day Rymer and I got up early for a practice round before setting off home. Rymer pulled my tour bag along with my trademark boxing gloves used as head-covers for my woods and just across from us was another man and a boy pulling a similar bag with boxing gloves as covers. The young boys eyed each other curiously and suspiciously. The other pair were talking fast to each other in what sounded like Spanish. I told Rymer to shadow box for the crack and the 'Spanish' man started laughing and approached me.

'Hello, I'm Esteban Toledo,' he smiled.

'And I'm Joe Smith, pleased to meet you.'

'I used to be a boxer too, did you?' explained Esteban.

'Not used to be, I still am,' I said.

Esteban went on to tell me how he had literally boxed his way out of poverty in Mexico, living in his car and finally getting over the border into America and taking up golf and getting himself on to the US tour. It was a story that mirrored my own to an extent and we laughed and joked together like old friends. He said he started working on a golf range near the US border and told how he used to find the golf balls and sell them back to the players. It was the boxing though that got him over the border and he fought once in Las Vegas for a $5,000 purse. He cringed when I told him about some of my bare-knuckle escapades and my descent into crime, and I sympathised when he told me how he believed his brother had been murdered and his body dumped into the river when his family lived in a steel hut back in Mexico. We had a lovely photo taken of the four of us. A nice man, and I admired how he overcame the odds to become successful. This tough little Mexican is a great example to anyone at the bottom of the pile.

Alan Mortlock had me matched with a mad biker from Sheffield next, who went by the name of Micky Hard As Steel. On the day of the fight news reached us that Micky and his gang had all been lifted on firearm offences and he therefore would not be turning up at the old Bailey's nightclub in Watford, our venue. One thing I was learning fast about the unlicensed scene was that it meant very little who you were scheduled to fight because on the night there was an even-money chance that you'd be matched up with somebody else.

Alan desperately pumped his mobile phone trying to rustle up an opponent who would get in a ring with just a few hours' notice as he had sold out the place and didn't fancy refunding everyone. I, alone, had sold three hundred tickets and did not wish to let those people down or return money that was as good as spent. Also having taken the money he had to come up with someone credible. I suggested an old friend of mine, Brian 'Sonny' Nickells, who had enjoyed a solid professional career before copping a lifetime ban for headbutting his opponent and then the referee in a British Heavyweight title eliminator. Brian had picked up work in films as a bit-part actor and a stuntman and was trying to get back into the game via unlicensed boxing. Alan offered a grand and Brian agreed. We spoke before the fight and agreed to go gently on one another. He said he would fight under the name Brian Clark because he was worried about his reputation from the past.

'Brian, this is unlicensed. Your reputation is the best thing you have going for you,' I told him.

The bell sounds and I am tip, tap, tip, tip – nice and fast but without power. He is a tear-up merchant and allows me to dance around and literally pull my punches. On the stool my team tell me to step it up a bit. The crowd are getting restless. Brian grabs me in a clinch and shouts to the ref to tell me to stop grabbing him. He laughs and so do I. We shouldn't have done that. A big lump ringside jumps up and jabs his fingers. 'Fucking fight you pair of fucking wankers,' he screams.

Brian lets me go and scrambles under the ropes and confronts this bloke. 'Who you calling wankers? You cunt. Here borrow my gloves and you go and fight him. Or do you want me to smash you up?'

Brian cocks his head to one side waiting for an answer and the bloke fucks off. We take the fight up a level and the crowd start to enjoy it. At one point he unleashes a crack to my ribs that has the crowd on their feet. 'Go easy, bruv,' I whisper in his ear at the next clinch.

The ref gives me the fight.

I am relieved that Brian and I were not fighting for real because we are really good pals. Six months later he caused uproar in another match when he launched the referee out of the ring, knocked his opponent clean out and then kicked his teeth down his throat. I happened to be in his corner that day. Brian is full of surprises. He is the only fighter, who I know of, to be banned by the British Boxing Board of Control and by all unlicensed promoters. He's nice to his cats though and I love him to bits.

Next up I was offered a crack at the London Unlicensed Heavyweight Title in the spiritual home of boxing, Osterley. My opponent was a 6ft 4in Irishman introduced to me as Seamus. We shook hands.

'How come you qualify as a Londoner?' I innocently enquired of him.

'I have lived here now for three weeks,' he returned in an almost unintelligible Belfast brogue.

'That long?'

Far be it from me to question the 'rules'. Steve Holdsworth, the Eurosport boxing commentator came into my dressing room and cautioned me not to underrate the Irishman. Steve had seen him fight and said rather mysteriously: 'He's useful, Joe. Be careful.'

The place was packed and I came out second wearing a red-silk dressing gown (sorry, Christine) and to the tune of 'Eye Of The Tiger', the *Rocky* theme. It was my biggest occasion yet.

I plonk a sweet left jab. Then another. I'm hesitant to go in with my right as I know nothing about his style and power. I'm starting well. Working hard in the gym is paying off. My left hand is set further from my face and nearer to his. I've been working on not pulling my jab at all back before throwing it just straight forward at his face and it is working wonders. He's younger than me by ten years yet he can't match my speed. I feel good. I move back, drop my guard and goad him in. Jab him. Move. In the middle of the ring now I show him my left to his head and he instinctively tries to block, opening the door to his body. Thud. The crowd are thinking what I'm thinking.

'Go on Joe. Knock him out.'

Someone in my corner tells me I'm out of range and to close in. Correct. I'm out of range but my left hand isn't. I'm hitting him and he ain't hitting me. That's the fucking idea, isn't it? Jab, double jab, double jab, right cross. I rock the Irishman and the crowd are screaming for me to move in and finish him. But I'm taking no chances. I've seen so many get suckered in for the knockout and get sparked themselves in their enthusiasm. I'm not going to let this one slip. I want that belt in my cabinet – London Unlicensed Heavyweight Boxing Champion to stand next to my London

Junior Open Champion at golf. However, this twenty-two-year-old, sixteen-and-a-half-stone and now half-mad Paddy isn't finished yet. He's rushing me in his frustration. I tie him up and hit him on the blind side of the referee. He's yelling as he throws his punches. He whips out an almighty right that cracks me on the jaw and I bang, bang, bang him back and we clinch.

'Someone told me you had a punch, Seamus,' I say.

No reply. He's huffing and puffing. 'Are you OK?' I ask.

He gets me with some more decent shots but I am returning in kind. I'm waiting for the final bell now because I know if he doesn't knock me out, and there's no chance of that, I've won. I've dictated the fight from the off. Ding! Ding!

I hugged Seamus. He was a nice young chap and had fought well. To my surprise Gypsy Johnny Frankham was introduced over the mic as the man who was going to present me with my belt. Johnny is the greatest gypsy fighter of all time and an all-round legend. He was once British Light Heavyweight Champion and there is also a famous picture of him standing over a floored Muhammad Ali in a publicity shot. Steve Holdsworth came over and complimented me on my performance and we all went off and had one big party.

CLOSING UP

My boxing career was looking up though I knew that as I was now in my thirties I had no real prospect of turning professional and the London Heavyweight Unlicensed Championship would likely be the peak of my achievements in the ring, but I would have a few more fights because I was enjoying my growing reputation and the money was more than welcome. I was still nursing my golf ambitions and had appointed Alan Barber of Windlesham Golf Club as a part-time coach. He helped eliminate a problem I had where I was getting too much leg movement when swinging and encouraged me to hit the ball with an extra-wide stance. I became thirty-five yards longer and much straighter. Around the same time, playing in yet another Open Regional Qualifier, I picked up a book called *The Dave Pelz Putting Bible* by Phil Mickelson and it really did become my bible in helping me rid myself of the dreaded yips

Back on the unlicensed front a night's boxing had been scheduled against a bunch of Eastern Europeans at Uxbridge, West London. My opponent was a German called Alex Heinz who was a former light heavyweight champion in his own country. It was a hot night and the doctor who checked my blood pressure before the fight told me I was eighty-five over seventy and said that was the best of all the fighters on the bill that night. I bet he says that to all the boxers. I bossed this one from the start, coasting a little, because the guy was struggling to go up a weight and he couldn't do it.

Some spectators thought I was clowning a bit, but I was pacing myself for the six rounds in the sweltering heat and in the third I let off a combination that rocked the German. I asked the ref to stop the fight, telling him I could knock him out my opponent at will. In a flash, and delivering a lesson to me about the counting of chickens, he unleashed a punch from the floor that everyone saw coming, bar me. It connected flush on my jaw and I felt as if I had been wired to the mains electricity and the switch had been thrown.

I shook from head to toe and like an Old English Sheepdog emerging from water and went back and promptly dropped game old Axel before he could spring any further surprises. He got up at a count of six and I moved in on him again. This time the ref took my advice and stopped the fight. However, the real fireworks were about to come.

My cousin Wally Stockin was on the bill in an attempt to make a boxing comeback. Wally was now in his forties and it may not have been the wisest decision he has made, but there is nobody gamer than he around. Minor things like age do not occur to Wally. His brother Jimmy is renowned as being one of the best bare-knuckle fighters of his era but Wally enjoyed a very successful boxing career fighting professionally in the late 1970s and early 1980s as a clever and determined lightweight. He famously and poignantly fought on the night that his father was murdered and this tragic episode is recounted in Jimmy's excellent book *On The Cobbles*. He lost, understandably, and the man he competed with that fateful night back in 1979 up in Dudley in the West Midlands was Ian Kid Murray. Ian went on to fight Lloyd Honeghan and Terry Marsh among many others. The fighter Wally had been matched against this balmy night was a classy Russian and fifteen years Wally's junior.

Around the ring there was a buzz of excitement and a lot of people thought, but dare not say it, that it was a mismatch. One well-known and respected businessman tried to get a bet on Wally and when he could not get one switched and said he would take money on Wally getting beat. He then changed his mind again and said he would not take bets against Wally in case the judges were 'hookey'. Wally's brother Jimmy was down in the thick of this and whether he had planned something or his blood was up I don't know, but he challenged the man.

'My Wally will knock the man out,' Jimmy growled.

'Never in a million years. I will lay you two to one.'

'Done,' said Jim. 'I'll have five grand.'

The man took a sharp intake of breath at this but nodded his agreement. Someone then discreetly spoke to the Russian and said he would double his wage for the evening if he took a dive. The Russian nodded. So we were now looking at a fixed fight.

Wally was not involved in the negotiation and steamed out from the bell peppering the bigger man with punches and boxing well, but by the second round the Russian was still standing and Wally was already huffing and puffing. He did catch the guy with a peach of a punch yet the Russian did not flinch and then moved into gear and started to box cleverly and accurately. By the time Wall was back on his stool before the third and final round one of his eyes had completely shut and the other was swelling up as we studied it.

'He's in trouble,' said Wally, a touch optimistically.

Like an injured terrier Wally roared out and despite his impaired vision was landing more punches than he was taking. Sheer determination this time was winning over the Russian's superior skill but our joy at Wally's blast-from-the-past performance was tempered by the growing realisation that his opponent had no intention of taking a dive. The bell went and the referee without hesitation lifted Wally's arm aloft as he squinted around the ring trying to work out where everyone was. His eye needed treatment, but more worrying is that Jimmy Stockin had been misled and had to pull up five grand because even though Wally had won, it had not been by a knockout and therefore he had lost the wager. The Russian was standing in his corner in conversation with his team and suddenly Jim was approaching them with a sharpness about his walk. I knew what was coming. I'd seen it before. He smashed the Russian with an almighty right-hander and the big man tumbled out of the ring. Within seconds, and it was seconds, a fearful fight was raging in the ring and spreading like a field-fire across the audience. The entourage with the Eastern European fighters on the bill were no slouches and were fighting with about thirty members of our family. Chairs, bottles, fists, heads and feet flew all over and people who had no connection with us, or the Russian, set about each other. It was a proper Wild West London brawl in which the ex-communists came off worse. It only ended when the police burst in from various doors truncheons drawn and being pulled along by excited Alsatian dogs.

Jim told me after that he hadn't gone for the Russian over the bet but because he was mad seeing his brother hurt even though he had fought out of his skin and won. He said he knew that the Russian was not going to take a dive. 'How could he? He couldn't speak a word of English. He didn't know what was being said to him.'

The local press relished the incident, pointing out that it was the first time boxing had been staged in Uxbridge for fifty years and because of a riot involving 'the gypsy Mafia and the Russian Mafia' there would be no more for another fifty years. The law may have made some arrests that night but to my knowledge nobody was charged. That was because nobody saw anything. How could they with all that going on?

My next fight was against a former US marine who borrowed the names of two American heroes – one real, one not – and went by the title of Rambo Patten. He was a mixed-race, very fit-looking man, but after forty-eight seconds of the first round he was fit for fuck all. I put him down three times before switching him off with a crunching right hand that sent him unconscious before he hit the canvas. Thankfully, he came round and was OK. I decided to retire from boxing after that night, although there would be a couple more fights before I actually did. I had gone as far as I could and had nothing left to prove at that level and now was only fighting for money. Sooner or later someone fitter, younger, stronger and better would come along and knock my head off my shoulders and would it be worth it? I could get out with my dignity and faculties intact.

Financially, even though Christine had given birth to my second wonderful daughter, Louisa Mary Marie, things were improving and the scrap-metal business that myself, young Trevor and my pal, Danny Shaw, had set up was starting to make us a living. Also Danny was happy about minding the shop when I went off to play tournament golf. Although I had mentally accepted that I had gone as far as I could in boxing, I had not reached that point in golf. A close friend of mine, Graham Stevens, also had confidence in me and he gave me invaluable financial support at this time. Graham owns the successful Ram Golf and Stubbert Golf businesses and he is a former European Tour player himself. He knows I have this dogged determination to force myself into the highest level.

I went to the European Tour School at St Anne's old links where I scored seventy-three, seventy-four and seventy-three to miss the cut by two shots. Then in the Open Regional Qualifier at Hindhead something was wrong with my technique but I could not put my finger on it. I struggled from the first tee to the last green and in the middle was a four-hour rain delay yet I battled on even if I was missing most greens and having to chip and putt to save par. It was nine hours before I reached the eighteenth hole where I was in the Greenside Bunker. Almost dark and I splashed out to within four feet and rolled in the putt for my seventeenth par of the round with only one bogey for a score of seventy-one. It wasn't a bad tally on the very tough Surrey course but not enough to see me through though, but enough to get me into an eleven-man play-off for four final qualifying spots. The following morning it was a two four-ball and three-ball sudden death play-off, last to play was our three-ball. I drove my ball straight down the middle and struck my wedge over the flag to within twelve feet of the hole and rolled in the most tricky of putts for my birdie three. It became apparent that only two others had made birdie three and I was through.

If I could get through playing not so good then I must be doing something right. Alan Barber diagnosed my niggling problem as me being too active with my hands and he was right. I booked my Heathrow-Edinburgh flight thinking... this time... this time. On the morning of the day we were flying I went to the local shopping centre to get some bits for myself with money my family had gifted me as it was my birthday. When I got back I heard the news. It was the 7th July 2005. Some lunatics had blown parts of London to bits. Much of the time the news washes over you. There is too much of it, for one thing. But bombs in Lebanon, suicide missions in Israel, genocide in Africa, another British soldier kops it in Afghanistan – they are everyday fare and if we are honest we barely ever give it a second thought. It's happening somewhere else. Someone else's problem. Then 7/7/2005, my birthday, it's on our doorstep; it is not somewhere else and it is *our* problem. That, obviously, was the idea. My reaction was the same as anyone's: firstly, are any of our family and friends up there? Then, those poor, poor people. Then, fucking murdering bastards. Then, where does all this end? If I hadn't qualified to play I remembered that I would have been in London for a meeting. It stops you in your tracks. And I felt sad for London and realised how much London means to me. I know London is not a person but that day I felt sorry for it and wanted to wrap my arms around it. Being blown up like that. Now in fear of what bit of it will be attacked. And I felt sorry for me as one of London's people. Would anything be the same again? It was in that frame of mind I boarded my plane to Edinburgh.

I had young Rymer and Trevor with me. Trevor is my wife's cousin and tragically his mother died in her sleep at the young age of forty-seven and his father is serving fifteen years for armed robbery. Christine and I took him in because that is what families do, or used to at any rate. At Edinburgh we plucked our luggage from the conveyor belt and I went over to outsize luggage to fetch my golf clubs but they were nowhere to be seen. I eventually found someone, an airport worker, who admitted to having some responsibility and he told me that my clubs were nowhere to be found. He expressed no regret, no concern, and just delivered the news that they were lost in a monotone, deep Scottish accent. They may come up on the next flight he suggested. 'What sort of service is this? I need my fucking clubs.' I raised my voice as my eyes blinked through a descending red mist.

He had his hands behind his back and rocked back slightly on his heels. He reminded me of the pompous screw out of TV's *Porridge*.

'Stop feeling sorry for yourself, big fella. You could have been on a train in London today.'

I couldn't believe he said that. I flipped. Instead of launching him I squared up to a supporting pillar about to bash my fists into it as through my rage I knew there was less chance of the pillar getting me nicked for assault. I did not want to smash my hands to a pulp, though.

'See this fucking pillar. Get me a man in this airport this big and I will spread him across the floor. Get me someone proper to fight you snivelling fucking tosspot. Half of my city has been blown up, you lose my fucking golf clubs and you tell me I could have been on a tube train in London. Who do you think you are you? You Jock cunt.'

I was screaming. Foaming at the mouth like a rabid dog. I threw my luggage into the air like missiles and kicked the trollies all over. All eyes had turned to us and hopefully the nosey bastards had missed their suitcases whizz past them on the conveyor belt.

'You open your mouth again and I'm going to fill it,' I warned as the man looked like he was going to protest.

Calming down slightly we went out to sort out our car hire when two policemen approached.

'I am arresting you for threatening behaviour,' said the first one.

It was going from bad to worse.

'Officer, please give me a break. I am not here to qualify for a court case. I'm here to qualify for the Open Championship. At least that's the plan. It hasn't started well because those clowns in there have lost my clubs and they wouldn't even apologise or offer to help.'

'Are you a golfer?'

'Yes, I'm a golfer.'

He examined my passport.

'It's your birthday?'

'That's right.'

'It's not a good birthday, is it?' his expression said it all.

'It's a tragic day,' I replied.

He handed me back my passport and gently touched my arm.

'Let's say you've had a verbal caution. Hope your clubs turn up and the best of luck in the tournament.'

'Thanks, officer.'

We made it to our bed and breakfast overlooking the Tamar River near Dundee and my kind hostess lent me her set of clubs to practise with. That was a touch. Mine turned up the next day and I got stuck into the task ahead. After carding a first round of seventy-six, when my putter was really cold, I followed with a solid round of seventy-one which included a lost ball on my second hole. I had played well but was left outside the qualifying mark ensuring that my dream remained a dream. I knew time was running out but did not and do not despair as some golfers can peak as late as forty-five years of age.

As I write I've had my most successful golf year yet. A fourth place in Portugal, a second in Spain and my best ever tour event in England finishing third on the Jamega tour. My stroke average is lower. I remain confident that I *will* qualify and play in the British Open.

Fighting is another matter and I grabbed a bit of glory in my penultimate fight. It was against Steve Yorath, a Welsh veteran with a long professional career who had made his home on the Gold Coast and had only recently challenged for the Australian Heavyweight Title. Earlier in his career he had lost on points to Chris Okoh, a former Commonwealth Cruiserweight champion. I knocked him out in the third round with the help of a little dose of trickery. I kept shouting at the timekeeper as we grappled and eventually Steve looked over to see what all the fuss was about and I smacked him with a couple of beauties which took his legs away. People asked me if I could have finished it without doing that. Who knows? He has asked for a rematch but I'm retired. That's my story and I'm sticking to it.

My final venture on to canvas was more satisfying. After the Steve Yorath fight I had kept out of the ring but was coaxed back to fight a guy called Sheridan Davey, who had decent form. He had gone the distance with

Dominique Negus who is well-known for headbutting Olympic gold medallist Audley Harrison on live TV while giving him all sorts of other problems. It was satisfying because all proceeds of the fight were to go to the Shooting Stars charity, a wonderful organisation that provides support to terminally ill children and their families. We put on four good rounds of boxing and the ref was about to raise my hand to the audience but I said he should not give a decision. Winning or losing was unimportant. Joey Pyle and his partner Warren were impressed with the fight to the extent they wanted a ten-round rematch and make it the British Unlicensed title. It was tempting but I had made my mind up to retire and that this time it would be my very last venture into the ring. I held my new baby boy aloft and told the crowd his name: Joseph Bradley Stone Aaron John Neville Jim Amos Bill Smith. When I registered him the lady from Uxbridge Registry Office said it was the longest name they had recorded in a hundred years and then phoned The Samaritans.

I am glad to say that my dark days of violence and criminality are behind me and I thank God that I was allowed to come through it and out the other side. Many do not. I hope that this story will show young men who feel that their lives have been mapped out for them and despite them, whether they be gypsy or not, that you can follow your dreams. You *can* make things happen. Positively. It heartens me that gypsies are now coming through in other sporting walks of life and not just boxing. There are a bunch of young gypsy golfers out there and one of the bastards will beat me to becoming the first Romany British golfing champion. In football we have seen Lenny Pidgeley keeping goal in the Premiership and Freddie Eastwood bursting through at Southend United and at present playing for Coventry City via Wolverhampton Wanderers. They are both great blokes and there are plenty more waiting in the wings. Just recently we had the young boxer Billy Joe Saunders acquit himself well in the Beijing Olympic Games. Billy's great-grandfather is Absolom Beeny who is now in his tenth decade but in his day a noted bare-knuckle man and a regular feature in the fairground boxing booths. Doors are opening and Romanies are cautiously stepping through them.

Gypsies are the last ethnic group resident in this country to be alighted upon by equality crusaders. This is because fundamentally we do not want 'equal rights' and therefore those who want to work on our behalf have to walk a tightrope of fighting for a fairer deal for a community that largely does not want them to. Gypsy culture is all about being apart from mainstream society. Traditionally we have made few demands on 'normal' society in exchange for a blind eye being turned on us maintaining a way of life that sits outside modern thinking. We have traditionally shunned schools, social services, conventional employment and housing, and because we are relatively few in number and, used to, at least, never stay in one place long, we have deliberately ducked under the radar.

Times have changed. The country is managed tightly. Every fart is logged, classified and monitored. Having an indigenous group of people, some of who may have never ever had their births or deaths registered, or who don't appear on a database and may not pay tax or draw benefits, is an affront to modern, meddling governments. Every inch of land is owned, recorded, watched and can be zoomed in on by Google Earth. You can't disappear and pull up your caravan behind a tree in the middle of nowhere any more. In a country where you can be fined for smoking a cigarette or dropping a Toffee Crisp wrapper, how long will gypsies be able to continue scraping a living doing building, repair and garden work without the requisite health-and-safety certificates, public liability insurances, Uncle Tom Cobley and all?

The fact is that my generation were probably the last to experience and enjoy the traditional Romany outdoor lifestyle. My children's children for sure will never live full-time in a caravan. They *will* go to school and will take conventional employment. In short they will be the same as everyone else. It is sad, but at least the ingrained prejudices and fears that exist between gypsies and Gorgios will dissipate. We are all seeing our heritages, whoever we are, become memories and exhibits in a museum in our lifetimes. That is how fast things are moving now.

I do not regard myself as part of an ethnic group, by the way. That is how others choose to present gypsies. Not me. I am English, first and foremost and proud. I love England. I did not know what an ethnic group was until people started talking about it so much in the last twenty years. In fact the whole thing about us an ethnic group makes me feel uneasy as if we have just turned up or something. We've been part and parcel of England for five hundred years or more. We were here before the Jews, the Huguenots, the West Indians, the Asians and the Poles. Romans, Vikings and others came before us but we arrived less noisily. There was no raping and pillaging that I am aware of yet somehow a law was put on the statute book that stated the penalty for being a gypsy was hanging. We were part of the scenery before

America and Australia were 'discovered'. I am English and I am a Romany. I am as despairing as the next man when I see how various groups try to make us feel ashamed of England and its past. I'm an ordinary gypsy man without an education and I don't understand why people want to say this is not a great country. It is. The proof is in the pudding. Why does nearly every bastard want to live here?

We gypsies have always had our own heritage, but now it makes me laugh to see others trying to create one for us. Recently there was a lot of press coverage over some press release that claimed various celebrities were gypsies or had Romany extraction. The most famous of these was Elvis Presley. What is the point in all this? Oh, if Elvis was one, then they can't be all bad? Is that it? If Elvis was a gypsy then I *am* actually Dusty Springfield. We have genuine people that can be celebrated if they just looked hard enough rather than making up ones.

Yul Brynner, star of *The Magnificent Seven*, definitely had Romany blood in his veins. Why else would he have financed a school on one of the first permanent gypsy sites in Hainault, Essex back in the 1960s? Also from the world of acting was Alan Lake who boasted classic black curly hair and dark-skinned features. He was never out of work for long either on the big or small screen, and achieved real fame when he became the husband of Diana Dors, a 1950s screen idol. Diana was a lot older than Alan and when she succumbed to cancer in the 1980s he put a gun in his mouth and shot himself.

George 'Digger' Stanley was another. Born in a vardo at Kingston-upon-Thames in 1876 he too plied his trade in the boxing booths before becoming British and European Bantamweight Champion. He famously sailed to America to fight their middleweight champion in what was considered to be a formality for the Yank. Despite taking three months to get there and being ridiculed in the local press he smashed the middleweight to smithereens. Staying with boxing there was Johnny Frankham and Jem Mace, both discussed earlier. More recently there has been Tony Sibson, a gypsy boxer from Leicester, who challenged the great Marvin Hagler for the World Middleweight Title and Gypsy Henry Wharton who went up against both Nigel Benn and Chris Eubank in world title fights.

From the world of music David Essex is proud of his Irish traveller roots and served as a patron for some time on the National Gypsy Council. Django Reinhardt is a celebrated jazz guitarist. He played the violin until his gypsy wagon caught fire. Django went in to retrieve his instrument only to lose two fingers on his most used hand. However, the Frenchman took to playing the guitar with only two fingers. He became a legend. Ronnie Wood of the Rolling Stones and West Drayton was the first generation of his water-gypsy dynasty to be born on dry land and Joe Longthorne, brilliant cabaret artist, is gypsy through and through. His Uncle Tug Wilson was a bare-knuckle fighter and his grandmother a fortune teller.

I have talked about the footballers. Freddy Eastwood, who I mentioned earlier, is my first cousin and we share business interests. Romanies everywhere celebrated when he scored a thundering goal against the mighty Manchester United from a free kick for lowly Southend United in a cup-tie. It won the little club the game and Freddy was lauded in the press and on the TV. One paper called him The Romany Rooney and even Sir Alex Ferguson hailed him as an important new talent. However, maybe the most famous gypsy ever involved in British football is Sir Alf Ramsey, manager of the 1966 England World Cup winners and a skilful full-back with Tottenham Hotspur in his playing days. According to the biography by Leo McKinstry it was common knowledge within the game that Alf was of Romany extraction. Apparently on the team coach when they passed a gypsy site Bobby Moore would call out to him: 'Look Alf there's your family over there.' Alf and his father both had the nickname Darkie and it was said he went to elocution lessons to rid himself of his accent. Sir Alf denied this and did everything he could to hide his humble roots, whatever they may have been.

I hope and I am determined that I will add my name to this illustrious list because, although my heart and my granite jaw can be broken, my will to compete in the British Open at golf cannot.

I'm out with young Rymer on the golf course and we're practising. Having fun. Laughing and joking and talking. It's a blustery day and there is even a light drizzle now and then but I'm so happy looking at my innocent, sweet kid, enjoying himself running excitedly to retrieve his ball. I've been saying to him about getting down the gym and teaching him a bit of boxing. But I don't want him getting the wrong idea. I said to him I just wanted him to learn some self-defence, because in this world you've got to protect yourself, but he should avoid fighting. 'The man that walks away from a fight is no coward,' I had heard myself say to him and now thoughts of Rymer come rushing into my mind. He had said something similar to me all those years ago, when I was a kid too. I'm picturing him now. Such a big strong man with a smile that defied anyone not to love him. His big heavy hand on my shoulder saying these things as we played golf together thirty years ago and I'm realising more and more that these weren't passing remarks. He was deliberately trying to steer me on a course as he had done my dad and how I am doing now, today, to Rymer. My grandfather, that battered, lovely old boxer is here now. Rymer is talking to Rymer. Through me. I know it. And a picture that I had suppressed for years flashes into my mind. Rymer, my grandfather, is lying on the ground on the golf-course. The man they could not fell is dead. The horror and the fear comes back and I'm like a little boy again. My eyes are filling with tears and I'm blinking fast trying to break them up. Stop them forming. I grip my club tight for support. Young Rymer runs back to me and looks up.

'What's up Dad? Why you crying?' he asks.

I look down at him and smile and place my hand on his shoulder.

'I'm not crying son, it's this wind. The bloody wind.'

BIG FAT REFLECTIONS: 2020–1

It's been more than a decade now since *Gypsy Joe* was first released. A great deal has happened in that time, for me, my family and in the wider world. In this new chapter I will try and recount the good and the bad, the happy and the sad. It all goes to show that an autobiography written during one's lifetime – and it would be bloody hard to do it after you're dead – is a mere snapshot in time. Things change and your outlook changes. If you stayed the same way throughout your life that would be a worry. Because there would be a lot of daft people out there. Most of us are daft in our younger years. I've not met too many wise heads on young shoulders. Have you?

Gypsy Joe was released in the summer of 2009. Barrack Obama was President of the USA. He was the first man of colour to ascend to leader of the free world – a marvellous achievement, giving hope to minorities across the world. His election heralded a more tolerant, integrated world. What happened there? Manchester United dominated the Premier League in football. What happened there? Roger Federer won Wimbledon (again), a great racehorse Sea The Stars was the Epsom Derby winner. Michael Jackson died. Ronnie Biggs was released from prison. The final, brave survivors of the First World War trenches left us. Kings Of Leon were riding high in the charts with 'Sex On Fire'.

But for me, the key event was my book coming out, and the esteemed *Observer* newspaper named it as Sports Book of the Year. Can you imagine how I felt? Not only was it a huge boost for my ego it was a humbling experience. This newspaper that is read by the great and the good of the nation decided my old life story was worthy of recommendation, deserving of plaudits and awards.

'One of the best golf books written this year; although the cheque books come out for the scandal, this true story of thwarted ambition, criminality, violence and redemption has substance. A courageous story shot through with intelligence and humanity,' the *Observer* commented.

I thought back to the days when a kind man came to our caravan and painstakingly taught me to read and write, and here I was a published and accepted author. Those words I learnt with great difficulty but enthusiasm were now being read, enjoyed and appreciated by others. Of course, my writing partner in this endeavour, Martin Knight, played a key part. If he hadn't guided and encouraged me it would never have happened. He edited me, because I can go on – have you noticed? He tightened things up, eliminated many of the grammatical and spelling disasters, provided context and generally polished the whole thing. It was a joint effort in every sense, but Martin will tell you it was my original manuscript, carefully handwritten in exercise book after exercise book.

Of course, I wanted to earn from the book. I fantasised about a film or a documentary. But also I wanted to change perceptions about gypsies and gypsy life. I hope my book shone a light on our culture and banished some of the myths that swirl around us. We were, and sadly still are, the only ethnic minority where it is still permissible to demonstrate open prejudice against us. The attitudes discussed earlier in the book persist. I like to think *Gypsy Joe* persuaded some people at least that those attitudes and those prejudices should be reconsidered.

Our cause – and you can't really call it that because gypsy people don't have a driving urge to be accepted by the Gorgio world – has not been helped by allowing the cameras into our lives. If anything, it has entrenched an inherent racism against us. A couple of years after the book was released, Channel 4 aired the first series of *Big Fat Gypsy Weddings*. It triggered great interest in our community and attained huge viewing figures. However, it did us no favours, in my opinion. The title is a giveaway to the approach. It was going to be poking fun, ridiculing rather than rationalising, and it did just that. Look at the money these people spend on weddings. Look at the girls and boys in their ill-fitting suits and bling. If they had showed a true Romany funeral, viewers would have seen our intense relationship with death and passing. There was no real attempt to address the hurdles gypsies face in a world that is changing faster than we can keep up with. No Romany role models or success stories were featured. The early episodes centred on Irish travelling families, and I don't think the producers explained the distinction between that group and Romany British gypsies who have lived in the UK for generations. From this show the first gypsy reality TV star emerged, Paddy Docherty. Paddy did move things beyond the stereotypes, and he was more than a match for Sally Bercow, the politician's wife who hitched herself to Paddy's rising celebrity. I read recently that Paddy is suffering with prostate cancer and I wish him a full and speedy recovery. My conclusion, though, is that the media have yet to explore and explain our culture and way of life in a sensible and measured way. Until that happens, better social mobility for gypsies and integration of communities is unlikely to be achieved.

However, in the decade since my book landed on the shelves we have had some break-out personalities that have done more than any mock TV 'documentaries' to win over the public at large. Step forward Tyson Fury and Billy Joe Saunders in the world of boxing. Great achievers with their best years ahead of them. Tyson, particularly, has it in his gift to become the most famous gypsy Englishman ever. Cher Lloyd and Scarlett Lee both had great success on TV's *The X Factor* and have developed singing careers. Mikey Walsh wrote the ground-breaking book *Gypsy Boy* and Alfie Best has excelled in the world of business. I pray that the them-and-us wall that exists between Romany and Gorgio cultures continues to be dismantled steadily by both sides. I think it will. God willing.

The years 2008 and 2009 saw my business develop from a backyard, black economy, father-and-son scrap business into a respectable, legitimate and fast-growing metal trading concern. I realised that in business you can think big or think small. Or in my case think big and stay small. To break out I needed to become fully legitimate and surrender to the ever-growing weight of red tape and regulation so hated by small-business operators everywhere. As is well known also, gypsies, generally, don't do red tape.

I traded in my steel-toe-cap boots for a pair of brogues, donned a suit and tie and hit the road. I met with government departments, councils, customers and suppliers. I wanted to put everything on a firm platform and not have to look over my shoulder. There was a short-to-medium-term financial hit in all this, but my instinct was correct. We were able to ride the tremendous high when scrap prices went through the roof as Chinese consumption drove metal prices skywards and just about weathered the recession when the price came back down to earth. This and a far tougher regulatory regime in our sector were the kiss of death for many unprepared, decades-old scrap businesses. We invested in new regulatory-compliant machinery when times were good. I was firmly set on my new course.

Father And Son

My family and I were enjoying a newfound affluence. Besides wining and dining I stepped up my support of Brentford Football Club, attended the top events in the horse racing calendar and got back into my golf. I was delighted to be invited, along with my son Rymer, now a very promising young player, to become members at the prestigious Buckinghamshire Golf Club, known affectionately as The Bucks. I had come a long way from the distressed young boy being booted out of Home Park for being a gypsy, but I stayed close to my West London roots by playing frequently at Wyke Green Golf Club.

In 2010 Rymer and I played as a team in the prestigious and highly competitive Father and Son Championship tournament in El Rompido in Spain. That year we finished fifth. Rymer played a good game, but I was tired and listless, and I felt I let the side down. I sat down afterwards and analysed my poor form and reached the following conclusion: I was a fat fucker!

Yes, I was carrying far too much weight, and because of my creeping arthritis was no longer able to hammer it in the gym and burn the calories. At least, that is what I believed. I looked around for options and decided to give Weight Watchers a try. I got some odd looks when I attended the first class of, chiefly, overweight women, but they were delightful ladies and seemed to welcome the light relief. The points system operated by the group suited me fine, and I looked forward to the weigh-ins and the approval and encouragement of my new friends as we battled to fight the flab.

Truthfully, I found it easy. Half a stone came off in the first week, and I got a little medal for being slimmer of the month for our region. My class-mates wanted to know how I was doing it. I told them that I no longer drank ten or twelve pints of cider when I went out at the weekend. I substituted that for white wine and soda. I danced whenever I could. Not in Tesco, but in pubs and at parties, and I walked much, much more. The first few bars of a good old song would emanate from the juke box and I'd jump up and dance. It got strange looks, but those calories inside me were screaming – Burn, Baby, Burn.

In a few months I dropped from twenty stone to sixteen. At first people that knew me but did not know about my regime asked if I was all right. What they meant is 'Have you got cancer?' But soon the shock wore off. I was in good nick, feeling strong and ready to go back to El Rompido for the 2011 Father and Son Championship.

We went into the tournament with a determined and disciplined mindset. We were not even drinking caffeine at night let alone alcohol, as we knew a good sleep was paramount. The approach paid dividends and culminated in being the best day of my life in golf. The climactic final day will remain with me until I draw my last breath – and earlier on in the competition I had told Rymer I would die a happy man if we were victorious.

On the last day we were in touch with the leaders but got off to a storming start by carding a four under par front nine to breathe down the necks of the leaders, the Pickfords from Luxembourg and the Carpenters from the USA, who had won the championship in the previous year, both of whom started the day on three under par. Rymer, who was then just seventeen and playing off a handicap of two, then stepped up the pressure by finishing with a beautiful three birdie flourish from the sixteenth hole. He finally rolled in a cool twelve-foot birdie putt on the last and the crowd went mad. It was a sweet moment. One of life's treasured gifts. A father and son joined in love and the sense of shared achievement. Rymer punched the air modestly and I looked skywards hoping my grandfather and Rymer's great-grandfather, to whom he owes his name, was looking down.

Unlike Rymer I couldn't contain myself. I danced a shadow boxing jig and performed a high-five slap with opponent David Mills that near-on removed his arm from the shoulder joint. When they presented us with the trophy on the green Rymer took a sip of champagne, but I lunged for the bottle and necked it to the amusement of the spectators. Be fair, I hadn't touched a drop of alcohol for a week. I made a short (believe it or not) speech to the media who were covering the event: 'This is one of the greatest moments of my life collecting the European Father and Son Golf Championship trophy with my dear son, Rymer. Coming from a gypsy community and from a former career as a bare-knuckle boxer I've had to fight all my life to get respect and acceptance in the elitist golfing world. Well, today I've won the biggest fight of my life and this trophy makes the twenty-eight years of hard work all worth while.'

Back in the room I phoned home. My father came on.

'Dad, we are champions of Europe,' I said.

'You what?'

I recounted joyfully the day's events, and we were both gulping back tears of happiness. Mum the same. Undiluted pride and joy for us Smiths.

Shortly after the euphoria of our European triumph the Smiths delivered again. This time my darling wife Christine gave birth to our new baby son. We named him Aaron after my dad. Also, Rymer reached a scratch handicap and became Club Champion at The Bucks. What could go wrong? I'd soon find out, as my old life was looking like it would rear its ugly head again.

Just The Ticket

Although my golf was good, I had not managed to qualify for the British Open but that did not stop me travelling up to Muirfield as a spectator in 2013. I rang my brother John to see if he was going, and he was already there.

'We have the best digs sorted, bruv, on the harbour at North Berwick. Get yourself up here.'

I was in two minds as I was suffering with gout. And suffering is the right word. Only those in the know will appreciate what I am saying. It is the worst pain I've experienced yet, and I would not wish it on my worst enemy. Why there isn't a network of gout support groups, I don't know. Still, I figured, if I could keep my foot raised and avoid banging it, I should get by.

John was already up there buying and selling tickets. That's what he does. The *Daily Mail* once described him as a 'Britain's leading ticket tout', as if it was some deplorable, nefarious crime. In many cases touts are part of the supply chain – the direct selling arm of the venues or promoters themselves, if you like. How else do you think people like my brother are able to purchase scores or hundreds of tickets at a time? Often tickets are purchased from punters who want rid and are sold on at a profit. It's trading, and most of the time all sides of the transaction are happy, that is why the practice persists.

So, imagine the scene. I'm in the rooms at North Berwick. The others, including John's pals Steve Bradley and Gary Nickells, are at the course, five miles away. I decided to watch the action on the TV after limping down the bookies and placing a myriad of bets. The slips were laid out all over the floor. I am not a habitual betting man, but when my two sports – golf and boxing – are concerned, and especially if I am partaking (albeit via a television set five miles away), I fully immerse myself. The financial tension replaces the adrenalin rush of playing. There is a gentle breeze brushing my face as I have the top half of the stable-type door open to enjoy the weather.

'Hi, mate, is this the fish restaurant?'

Two men and a woman were peering in as they asked this weird question. Did it look like a fucking fish restaurant?

'No, mate.'

I saw their eyes searching the room and knew immediately they were police. Even if they hadn't of been nosing around I'd have known. Those of us who have ever ventured on the wrong side of the law tend to know. The police, for all their skills, have never managed to blend in very well. They can wear T-shirts, bomber jackets and gold chains galore, but it just doesn't look right on them.

I was baffled. I'd nothing to hide. I was a straight businessman and upstanding citizen these days. If my brother and his mates were up to no good they'd never let on where they were staying, so I settled back into my armchair and tuned back into the golf.

But something nagged at me, so I rang my brother's phone and then his mates'. All were switched off. Now I thought something was amiss. This was confirmed a bit later when I had calls from Colin The Claw and Johnny Scarecrow to tell me the boys had been nicked. I know, I know, it's starting to sound like an episode of *Minder* now.

I gathered up the tickets that the boys had left in the house and shoved them up a disused fireplace. Sure enough my visitors were back, unsuccessful in their quest to find the mysterious fish restaurant. This time they were very direct.

'We are here to search these premises and we have a warrant on its way,' said their leader.

I saw no point in resisting, and I said I have not the faintest idea what you are hoping to find, and I invited them to search my room as I knew that, at least, was clean. They alighted on my cash. Quite a lot of it.

'What is this?' asked the female police officer.

'It's cash. Do you not have it in Scotland? We use it down south to buy things. Very useful.'

'I don't think you are in any position to be joking,' said the top man, rather ominously I thought.

The cash was for my spending, buying gifts for my family and for wagering on Phil Mickleson to defeat Tiger Woods, but I thought better of saying anything.

They didn't find anything, and just when I thought they were giving up the leader announced: 'I'm afraid I am placing you under arrest on suspicion of conspiracy to commit fraud.'

'You're joking.'

They wouldn't allow me to gather my belongings or explain anything more. I suggested we go to their police station and sort out this misunderstanding.

I've enjoyed hospitality in a few police station cells in my time, but the one they took me to in Kircaldy was harsh to say the least. In England you can normally count on a bench in the cell and a blanket and on most occasions the offer of a drink. I was shoved into a bare cell and sat on the floor like a dog. Twenty hours passed, and I slept intermittently on the stone floor. Finally, I was given a drink and some food and led to the interview room.

'Mr Smith, can you tell us what you know about these tickets that were purchased by Mr ? and sold to Mr ? at Muirfield yesterday?'

'Look, where did you arrest me?'

'North Berwick.'

'Correct. I have not been to Muirfield, at all. How can I know about any ticket transactions?'

After half an hour of backwards and forwards they stood up and said: 'If you do not co-operate with us we will charge you and remand you to prison.'

This was all getting a bit heavy.

I let my head drop into my hands and took deep breaths. The two detectives sat back down.

'OK, OK,' I said. 'I've been thinking about this and I'm prepared to say something... Can I have a drink of water, please?'

'Of course, Joe.' One jumped up and headed for the door. He came straight back with the water and I took my time sipping it. As I did they moved their chairs closer to mine.

I placed the glass on the table, looked them both in the eyes and said: 'I have nothing further to say.'

That didn't go down well and in hindsight may have been an error. I was under the impression they were bluffing, or incompetent, possibly both and that there was nothing to charge me over.

But they were back in my cell not so long later with my charge sheet. I was to appear at Haddington Magistrates Court on Monday morning. This Scottish legal system was so unlike the English one. I'd never have been charged without evidence at home.

On Monday morning I'm moved from my police cell to a prison van for the journey to the court. Inside the van I am reunited with John, my brother, and his friends. I knew better than to ask any questions. Before I could, anyway, the car radio and BBC Scotland caught my ear. I raised my hand to the others so we could listen.

'Three men are appearing in court this morning having been detained by police investigating the Muirfield Open Ticket Fraud. The men are not local to East Lothian and are thirty-four, forty-seven and fifty-two.' This news item was ahead of a story about the heatwave in Scotland.

Fucking hell! I was feeling the heat now. 'The Muirfield Open Ticket Fraud' – what was all that about? Some touting that I was not even part of had been elevated by the Scots into some sort of Great Train Robbery deal. I had a strong feeling that the press would be outside the court, and I told the others I'd be covering my face.

'I thought you liked publicity, Joe?'

How they could be joking, I don't know. I didn't want my boat race plastered across golfing magazines giving certain people the ammunition to shoot me down after years of trying to win acceptance in the sport. And, also, I was innocent of any wrongdoing.

Gary 'The Burger' Nickells decided to do the same thing. Not sure who he was protecting his identity from, but it backfired when, as he stepped down from the van, he missed his footing and fell straight into the arms of waiting photographers leaving me a route through and able to remain incognito.

In the holding cell below the court the gaoler, who politely introduced himself as Gary The Gaoler, asked if he could have my autograph, which threw me.

'You a golf fan, Gary?'

'No, Joe. I read all the hard-men books. I've read your one. Great book.'

'Well, thank you. I'll sign something when I get out later.'

Gary The Gaoler frowned. 'I'm sorry, Joe, but you'll be lucky to walk today, I'm afraid.'

And Gary was dead right. We were taken up to face the Sheriff, and without any further ado he remanded us into custody for one week at Edinburgh Prison pending further police enquiries into the crime of the century.

Saughton Prison has a formidable reputation, even down in England. Along with Barlinnie and Carstairs it is a Scottish name that resonates among criminals and not a place where Englishmen would feel entirely comfortable.

The first prison officer I engaged with addressed me as if he were Mr Mackay from *Porridge*. So, I responded as if I was Ronnie Barker in full Fletcher mode.

'Here they are,' he announced, 'the rip-off laddies from London. Selling people dodgy tickets.'

'Are you serious, mate?' I said. 'This place is full of murderers, junkies and thieves and you're excited about some unofficial tickets being flogged?'

He sniffed and stood up on tiptoes, hands clasped behind his back. 'Well, I would not have been very happy if I'd bought one.'

'You didn't, though, did you?'

Officer Mackay backed down after that and for whatever reason became almost apologetic.

However, Mackay was likely to be the least of our worries. We were, on the surface, Jack the lads, cockneys and gypsies being parachuted into a volatile, close-knit Scottish criminal community.

On the second day we were sitting around, us three, carefully minding our own business when we were approached by a Scottish gypsy man. He addressed my brother.

'Are you John Smith?' he asked.

John nodded.

'Big John Smith from London?'

John is about six feet eight inches tall and twenty-six stone, so that question didn't really warrant a reply.

'I've been looking for you for years,' he said.

I'm not very pleased with the way this is developing and new from experience that in an enclosed space, in a possibly hostile prison, to show weakness could mean our remaining six days would be very dangerous indeed.

Still handicapped by the pain from my gout I looked straight at him but kept my body language very still. It's a fine balance between holding your own and escalating a situation.

'Well, mate, you've found him. He's sitting there a foot away from you. What you going to do?'

The gypsy lad then broke into a broad smile. 'Och, I was only winding you up. It's a joke, bruv.'

Personally, I don't think it was. Our friend here was trying to earn some brownie points. He was banking on us backing off and him climbing the ladder in the prison hierarchy.

Later an altogether more genuine gypsy guy, Tom Henry, introduced himself.

'I've heard of you lads – the Stockins and the Smiths. As far as I'm concerned, we're cousins. Anything I can sort you boys? Money, clothes?'

That was more like it. We politely declined Tom's kind offer because John had a mate on the outside, Stuart Wiermouth, who was co-ordinating the essentials behind the scenes.

I had tried to get some bail sorted out but was rebuffed, being told that the security bail system was different north of the border. I spoke to my wife, Christine, on the phone, and despite the predicament I was in we couldn't stop laughing at the ridiculousness of it all.

'I should be home by Christmas,' I told her.

At one of our meal times the guy serving was reprimanded because he gave Big John a big portion when all prisoners were supposed to be served equally.

'How the fuck am I supposed to give that eight-stone smackhead the same amount of grub as this man,' remonstrated the prisoner. 'This man wants drugs. This man wants food and lots of it.'

We all laughed.

Back in court for the third time common sense finally prevailed. Witnesses had been found who had seen me limping to the betting shop, and it was proved I had been nowhere near Muirfield.

'My client was simply on holiday and has found himself incarcerated in prison,' concluded my brief.

After further negotiation between the brief and the bench my brother and his friends pleaded guilty to a £90 fraud charge, and all were released with a small fine to pay. We decided not to explore the delights of North Berwick, or even Edinburgh Castle and the Royal Mile, and headed south before we could be re-arrested on suspicion of bagpipe theft.

Shortly after I was arrested for a second time. About thirty police officers arrived at my yard. They had a warrant and were acting on 'information received'. They found some cable with Virgin Media stamped on it.

'This is stolen,' one declared. Happy with this booty, they told me the warrant extended to my house, and we travelled there and now they found some cash. A few thousand pounds at most. I was taken down to the local police station read my rights and charged with receiving stolen goods and money laundering.

Fancying a stab at being Rumpole Of The Bailey I defended myself in court. I was very confident and was not going to miss the opportunity of showing the police officers up for being prejudiced and incompetent. Virgin Media confirmed to the court that the cabling was worthless beyond recycling value and I had acquired it legally. I explained to the judge that the nature of the scrap business involves the ability to be able to purchase material at short notice and for cash. I proved that cash purchases were being recorded and declared. I provided further confirmation that my taxes were paid and in order.

The judge was straight down the line when he addressed the court, and specifically the police.

'Mr Smith has attended court today armed with evidence and information to support his case that he is innocent. You have attended court with no credible evidence to support your case that he is guilty. May I suggest in future that you assemble a credible case before charging your target. And I use the word target quite deliberately. I believe that Mr Smith was targeted, for whatever reason, without any supporting evidence. I cannot help but wonder if there are better uses of police time.'

Soon after this case, new legislation was introduced that meant cash could not be used in scrap metal transactions and stringent identification rules had to be met. It meant a difficult transition, and I wondered why casinos or supermarkets were not subject to similar rules, but, ultimately, I welcomed the change. Scrap was now a fully legitimate business. I was hoping I could now build and expand a transparent business that perhaps could one day be sold to a bigger concern.

I was fully vindicated, but both these episodes demonstrate how difficult it can be to stay on the right side of the law even after one has led a straight and honourable life for several years.

Son And Father

It was on the way to the funeral of a cousin that I got one of those phone calls that hits you like a blow to the solar plexus and sometimes means life will never be the same again. My sister Maria called and said that Dad had undergone a routine blood test and the doctors had found an abnormality. Shortly after we were invited to West Middlesex Hospital, the place of my birth and the place that saved my dad's infant life when he had been stricken with meningitis, to discuss with him the diagnosis of that blood test and further investigation.

We all knew it was bad news. You don't invite the family in to tell them the patient is as fit as a fiddle. We just hoped there was a condition that could be cured or, at worst, managed. A very tall doctor in his late fifties sat us down and remained expressionless as he began to ask some questions. Had Dad worked with asbestos? Had Dad ever smoked?

'Yes,' said Dad.

'And when did you stop?'

'About ten past one,' Dad replied, and we all laughed, but the po-faced doctor was not even smiling.

Then the doctor delivered the worst news. I know it's his job and he has had to communicate these awful tidings many, many times, but we all felt he could have been gentler and more sympathetic.

'Mr Smith has cancer in his lungs and liver, I'm afraid to inform you.'

It was the opening shot of a heart-breaking and traumatic final journey for the old man and his beloved family.

At a later appointment I was with him, and something that was said made me cry. I dropped my head so he wouldn't see, but he had clocked it. From his chair he stuck his lovely old thumb up.

'Don't worry, son. I'm not the first man to get this and I won't be the last. It'll be all right.'

That was the measure of the man. His life was ebbing away, and he was undergoing all sorts of invasive tests and enduring the most debilitating treatments, but his first thoughts were for us, his family.

I had a golf tournament booked which I honoured. But on my return Dad had taken a turn for the worse and I decided to leave the family home and move in with my parents and give my mum the help she needed as Dad's illness demanded more and more care. My wonderful wife was, as always, fully supportive.

Watching close up my big strong Daddy weaken every day was the most painful experience, but I am so glad to have had those precious hours, days and weeks with him. The feeling of helplessness tore me apart. I couldn't grab his disease by the throat and fuck it off out of it. I couldn't reason with it. It's a horrible, one-sided battle, and it jars me when people talk about losing the fight to cancer or winning the battle like it's a competition.

Dad was so brave. He'd call me up to his room in the morning to help him dress and get ready, for, unbelievably, this courageous, loyal man was still going to work as the illness ravaged his body. He wanted to see his clients, some of whom he had been serving for forty-five years or more. He regarded them as close friends and they him.

On Sunday 7th September 2014, following a family conference, I was persuaded that my helping my mum was not enough to give Dad the care he needed and we all agreed we would admit him to hospital. Poor man felt every bump and pothole as we drove him. In his prime Dad was a six-foot-two-inch man carrying sixteen stone. He protected, nurtured and nourished me as a little boy, and now it was me in my prime, yet I could not do the same for him. I felt distraught and powerless as the chain of events raced ahead. At the hospital the doctors confirmed we were correct to pass Dad into their care. They said his life expectancy was now being measured in days.

His last surviving uncle, Jukebox, came to visit. Jukebox was a link to a Romany life and a life Dad and he had lived that already was unimaginable, faded into a past that survives only in old and rare photographs. Jukebox stood by the bed and sang 'Smile' by Nat King Cole: 'Smile, though your heart is aching'. It was a sweet moment. Dad could not respond. He was too weak. But a smile twitched on his dry lips.

The medical team expressed astonishment as Dad survived beyond the forty-eight hours they had estimated. September was Dad's favourite month. It was the main hop-picking month, and those hard-working, hard-drinking and hard-playing days among the vines and bushels of Kent were his best of times. He also loved his real ale and especially Young's who like him were proud of their south-west-London roots.

On Sunday 14th September I gave Dad his last sip of Young's. There were thirty or forty family members gathered around his bed. At around 10.30pm, as they were calling last orders in pubs around the country, Dad took his final breaths. I shouted his name loudly, and we could see he tried to speak. The words were in his mouth, but he was unable to form them. Had he of spoken he would have said 'See ya' and 'Look after yourselves' because even now in these final seconds on earth he'd have been worried about how *we* were.

When it was clear Dad had passed, I roared like a lion and continued to do so for what seemed like minutes. I make no apologies and had not intended to do so. It just happened like a balloon rapidly deflating. All the frustrations, the fears, the misery, the regrets and the pain came rushing out, and I am glad it did because I became completely calm when I was done.

I leant over and kissed my daddy's forehead. We would not be walking the fairway together at the British Open as we had both dreamt and discussed. But we chased that dream. We tried. Boy, did we try. We tried to conquer his wretched illness. We tried, we fucking tried. But, we will walk a fairway together. I know we will meet again and in the scheme of things – ten, twenty, thirty, forty or fifty years is a blink. A mere blink.

Dad's funeral was a big occasion. The local paper reported that upwards of eight hundred people followed his coffin from the house to the church. People had come from all over the country to pay their respects to dear modest, humble, decent Aaron Smith. Graveside in Hounslow, the equivalent of a mid-week Fulham FC home crowd toasted him with cans of Guinness and John Smith's – even the vicar joined in. Dad's requested song, Queen's

'The Show Must Go On', blared out, stirring every other resting soul in the entire graveyard. Aaron Smith, our great dad, had arrived.

Final Round

I eased my sadness at Dad's passing by throwing myself into the purchase and development of my dream house. Christine and I found a property that suited our needs and had the space and foundations to remodel it how we wanted. It had a spacious garden for the children to play in and room for the gym and bar I always fancied. If I got fed up or down I could storm off down the pub and it was just out the back door. As a rule, I was the only punter – but I don't mind my own company.

At work the trials and tribulations continued apace. The council served me papers to move premises claiming our yard was on Green Belt land. Maybe it was, but the council had never raised this before and had been happily taking business rates from me for ten years. At the same time the scrap business was sinking into another recession. I was battling officialdom again, struggling to keep the business afloat and project managing the redevelopment of my house (I had no choice; others were spending my money like water) with money that was becoming more and more elusive. I started drinking a lot of red wine.

Alcohol has it uses. It can ignite parties and social gatherings. It can encourage people to do outrageous things which can be quite funny at the time, but one thing it most certainly cannot do is make problems disappear. I decided that I needed something else to take my mind off my woes. Then it came to me – I'd fight again.

Christine was not thrilled by the idea. It was ten years since I last fought, and I was now in my forty-fifth year and she worried I'd get hurt, but my mind was made up. I got training and started sparring with my old pal and former professional boxer George Carmen. It was soon apparent that age had caught up with me and my former style of dancing and moving quickly around the ring was no longer an option. I had to stand and trade, and I found I wasn't bad at that.

I moved on to training and sparring with Queensbury League boxers under the auspices of Ross Minter, former world title challenger and son of legendary Middle Weight World Champion Alan Minter. Soon I was ready to fight in a bona-fide competitive match.

My opponent was to be a man called Dan Lovett. Dan was a veteran of the unlicensed scene having fought 119 times. He was known as a tough and unforgiving fighter who topped eighteen stone. From North London he had massive support. Dan had announced his retirement and intention to become a referee. It goes without saying he'd be wanting to bow out on a convincing win.

The fight was being staged at the good old Circus Tavern in Rainham, Essex. Alan Mortlock was the promoter. The phrase spit and sawdust could have been originally describing this place. The atmosphere was visceral and confrontational and that was just the crowd. In my corner was my son Rymer and Trevor 'Scrappa' Smith, who I had raised from the age of eight (him, not me). As we exchanged final words of encouragement I told the boys I would box Dan's ears off and knock him out. I felt supremely confident.

My plan was to tire Dan out, or let him tire himself out, and then finish him when the tank was empty. I think I executed this well as I ambled around the ring forcing Dan to follow me. I let him push me to the ropes, and inevitably we spent some time grappling each other. All the time I was landing some punches to help me towards a points win should I need it. It probably wasn't the best entertainment and the crowd were becoming frustrated, and I think Dan felt the pressure to turn the fight. Even the referee Mark Potter, a former British Heavyweight title challenger, urged us to get on with it.

Dan's frustration got the better of him when he came at me hands down. I landed a peach of a punch on his chin that shuddered his body from head to toe. I moved in to cement my advantage, but the bell rang. Turning to my corner with my hands down I walked away with my back to Dan. The effect of the punch may have scrambled him a bit because he launched an after-the-bell attack on me. My corner boys, alarmed by the turn of events, jumped into the ring and threw punches back at Dan. It was one of those explosive moments in a boxing match when the violence can spill over into the crowd, but thankfully Mark Potter somehow calmed it down and soon we were back out for the final round.

Dan was in a dangerous mood and I was worried. I knew if I made one slip-up he'd show no mercy whatsoever. I slipped one of his punches and managed a left hook to his body which sent him through the middle ropes and into the dining table of some VIP spectators. The clock was running down, and I welcomed the bell when it came. It was a split decision, but I was the points winner.

Dan was gracious in defeat and came into my dressing room.

'Joe, I don't know what came over me. I have never fought dirty in all my fights.'

'I know what came over you, Dan. I goaded you and frustrated you to the point you lost your self-control. That was my plan, mate. The difference on the night was that I could see your cards, but you couldn't see mine.'

'Yes, mate. I give you that. You outfoxed me.'

We smiled at one another and slapped backs.

I was pleased with some of the comments I saw online. One ex-boxer wrote: 'Whatever Smith has lost to Father Time, he certainly has kept his ring craft intact.'

Alan Mortlock arranged another couple of fights of me. One pulled out and the other I turned down because I could not study my would-be opponent. I was confident but not completely stupid. Then Alan told me about a fighter from Bristol who, at forty-nine, was even older than me and unbeaten. It was his dream to fight at the York Hall in Bethnal Green – the pinnacle of a hard, long career. York Hall has a special place in boxing and a unique atmosphere. It's in a part of London that is rough, and the Kray Twins and Freddie Foreman were among the very hard men who have fought there. Boxing, it is often said, has often walked side by side with villains and gangsters, and if that is true then York Hall captures that mix well.

But I decided to use this fight to make a stand against violence and encourage youngsters away from the streets and a life of crime. At the weigh-in there was a man raising money for a charity in the name of a young boy who had been stabbed to death. I told the man I would use the fight to raise awareness. I decided there and then that this would be my last fight. It felt right as Rymer, my son, had fought earlier on the same bill and had achieved a good points win.

I told the promoter that if the old boy is good enough to bash me up then I was prepared for war, but if I had the better of him I would not be taking any liberties and I will ensure he gets through to the end of the fight and that if I was the clear winner I wanted the referee to call it a draw. I told the promoter to tell the ref, however far ahead I am (if indeed I am), to raise both hands at the end. A plan had formed in my head.

I entered the ring to the dramatic music of *The Sweeney*, the iconic 1970s police TV show and wearing a balaclava. The crowd were confused and amused. As I hoped, although the Bristolian man was a unit, big and strong, I was able to outbox him comfortably. I danced around him peppering him with good punches, well pulled. When the final bell rang I walked over and raised my opponent's hand along with my own. Referee Wayne Alexander declared a draw.

I took the opportunity to grab the microphone and spoke to the crowd. I had my balaclava in my hand.

'See this nonsense,' I said, 'this balaclava. This is rubbish. All you youngsters you need to throw these things away and replace with sport. You will never regret it.' I dramatically tossed the balaclava away. Hopefully my theatrics raised a little more money for the charity in the name of the tragic boy that was stabbed to death and, you never know, it may have made someone in that crowd think twice. I hope so.

Back in my dressing room *Get West London* interviewed me.

'What's next, Joe?'

'Nothing, mate. That's it now. My boxing career is over. I've never hit the canvas or the floor, and I've fought and sparred with some good men. I'm quitting while I'm ahead. Goodbye boxing and thanks for the memories.

I'm A Believer

Around this time, I surrendered my professional status as a golfer and went amateur so I would be able to play more. I was delighted when me and my team consisting of Alan Feltham, Roy Thomas and Andy Parker played in a pro-am tournament in Mar Menor in Spain. I won the individual contest with scores of sixty-nine, seventy-one, seventy-seven, which boosted me no end. I was playing out my skin and feeling chilled. However, my relaxed state of mind was soon to be shattered.

In March 2018 I was enjoying my daily phone call with Mum. We would have a chat and wind each other up a bit. Then I realised she was not replying. I thought perhaps she'd left me jabbering while she had moved across the kitchen to make a sandwich. That was well within possibility. Then I could hear my niece saying 'Gran, Gran, you OK?' and the panic in her voice alarmed me. My other niece picked up the phone and said she thought Mum was having a stroke.

Without further ado Rymer and I jumped in his car and sped at breakneck speed from Denham to Mum's place in Hounslow. Adrenalin and a nippy BMW carried us across in record time. When we arrived it was clear she had had a stroke, and although an ambulance had been called I put her in the adapted van my sister-in-law Mandy has for their disabled niece Anna Marie and charged off again to the West Middlesex Hospital. I'm no medical expert, but it had been drummed into us on the television and elsewhere that in stroke situations time is of the essence. Receiving treatment can be the difference between recovery and a lifetime of disability – and that's if the patient survives.

At the West Middlesex I banged on the doors frantically, and thankfully Mum was admitted and treated. She was then dispatched in another ambulance to the Charing Cross Hospital in Hammersmith. Mum was responding and seemed to have her memory intact. The family breathed a massive sigh of relief.

Alas, the relief was short-lived. The next day Mum suffered a heart attack and then, following a rally, another. The doctors informed us that her condition was now 'critical'. How did it come to this? Mum was not old. She was as strong as an ox. We were coming to terms with losing Dad. This could not be happening. But, it was.

Visitors surrounded her beside all willing her to recover. And she fought like a warrior. If I thought my fighting spirit came from my dad only, Mum's courage and sheer stamina at the end was a lesson. She had the heart of a lion. She did not want to leave her beloved family and friends.

Me and my brothers and one of Mum's brothers were strolling alongside the Thames, allowing other visitors to share her moments bedside when the phone rang. She's going, we were told. We charged back to the hospital like men possessed. Bursting into the room I ran up and laid my head on Mum's chest, crying her name. Just like when I was a little boy. Her little boy. I looked up at her face and she gently closed those beautiful blue eyes for the last time and the machines that she was linked up to stopped beeping and flashing. The room went quiet save for sobbing. Big, loud sobs emanating from deep inside all of us as one.

Mum's funeral was a send-off and a half. Not far off a thousand people came to the house and followed the coffin to the church to pay their respects and remember their friend and loved one. My sisters and nieces captured her personality beautifully by putting together a tape of Mum in her own environment at the kitchen table talking, joking, taking the mickey. Mum being Mum. It had the mourners laughing and giggling. Mum was running this funeral, make no mistake.

I spoke at the funeral, something I was determined to do. I feared breaking down, but I felt Mum behind me telling me to get on with it. That day the sheer, gut-wrenching grief that I had felt since she died was gently replaced by a happiness. A thankfulness that took over. I felt blessed that I had had Mum and Dad in my life, and from then on the good memories and the love and laughs replaced those dark final days. It's a glorious feeling. When I think of Mum and Dad now I celebrate their lives and what they did for us.

Just three months of Mum's passing we lost baby Jimmy. He was my niece Stephanie's brave little twin. He was born with a faulty heart and finally succumbed to it. Doctors were gobsmacked at the fight the little fella waged. His lovely little grave is just behind Mum and Dad's. I remember at little Jimmy's funeral looking at the picture of Dad surrounded by beer bottles, smiling, at ease with the world and thinking how quickly it all changes. The fragility of it all! My adopted son Trevor had had a child by now, and soon Rymer and his wife gave birth to Skyla, so becoming a grandfather also contributed to this growing awareness of the cycle of life. This awareness deepened my religious awakening.

I don't go on about being a Christian. It's not something I feel the need to push on others. You won't find me at Fontwell Park standing on an upturned crate shouting at drunken punters about how much Jesus loves them. But it gives me comfort and I am glad for it.

The religious awakening happened in 1994. Don't lob this book across the room yet, thinking I've gone off my nut. Hear me out. My gran, Ria, had died, but she was still with us in the coffin, in the house, before she was to be buried as is a gypsy custom. In fact, it used to be a Christian custom – being traditionalists, we've kept it up. Aaron, my brother, and I were alone with Ria holding a hand each. We were cut up real bad as we were very close to our gran. The room was dimly lit with some crosses and candles burning in one corner. There was also a statue of Jesus that belonged to Ria. She had experienced an out-of-body experience when she was about thirty-five and quite unwell. From then on, she was an avid follower of Jesus.

When Aaron and I left the room, I stepped quickly into the corner on impulse and kissed the Jesus statue on the forehead.

'Please, Jesus, look after my gran. She loved and worshipped you.'

As I turned and left the room my steps were slightly unsteady. A warm glow enveloped me. I felt like I had been taken into a beautiful embrace. It was a feeling I had never had before or since. My tears of sadness turned into tears of joy. I knew without any doubt that my beloved gran *was* in good hands, *was* going to be looked after. The high I was experiencing from tip to toe was so intense and surpassed any high or emotion I had felt before whether it be in my personal or sporting life. It was what the word beautiful was made for.

My partner on this book, Martin Knight, told me of a similar experience. Perhaps not religious but indicative that these things happen. Martin's father died, and they were very close, and Martin was understandably very sad and down. However, he said, he never really cried and didn't deal with it very well.

One day, a few years later, he had a dream, but as he says dreams are not dreams when you are having them, they are real. They only become dreams when you wake up. In the 'dream' his father came in from work as he did when Martin was a teenager. Martin described his clothes and even the pen in his breast pocket. His dad took him in his arms and hugged him.

Back outside the dream, as Martin's wife Val will testify, he sat upright in bed and cried aloud huge great sobs and she had to calm him. Then Martin was fine as he remembered the dream. He is convinced that his father came to him that night, knowing he was unresolved and unhappy, and told him not to worry. Dad was all right and Martin should be happy. Martin says, and I believe him, that from that day he has perfect peace about his father and just remembers his life positively and looks forward to reuniting.

I am not a poet or a classical writer. I can't write songs. So I cannot adequately convey what happened in those few minutes, but it happened, and it changed my life. Why should I not tell you? I don't want to preach, but I say to you give it a chance. Open your mind and your heart and, you never know, you might experience something like I did. When it happens it's so real that doubt is banished from your thinking. Take the plunge and walk into a church and have a chat with someone. Half an hour out of your life and it may enrich however long you have left on this earth. Half an hour? If nothing changes what have you lost? Trust me, you're going to meet nicer, more interesting people in a church than you will in a pub toilet bending over a shithole sniffing cocaine off the window sill.

It pains me to see how this drug has entered the mainstream. What does it do? Makes you talk bollocks, that's about the strength of it. Under what circumstances would you normally go into the cubicles of a public toilet with another man? We simply don't think anything of it now, do we? Have a livener? It's a deadener. Cocaine is no livener. Slowly but surely it will ruin you. Be yourself. You don't need that shit. And, although much of my life has been involved with and around violence, my advice is to keep away from it. Nothing good comes from it.

I feel so strongly about how young lives are being wasted, destroyed and blighted by drugs, violence and crime. The three are inter-linked, and I despair how this depressing cycle repeats itself generation after generation. I see it in my community now, but I see it all over. I have spoken in schools to young people in the hope that I can demonstrate that whatever your beginnings, whatever your race or religion, whatever your financial foundations, there is hope. There are opportunities, and if you work at it you can succeed, you can flourish.

It saddens me that more people who have made it with a working-class or inner-city background have not given back more. With a few notable exceptions, few professional footballers, boxers, pop and film stars and athletes, for example, devote much of their time, wealth and life experience to help those they left behind. Years ago the singer Frankie Vaughan set a great example by donating loads of time and money to the boys' club movement.

Life is a gift. It's a wonderful gift and we should treasure it and maximise the pleasures it has to offer and minimise the miseries. If you are a man find a good woman. Try not to fall in love with a lady who gives you sex before you've hung your coat up because if she gives it to you so easily she is likely to do the same to somebody else. Therein lies grief.

I have been so lucky with my lovely wife Chris. We have our ups and downs – we'd be strange if we didn't – but our love deepens as we age. My children have all been a delight. Rymer and Trevor have joined me in this book, but my younger sons Aaron and Joe Junior have great futures ahead of them with both showing flair in sport. I won't risk ruining things for them by making any predictions here, but I think both will achieve big things in sport and life. And my darling girls Christina and Louie. Christina is already out there working in an office and I think Louie will follow her. They are beautiful, feisty blonde girls and I love them deeply and dearly.

Thank you for reading my book and indulging me in bringing it up to date. I hope it has entertained you. Whatever you do, whether sporting or not, box clever – and, above all, enjoy yourself.

Covid

If I had a pound for each time somebody said to me, 'I bet you preferred golf to bare-knuckle fighting. Bollocks to that. A gentle round of golf or getting your head punched in? No contest,' they'd say. If I had, I could have paid my mortgage off early. But throughout all the scrapping years the worst that ever happened to me was a couple of broken bones and some cuts and bruises, and it was when the blood flowed and the bruises swelled that I experienced some of the best adrenalin rushes imaginable. Hard to believe, but I, like many fighters, got off on the pain and grit. I'd gone from a boy who wanted to play to standing in a ring, at times fighting for my life, and to do this you are swimming in adrenalin. It's a buzz like no other.

However, if I told you that it was a gentle round of golf that nearly killed me just recently, would you believe me? Late last year I played a round of doubles with friends John Black, Matthew Ball and Jimmy Hearn. I played OK. Broke par. Won the game. Gentle fist pump. Happy days. Next morning I get a call from Matthew. He says that John Black has tested positive for Covid. I was not too fussed. I felt well. John seemed well on the course. A few days later I woke up at 3am in my bed with a cold on my chest, so I switched on a heater. I had all the symptoms of a cold, but two days in thought it sensible to take a Covid test. I was positive. I didn't panic. I was not at that dangerous age. Fairly fit. No underlying conditions I knew of.

Almost on cue, six days on from my first symptoms I began to feel really unwell. Really, really unwell. I couldn't move. My temperature hit 41, and, although I was loath to take that scary step, on Christmas Eve I went into hospital. They sent me for an X-ray and delivered the shocking news that I had severe double pneumonia on both lungs. They didn't say I was going to die, but neither did they say don't worry, you'll live. I thought this could be it. I wasn't going to see my fiftieth birthday – and then I thought about my wife, my kids and grandkids. They were distraught and they couldn't even visit because of Covid. If this was curtains, they were going to be pulled around me all alone. It was a bleak prospect. I sat on the bed and decided that even if the doctor said there was nothing they could do for me I would walk the three miles home and fight it there. I wanted to reach into my chest and rip the pneumonia out with my bare hands. A doctor came, and before he could speak I said, 'Tell me what I need to do. I cannot lose this battle!' and he replied calmly that they would put me on the Covid ward and that the next few days would determine my fate. I'd either rally or sink. I felt like a man wandering, battered and bruised, through a war-torn town, snipers holed up ready to shoot me down.

On the ward I met a nice man named Alan Green. He was opposite, arrived at the same time with all the same readings. He was local, and we talked football and other things. Each morning the nurses came and took our oxygen levels. Every now and then some poor bugger was told it had deteriorated, and they were taken off to be attached to a ventilator. Their chances of survival suddenly diminishing. There was a feeling of dread when they tested you. After three or four days my readings started to improve, and I knew they were because I started to feel better, but Alan's, sadly, were worsening. On New Year's Eve they let me go home, and I said goodbye to him. 'We'll have a drink on the outside,' I said.

My cousin and best pal Johnny Fagan rang me. 'Boy, I'm so proud of you. That was a result.'

'Too right, cuz – but you don't sound too good yourself.'

Johnny's voice was rasping a bit, and I advised him to get to hospital. He waited fourteen hours for an ambulance. Covid was confirmed when he got there. I was now the concerned friend, our roles suddenly reversed. I texted him and Alan every day as neither were up to talking. Then I stopped getting texts from Alan, and I feared the worst. This was confirmed by a call from his daughter a couple of days later. I only knew the man a few days, but I learned in that short time he was a good man.

Covid robbed us of Johnny Fagan on 22 January 2021. He was the most kind-hearted man and the best friend I ever had. He was in his seventies, and I looked upon him as a father and my children idolised him as a grandfather. But, most of all, he was a true and loyal friend. What he had he would willingly give, and I don't mean money. I say to Johnny I will see you up there, but I ain't rushing – and in the meantime: Alan meet Johnny; Johnny meet Alan.

Many years ago there was a series about nurses on the telly called *Angels*. I never really thought about the title, but I do now. I, we, all of us were cared for by nurses who were not only doing what they do but taking the place of families and loved ones in what, in many cases, were the final weeks, days, hours and minutes of our lives. They were surrounded by death and despair but managed to dispense love and comfort. I thank each and every one of you.

Joe Smith
Summer 2021

APPENDIX 1

THE SMITHS – MY TRIBUTE

Trevor is my stepson. He is a keen golfer but can also turn his hand to darts, football and boxing and is no slouch at any, but his real interest is running our scrap-metal yard. He is keen and everyone loves Trevor at work and his competence and enthusiasm allows me to pursue my golfing ambitions. Trevor and I have not always seen eye to eye and the boy had been dealt a poor hand in life, but we got through all that and I am as proud of him as any of my children that I fathered in the biological sense.

My son, Rymer John Daly, is a chip off the old block. He loves to compete at everything he does and he does it all well. Golf, boxing, football, rugby, pool, snooker, darts, tennis, you name it. He has had a couple of competitive boxing contests and did pretty well. This is not the sport I want him to take up, but thankfully he prefers his football and golf. When Rymer was from seven to ten years old he was nothing short of exceptional as a football player, but if I am to be totally honest his form dipped due to his reaction time and pace which has let him down yet his desire is still very much there and he is never afraid to put the work in, so I say all the time if you are enjoying yourself, then keep playing. As for his golf, he has a great mental attitude. He also plays his best on the occasion: a great thing to have in your armoury. One of my friends, Derrick Westly, has already placed money on him to be better than myself and achieve more in golf. Rymer and I have a special bond. We do everything together and are great mates. Just like his namesake, Grandfather Rymer and I, many years before.

When Christina Maria my eldest daughter was born my wife was so excited that she now had her little girl and was yearning to dress her up and show her off. Gypsy mums love their little girls and parading them. At one year old her baby beauty queen had no teeth, bright carrot-topped hair and you could not get a ring in her ear. A gypsy girl without an earring? Sacrilege! I would tease my wife that her angel would not be winning any baby competitions and she responded that any bad looks had been inherited from me. But just like the Ugly Duckling her hair went a stunning downy white, teeth appeared and lobes developed on her ears. She's now a darling. Knows how to work me. She's a Brentford fan and I take her to the odd game. At Griffin Park most of the games are odd. She has hit the occasional golf ball too but her sporting talent lies in running. My wife was a 1,500-metres Middlesex champion and little Christina looks like emulating her. Her school teacher tells us that she has a natural aptitude with a pen and paper and that is encouraging. She's a great kid.

The next one down is Louisa Mary Maria. I look at her and laugh. She's very much like me. If there was a sporting event in eating she'd be a champion. When I wander down to breakfast I sometimes have to break up a ruck as Louisa has eaten hers and decided to demolish Christina's as well. Food seems to be the most important thing in her life. When I asked her what her first full day at school was like, she said: 'Dad, I had dinner today and I liked it.' I love her so much.

Finally is our baby Joseph who as I have mentioned earlier has the longest name recorded at Uxbridge Register Office. At two-years-old we have not got a sport for him yet but I am sure he will not need too much pushing. Already he tries to take a swing of the golf club. I must say not on par with Tiger Woods who at the same age was embarrassing Bob Hope at putting. He's into everything. I'm looking forward to standing on the touchline on a frosty morning watching him play football. Joke. He's our baby and I say, finally, though he might not always be because I still like to practise making them when I am allowed.

And that brings me nicely to my wife Christine. She is down to earth and forever supporting the underdog. She is kind, thoughtful and soft-hearted but if someone upsets her she is a different animal or should I just say an animal? Recently I was playing golf in Paris trying to qualify for the French Open and after playing my practice round I rang home to discover that Christine had intervened between two women from around the corner, one who she felt was picking on the other. The younger woman turned on my wife for her trouble and Christina just flipped. She broke her nose and knocked her teeth out and the woman left the scene in an ambulance. When I returned my neighbour told me that she could not believe that someone my wife's size could dish out such a beating to such a bigger person. I used to think that other women never made a pass at me because I was ugly, but now I know that it is because they are frightened of her and I am a handsome bastard after all. We've had our ups and downs but what couples do not? Especially with five kids wrapped around you day and night. But she has remained loving, supportive and patient. And after bearing four children she is still as slim and sexy as ever. I am a lucky man and I could not wish for a better wife.

I would like to mention all of my family and friends here in this book, but it would extend to several hundred pages if I did yet I have to mention my Gorgio friend Bernie Watson. He was a great man and a great friend. He spoke his mind and I remember once when he said: 'I fucking hated gypsies till I got to know you and your family.' He died in a tragic accident and his wife Mandy asked me to be a pall-bearer at his funeral which I was delighted to do. He was a Brentford Football Club nut and I look forward to seeing him in heaven (I hope) and him waiting there with a pint of Guinness.

APPENDIX 2

IT'S NOT THAT MUCH DIFFERENT BEING...

A GOLF PRO	A BARE-KNUCKLE FIGHTER
I walk to the first tee and I think: 'Here we go again.'	I walk down the middle of a gypsy site to see a crowd of people and I think: 'Here we go again.'
Then I meet my playing partners and the starter says: 'It's nearly time lads.' I free myself up as best I can. A last few warm-up swings and a few deep breaths. With the adrenalin flowing, I am a bag of nerves, just as I was the very first time I played competitively, aged 12. But the only difference now is I have the experience to handle it. 'Match 14 on the tee Joe Smith.' Bang, I am doing battle.	I meet the fair-play man. 'OK then lads, when you are ready.' I shake myself down some last few warm-up punches. Some deep breaths trying to control what is a huge adrenalin burst. Then shitting myself. I hope I am going to win this one. 'Come on lads, let's go.' Time for one last thought, you are going to have to fucking kill me to beat me, then bang! I am doing battle.
When I am playing well it suddenly seems easy. I am two or three under, swinging well, putting well and even when I miss the odd green I feel great, then bang. I should never disrespect a golf course when a treble bogey almost brings me to my knees. Suddenly I am just another golfer.	I start to fight – jab, jab, double jab, right cross, right to the body, left hook to the head; everything is flowing and is going so right. I am like Sugar Ray Leonard, dropping my hands, chin in the air and this poor man in front of me is bleeding badly and he is a warrior and is desperate to pull something out of the bag. Low hands and a high chin, he senses something, then smack, from nowhere he throws a desperate one that everyone sees coming, except me,

I start a round with a three-putt bogey, hit a drive into the trees, another bogey follows. I hit my iron shot in the water. I am four over par. I mishit my drive on the fourth tee and think: 'What the fuck am I doing here?' The easy route always crosses my mind. 'Let's pick the ball up and go straight to the bar,' and then the other half of me says: 'I have travelled a thousand miles to play here and I want to make it easy for the rest of the field? They are hard enough to beat as it is, without me making it easy for them by quitting.

Suddenly I find myself talking to myself. When I was a kid and saw someone talking to themselves, I would have thought that person was a nutcase. Then I make my first four-footer for par, back to basics on every swing, evenly putt every chip, every bunker shot, I know this is not my day and I have to dig as deep as I possibly can. I will not break. I am hoping to pull something from my socks. I need to play a fancy lob shot to try and make a birdie but I know my play is not flowing.

Then a conservative punch and spin shot to within 20 feet, lag my putt and take my par. Suddenly I hit a seven-iron – a bit smelly, it's going towards the pin and the bunker, it takes a decent bounce towards the hole. To within four feet my putt just drops on the edge of my first birdie. Some more pars and I finally hit a couple of good

and it brings me almost to my knees. Suddenly I am just another fighter.

You start to fight again. We both jab at the same time. My jab lands right on his bony elbow. But his jab glides perfectly straight past my elbow and rips straight through my right eyebrow. Blood pouring from my face I then do not know what to think about first my poor hand that struck the bony elbow or my poor eye. While I am making my mind up my opponent has already made up his: huge left, right to the head. More blood as I steady myself and try to focus. He switches – a left to the body, a right through the guard and suddenly I am in trouble. I am thinking: 'What the fuck am I doing here?'

Within the slightest split-second, I think to myself: 'This is hurting, go and shake the man's hand. Give best. Pack up.' Even quicker than that I think over myself 'Come on you cunt, fuck you, give fucking in and let everyone around down, including yourself.' By now I have done with talking to myself, I have turned my talking towards my opponent. I say 'Good punch' whenever he lands and stuff like 'This is fun mate. Come on people told me you could punch hard.' Then as I try to force home some punches, I start to breathe heavily so I hold on with blood flowing from my mouth, it's a job not to gargle blood.

It's back to basics, hands high, working cautiously behind the jab, trying to find something to turn it my way. Suddenly I land a decent one or two and for the first time he is slowing down. Now it's there, shots onto a par-five in two – a two-putt birdie suddenly – I am faced with a twenty-foot birdie putt and I think I can make this putt to finish only one over.

not so much between us. He too is bleeding. I think momentarily to move in and apply some more pressure only to decide: 'Last time I relaxed at the start I was in all sorts of trouble. I am going to stay focused and stick to basics.' There's no time limit, just keep going and grinding, then some good punches from me and it's now in my favour and soon my wilting opponent quits.

The wind is blowing and the other side of my mind I lag this putt hole-side and get my arse out at the two over. After five hours without blinking I am not knocking three feet past and missing the return. After all, four and a half hours before I did not think I was going to break 90, two putts later and I am finished. No I am not – make sure my card is marked and signed correctly – now I am finished. I feel like a beer and cigar but what I need after that battle is a big double bed to lay and ponder just how well I have grinded, it's then that I enjoy what I have done. And then sleep like a baby.

I shake hands and feel like a beer and a cigar, but all I need is a big double bed and a pretty woman to help patch me up and then to sleep like a baby. There is no better sleep than the one you have after a bare-knuckle fight.

Playing golf sometimes is the most hurtful experience mentally I can have, other than losing a friend or family member. Surely no-one would naturally think if you were not a golfing pro with a passion to compete you need a four-and-a-half-foot putt to make a cut. I hit what you think is a good putt, but somehow it misses or I think two putts from 15 feet and I am through to the next stage for a major championship. I leave my putt three feet from the hole. I miss it then I check the scoreboard only

Bare-knuckle fighting is surely much harder than golf, one would naturally think. If I were not a bare knuckle fighter and a golf pro the physical pain of a punch in the face would be hurtful, no doubt, but when the adrenalin is pumping and the juices flowing, it does not hurt a tenth of what the average person would imagine. To give you some idea about adrenalin I have done things like head butt my putter after missing a short putt causing a bump on my forehead, or I have to confirm I have failed with that very one shot.

That is painful, at that very moment I would exchange that pain for one almighty right-hander in the face, any time. No question about it.

punched my leg so hard after missing a putt which I thought was in and it would be only later that I would discover a massive bruise on my leg or the bump on my head.

Because at the moment of impact the punches do not hurt. The body and brain have taken over to get you through and therefore I will conclude that golf is a harder sport than bare-knuckle fighting by a points decision.

When it comes down to it there is not much to choose between mental and physical pain.